E-Commerce Law

Doing Business Online

Simmons & Simmons
Communication Practice

Palladian Law Publishing Ltd

© Simmons & Simmons
2001

Published by
Palladian Law Publishing Ltd
PO Box 15
Bembridge
Isle of Wight PO35 5NQ
www.palladianlaw.com

ISBN 1 902558 45 6

Typeset by Heath Lodge Publishing Services
Printed in Great Britain by The Cromwell Press Ltd

· E-Commerce Law ·

· Contents ·

About the Authors   ix

Acknowledgements   xi

Table of Cases   xii

Table of Statutes   xiv

Table of Statutory Instruments   xv

Table of EU Legislation   xvi

1. Introduction   1

2. **Online Contracts**   6
    Introduction   6
    Can contracts be made online?   6
    Offer and acceptance   8
    Standard terms   10
    Standard terms – reasonable terms   14
    Evidence of the contract   15
    Dealing with consumers – special considerations   16
    Terms of use of a website   24
    Summary   26

3   **Electronic Signatures and Encryption**   27
    Introduction   27
    What is an electronic signature?   27
    What is encryption?   28
    What does English law say about digital signatures?   31
    International legislation applicable to electronic signatures   34
    Summary   36

4   **Jurisdiction and Governing Law**   37
    Introduction   37
    Jurisdiction   37
    Governing law   39
    Enforcement of a judgment   39

	Brussels & Lugano Conventions, Brussels Regulation	40
	Rome Convention 1980	44
	Outside the European Community	46
	Practical considerations	47
	The *Yahoo!* case	49
	Summary	51
5	**Electronic Money**	52
	Introduction	52
	Electronic money and the Internet	52
	Terminology	53
	European Union developments	55
	Summary	62
6	**E-Commerce Directive**	63
	Introduction	63
	Background	63
	Home state regulation (the "country of origin" principle) – Article 3	64
	Electronic contracts – Articles 9-11	66
	Identification of commercial communications – Articles 6-7	68
	Status of intermediaries – Article 12	68
	Dispute resolution – Article 17	71
	Summary	73
7	**Domain Names**	74
	Introduction	74
	Domain name registration in UK	74
	Resolution of disputes over generic top level domains: UDRP	75
	Resolution of disputes over UK domain name registrations	76
	Practical points	85
	Conclusion	87
	Summary	88
8	**Data Protection**	89
	Introduction	89
	Data Protection Act 1998	89
	Notification	96
	Obligations imposed under the Act – Eight Data Protection Principles	97
	Fair and lawful processing (1st Principle)	98

Data subjects' rights under the Act (6th Principle) 103
Special rules on the use of data processors (7th Principle) 106
Special rules on the transfer of personal data outside the
  EEA (8th Principle) 107
Enforcement 112
Privacy policies 113
Summary 118

9   Advertising and Direct Marketing 119
Introduction 119
Advertising 119
Direct marketing 121
Spamming 131
Summary 135

10   Intellectual Property 136
Introduction 136
Copyright and associated rights 136
Trade marks 142
Patents 145
Confidential information 148
Exploiting intellectual property rights 149
Summary 151

11   Linking and Affiliate Deals 152
Introduction 152
What is linking? 152
Linking in US law 153
Linking in German Law 154
Linking in English law 155
Linking – practical advice 156
Metatags and banner ad keying 158
Linking and affiliate contracts 159
Summary 163

12   Tax 164
Introduction 164
Structuring an e-tailing venture 164
International perspective – "permanent establishments" 165
Going offshore? 166

	VAT	167
	Customs duties	168
	Summary	169
13	**Employee Benefits**	**170**
	Introduction	170
	Inland Revenue approved share schemes	170
	Unapproved share schemes	175
	Employee share ownership trusts	178
	Further information and advice	178
	Summary	179
	Glossary of Internet Terms	180
	Useful Internet Sites	186
	Appendix 1: E-Commerce Directive 2000/31/EC	203
	Appendix 2: Electronic Cash Directive 2000/46/EC	230
	Appendix 3: Copyright Directive 2001/29/EC	239
	Appendix 4: Personal Data Decision 20001/497/EC	260
	Appendix 5: Draft Standard Clauses Decision	275
	Index	287

· About the authors ·

Simmons & Simmons is a major international law firm whose Communications Practice in London comprises over 30 partners and more than 35 other lawyers across various legal disciplines. Simmons & Simmons has developed considerable experience in the field of e-commerce law in recent years and has advised on issues as diverse as online contracts, branding, linking and framing, data protection, copyright and consumer protection. Simmons & Simmons' e-commerce experience covers not only the Internet but also new media such as interactive digital television and WAP.

In addition to advising Internet ventures, Simmons & Simmons has also established its own in the form of elexica.com. Elexica is the award-winning online legal resource powered by knowledge from Simmons & Simmons. One of the facilities offered by elexica is regular email updates on legal developments in the IT and e-commerce field.

For more information about Simmons & Simmons visit: www.simmons-simmons.com

Main contacts

David Barrett – Partner
David joined Simmons & Simmons in January 2001 to lead the firm's IT practice. He is an acknowledged expert on technology work and has advised on a whole variety of e-business and e-commerce transactions.

Ed Lukins – Partner
Ed is a partner in the firm's corporate department focusing on the technology and communications sectors. He is listed as a top lawyer in "The Insider's Guide to Legal Services – IT & Telecoms" 2000 (New City Media) and also in their guide dealing with e-commerce, incorporating digital media.

Jeremy Morton
Jeremy advises on contentious and non-contentious aspects of intellectual property and in particular focuses on e-commerce and communications. The New City Media "Legal Insider's Guide to E-commerce" includes Jeremy among its leading E-commerce Lawyers.

Tom Wheadon – Partner
Tom has considerable experience in advising clients in the communications sector and in particular in the regulation and policy surrounding the industry. Tom has been recommended as one of the "Digital Dozen" in the "Insider's Guide to Legal Services".

· Acknowledgements ·

This book has been produced through the efforts of various members of the Simmons & Simmons Communications Practice and others within the firm. Without the contributions of the following people this book would not have been written or produced:

Jenny Barker, Kirsty Bartlett, Sahar Bhaimia, Nick Bolter, Alexander Brown, Sarah Christison, James Cotter, Bronwyn Donne, Sarah Hicks, Caroline Hooton, James Hope, Monica Ma, Jonathan Maas, Maria Reader, Mark Sheiham and Julia Whelan.

· Table of Cases ·

Avnet Inc v Isoact Ltd [1998] FSR 16   84

BiblioTech v Sam Khuri [2000] unreported   132-133
Britannia Building Society v Prangley & Others [2000] Lawtel
    12 June 2000   81-82
British Horseracing Board & Others v William Hill Organisation Ltd
    [2001] 2 CMLR 12   141
British Telecommunications & Others v One in a Million Ltd [1998]
    4 All ER 476   80-83

Carlill v Carbolic Smoke Ball Co [1893] 1 QB 256   4

French Connection v Sutton [1999] Lawtel, 2 Dec 1999   82

Glaxo plc v Glaxo Wellcome Ltd [1996] FSR 388   80
Godfrey v Demon Internet [1999] 4 All ER 342   69-71

Harrods Ltd v UK Network Services Ltd   [1996] unreported   79
Haymarket Group Ltd v Burmah Castrol plc [2001] unreported   156
Hotmail Corporation v Van Money Pie Inc, 1998 WL 388-389 (ND Cal)   12

Lee O'Brien v MGN Ltd, Chancery Div, 29 June 2000   11

MBNA v Stephen Freeman [2000] Lawtel, 24 July 2000   83

Pitman Training Ltd & PTC Oxford Ltd v Nominet UK & Pearson
    Professional Ltd [1997] FSR 797   84
Playboy Enterprises Inc v Netscape Communications Corporation, 55
F Supp 2d 1070 (1999)   153-154, 157, 159

Roadtech Computer System Ltd v Mandata (Management and Data Services)
    Ltd [2000] ETMR 97   158

St Albans City & District Council v International Computers Ltd [1996] 4
    All ER 481   14
Shetland Times v Wills [1997] FSR 604   155-157
Stepstone v OfiR, Landesgericht Koln, Case No: Az 28 0 692/00   154

Table of Cases

Ticketmaster v Tickets.com, 2000 CV 2000 CV 99-7654 (CD Cal)   13, 154
Timothy v Simpson (1834) 6 C&P 499   4
Totalise plc v Motley Food Ltd & Anr, *The Times*, 15 March 2001   104

Union of French Jewish Students & League against Racism and
    Anti-Semitism v Yahoo! Inc & Yahoo France [2000] unreported   49

Virgin Net Ltd v Prophoto UK (Adrian Paris) [1999] unreported   132

Watford Electronics Ltd v Sanderson CFL Ltd [2001] 1 All ER
    (Comm) 696   14

Yahoo! *See* Union of French Jewish Students & League against Racism and
    Anti-Semitism v Yahoo! Inc & Yahoo France

Zealander & Zealander v Laing Homes Ltd [2000] 2 TCLR 724   72

· Table of Statutes ·

Banking Act 1987   56
  s 3   57
  s 5   57

Consumer Credit Act 1974   6, 7
Consumer Protection Act 1987   9
  s 20   4
Copyright, Designs & Patents Act
  1988   137 *et seq*
  s 3A   140
  s 9(3)   138
  s 11   138
  s 17   139
  s 18   139
  s 21(3)   139

Data Protection Act 1998   24, 89 *et seq*, 122 et seq, *134*
  s 1   90
  s 2   90, 96
  s 4   98
  s 5   94
  s 7   103
  s 10   105
  s 11   122
  s 12   105
  s 13   106
  s 14   106
  s 17   96
  s 19   97
  s 21   97
  s 35   104
  s 40   112
  s 43   112
  s 47   112
  Sched 1   98, 101
  Sched 2   99, 101, 102, 108

Sched 3   102, 108
Sched 4   110

Electronic Communications Act 2000
  7-8, 31 *et seq*, 64, 73
  s 1   33
  s 2   33
  s 7   31, 32
  s 8(2)   8

Finance Act 2000   173, 174
Finance Act 2001   173

Regulation of Investigatory Powers
  Act 2000   100

Sale of Goods Act 1979   16
Supply of Goods and Services Act
  1982   16

Torts (Interference with Goods) Act
  1977   132, 135
Trade Marks Act 1994 79, 142 *et seq*
  s 10   79-80, 83, 84
  s 21   86

Unfair Contract Terms Act 1977
  14, 16-17, 45
  s 3   14, 17

Table of
Statutory Instruments

Companies Act 1985 (Electronic Communications) Order 2000　　　　8
Consumer Protection (Distance Selling) Regulations 2000　　17 *et seq*, 45, 66,
　　　　　　　　　　　　　　　　　　　　　　　　　　129, 133
　　reg 3　　　　　　　　　　　　　　　　　　　　　　17
　　reg 5　　　　　　　　　　　　　　　　　　　　　　18
　　reg 6　　　　　　　　　　　　　　　　　　　　　　18
　　reg 7　　　　　　　　　　　　　　　　　　　　　19-21
　　regs 7-20　　　　　　　　　　　　　　　　　　　　18
　　reg 8　　　　　　　　　　　　　　　　　　　　　19-22
　　reg 10　　　　　　　　　　　　　　　　　　　　20, 23
　　reg 13　　　　　　　　　　　　　　　　　　　　　22
　　reg 14　　　　　　　　　　　　　　　　　　　　　23
　　reg 15　　　　　　　　　　　　　　　　　　　　　23
　　reg 17　　　　　　　　　　　　　　　　　　　　　23
　　reg 25　　　　　　　　　　　　　　　　　　　　　17
　　Sched 2　　　　　　　　　　　　　　　　　　　　　18
Control of Misleading Advertisements Regulations 1988　　　　120
Copyright and Rights in Databases Regulations 1997　　　　　141
　　reg 13　　　　　　　　　　　　　　　　　　　　　141

Telecommunications (Data Protection and Privacy) Regulations 1999
　　　　　　　　　　　　　　　　　　　　　　　123 *et seq*

Unfair Contract Terms in Consumer Contracts Regulations 1999　　16
　　reg 5　　　　　　　　　　　　　　　　　　　　　　17
　　reg 7　　　　　　　　　　　　　　　　　　　　　　17
　　reg 8　　　　　　　　　　　　　　　　　　　　　　17

Table of
EU Legislation

Directives and Decisions

Copyright Directive (Dir 2001/29/EC)	140, 239 *et seq*
Data Protection Directive (Dir 95/46/EC)	89
Distance Selling Directive (Dir 97/7/EC)	66, 67
E-Commerce Directive (Dir 2000/31/EC)	63 *et seq*, 133, 203 *et seq*
Art 3	64
Art 5	66
Arts 6-7	68
Art 10	67, 68
Art 11	67
Art 12	68
Art 17	71, 72
Electronic Communications Directive (Dir 99/93/EC)	32-34, 36, 130
Electronic Money Directive (Dir 2000/28/EC)	56
Electronic Money Directive (Dir 2000/46/EC)	56 *et seq*, 230 *et seq*
Art 2	57
Art 3	58
Art 5	61
Art 7	60
Art 8	61
Personal Data Decision (Dec 2001/497/EC)	260 *et seq*

Regulation

Brussels Regulation (Reg 44/2001)	39 *et seq*, 71

Conventions

Brussels Convention	39 *et seq*
Lugano Convention	39 *et seq*
Rome Convention	40, 43 *et seq*

Chapter 1

· **Introduction** ·

When Charles Babbage began work on his "Analytical Engine" in 1833, the machine which is commonly credited with forming the basis of the logical structure of modern day computers, he can scarcely have imagined the impact that logical data processing machines would have on the world. Babbage's invention was a punched-card controlled general purpose calculator designed to perform a limited number of mathematical calculations. Today computers are integral to every aspect of our lives and by linking computers together over the telecommunications systems which span the globe, the Internet has allowed the distribution of information and services world wide as well as the creation of online communities. Since their inception the Internet and the World Wide Web have, of course, been adopted by business as cost effective means of selling goods and services to a large target audience. However, the Internet and the World Wide Web did not start life in the way we know them today. To look at their origins we have to go back to the 1950s.

In the midst of the Cold War the US Defence Department's Advanced Research Project Agency (ARPA) developed a military computer network (ARPANET) as a means of protecting vital information and data from nuclear attack. The computers within the US defence network were linked so that information and data was shared by all the computers and therefore if one computer in the network was destroyed by nuclear attack the information and data held by the network would survive.

In the 1960s academic institutions in the United States seized on the idea of networked computers as a means of sharing academic information and research amongst themselves. By 1969 ARPANET connected four universities: the Stanford Research Institute, UCLA, UC Santa Barbara and the University of Utah. This number grew over the next few years so that by 1971 ARPANET connected 23 universities and government research centres around the United States. It is perhaps not surprising, with hindsight, that by the early 1970s, although ARPANET was intended as a means of sharing data and information, e-mail was its most popular application.

In the late 1970s ARPANET became international, extending first to academic institutions in the United Kingdom and eventually ARPANET was opened to the general public as the first commercial version of ARPANET was made available. At this time we probably see the first formulations of the Internet – a communications tool which passed from the hands of the military and academic institutions into the hands of the general public. However, the Internet, as we know it, could not be said to have truly been born until the early 1980s when Transmission Control Protocol/Internet Protocol (TCP/IP) was created. TCP/IP is the common language of all Internet computers and allows files (whether text or graphics or otherwise) to be split into packets of data and sent across the network (by a variety of routes) before being reassembled by the computer at its destination.

In 1984 the number of Internet hosts numbered 1,000. By 1987 that number had grown to over 10,000 and this growth continued to accelerate so that by 1990 the number of Internet hosts exceeded 300,000. However, the large number of files accessible via the Internet were not easily accessible. There was no real structure to these files and so the Internet remained relatively difficult to use as there was no obvious and logical method for finding what one was looking for. However, that was about to change.

In 1991 "gopher" was released which was the first "point and click" way of navigating the vast number of files on the Internet. At the same time, Tim Berners-Lee working at CERN in Switzerland developed the computer code which would form the basis of the World Wide Web. His original system was designed as a method of sharing physics research with colleagues so that data could be accessed by all computers through the use of just one program. Tim Berners-Lee's concept had much wider application and it was not long before other people seized on the ability to combine words, graphics and sound on web pages as well as link web pages together in a coherent manner.

The fact that the two were developed separately demonstrates why there is a distinction between the Internet and the World Wide Web, although the two terms are commonly used interchangeably. The two were developed separately and are fundamentally different things. The Internet is a global network of interconnected computers using TCP/IP to transfer data between one another. The Internet is the infrastructure and is defined by reference to the way that data is sent from one computer to another. The World Wide Web, on the other hand, is a collection of text and multimedia files and other network services interconnected via a system of hypertext documents (the "http" which appears in the web browser is short for "hypertext transfer protocol").

If the Internet is the infrastructure, the World Wide Web is the content or application which sits on top of that infrastructure.

By 1996 the Internet comprised nearly 10,000,000 hosts with approximately 40,000,000 people connected to it. The bulk of traffic carried across the Internet was generated by the World Wide Web. Of course, this rapid take up of the Internet and the World Wide Web by so many people across the globe had not gone unnoticed by business. The original web browser, Mosaic, was swiftly overtaken by Netscape and Microsoft Explorer and many retailers were realising that they could sell products and services to a vast consumer base with apparently very low overheads.

The World Wide Web also became a major recreational tool with gaming and music sites becoming ever more popular. Little surprise then that the number of users of the Internet by the end of 1997 had reached over 100,000,000.

At the end of 2000 the estimated number of Internet users worldwide was 400,000,000. Also in 2000 the government estimated that 88% of businesses used e-mail everyday and 57% of businesses either allowed their customers to order online or order online from their suppliers.

We have come a long way since 1833! The real acceleration in technology and the use of the Internet can be seen if we chart the development of technology over the course of a day.

At 9am Charles Babbage draws up the plans for his Analytical Engine. Throughout the rest of the day the world is gradually developing computer processors of increasing sophistication but in terms of the development of the Internet nothing happens until 8.30pm when ARPANET is created. By 9.07pm ARPANET had connected four universities and by 10.27pm there were 1,000 Internet hosts. Shortly after this, at 11.04pm Tim Berners-Lee invented the World Wide Web which seemed to catch on since by 11.30pm there were 40 million people connected to the Internet worldwide. In five minutes that number grew to 100 million and by 11.51pm the total number of people connected to the Internet worldwide numbered 400 million.

Is it any wonder then that the legal and regulatory system in England has struggled to adapt itself at the same pace of change? It is worth remembering that at the same time as these momentous changes in technology were taking place the law was also developing and whilst legislation and case law could keep track of changes to commerce and social trends for most of this period, the acceleration in the use of the Internet and the World Wide Web has meant that the English legal system is, for the most part, having to adapt principles which were established by reference to different technology and business practices.

If we just take English contract law as an example, and in particular the rules surrounding the binding effect of certain types of advertisements, the classic case of *Carlill* v *Carbolic Smoke Ball Co* dates back to 1893. That case concerned an advertisement which promised to pay £100 to any user of the Carbolic Smoke Ball who caught influenza. It was held that the advertisement constituted an offer since the Carbolic Smoke Ball Co had stated that they had deposited £1,000 in their bank as a demonstration of their sincerity and since Carlill had caught influenza the court held that they had to pay the £100. Whilst this case may seem far removed from the world of websites and e-commerce the principles remain valid and so lawyers must apply the principles first established in a case from 1893 when establishing whether advertisements for the sale of goods on a website actually constitute an offer for the sale of those goods.

Similarly, there is a good deal of case law concerning the display of goods in a shop window and the case of *Timothy* v *Simpson* in 1834 starts off a line of cases which decide that a display of goods in a shop window or on the shelves constitute an "invitation to treat" and not an offer for the sale of those goods. As a result the shopkeeper is not necessarily bound by the price at which the goods are displayed in the shop window (although he may incur criminal liability under section 20 of the Consumer Protection Act 1987). These principles, established many years ago, are now having to be applied to the display of goods on a website. This is discussed further in Chapter 2 on Online Contracts.

Other aspects of the nature of the Internet are leading to legal issues that have not necessarily arisen in the same way before now. For example, the Internet is a global resource and consequently the multinational nature of the Internet has led to interesting questions concerning the governing law of contracts and the jurisdiction of courts to hear disputes over consumer (or B2C) contracts and the applicable law. Before the advent of the Internet consumer transactions across borders were relatively rare and when they did occur they were very often instigated by the individual (which affects the rules governing jurisdiction and governing law). Since websites operated by e-tailers are accessible in all countries national courts will have to consider questions of jurisdiction and governing law in respect of contracts between businesses and consumers based in different countries where the transaction has not necessarily been instigated by the consumer but arguably by the e-tailer targeting consumers in that country.

The international nature of the Internet has prompted the EU to begin a program of harmonising European Member States' laws so that those that provide services across the invisible national boundaries of the Internet encounter legal systems that are harmonised and, hopefully, seamless. Whether this objective can be achieved in time remains to be seen.

Finally, the Internet and the World Wide Web are extremely effective tools for the transfer of information and data between people and businesses. The use of individuals' personal data and in particular the collection and use of personal data in connection with the Internet became a very hot topic at the end of the 1990s and will continue to be so whilst e-tailers carry on collecting personal details from users of their websites and details regarding their usage of those websites. We discuss data protection in some detail in Chapters 7 and 8.

This book is intended as a primary resource and as such it has been written in a style and format which we hope will be useful for both lawyers and non-lawyers. We do not expect to have covered all the legal issues that an Internet company may encounter (such a list could be endless) but we have addressed the issues on which we are commonly called to advise and which we believe are most likely to be encountered by those conducting business online. Since European legislation can be difficult to find we have also included the texts of some important European legislation as appendices. The law is up to date to July 2001.

July 2001

Chapter 2

· **Online Contracts** ·

1. **Introduction**

An essential part of an e-commerce venture, whether it deals with businesses or consumers, will be the ability to contract online. But the e-tailer must not just focus on the ability to enter into contracts online but also the ability to make sure that the contract is formed at the right time and on the right terms.

In this chapter we will look at whether contracts can be formed online at all, the formation of online contracts and the incorporation of a business' standard terms into the contract with its customer. We will look at some of the issues that are faced by those Internet companies trading with consumers and also the terms of use that any Internet company may need to consider.

2. **Can contracts be made online?**

Perhaps only lawyers appreciate that a person enters into contracts every day and the majority of these binding transactions are entered into without any formality or a need for a contract evidenced in writing. For example, a person buying a newspaper in a shop enters into a contract with the newsagent for the sale of the newspaper. Contracts are also commonly entered into over the telephone such as when a person purchases concert tickets from a telephone booking line. Similarly, a contract can be formed online as easily as it can be formed by buying goods in a shop or over the telephone.

However, there are certain contracts which are required, by law, to be in writing. For example, the Consumer Credit Act 1974 regulates agreements for the provision of credit and hire and hire-purchase arrangements and imposes requirements on the form and content of the contracts establishing these arrangements. Principally, the Consumer Credit Act 1974 requires the agreement to be recorded in a document which embodies all its terms, which is signed by both the trader and the customer and which is readily legible when sent to the customer for signature. If an agreement does not meet these requirements then in the case of a dispute a court will declare that the agreement is unenforceable.

Whilst it might be thought that a requirement for an agreement in writing could be fulfilled if the customer is given the opportunity to print off a set of terms and conditions from a website or if an electronic copy of the contract is e-mailed to the customer, the consensus of opinion is that this would not constitute a written agreement. Where "writing" is not defined in the relevant statute the Interpretation Act 1978 comes into play which defines "writing" in Schedule 1 as "typing, printing, lithography, photography and other modes of representing or reproducing words in a visible form". The emphasis in this definition is on physical media for the conveyance of the contractual terms. Images on a website or within an e-mail merely constitute electronic data which of themselves are not physical media which can be viewed by a party to the contract.

The requirements of the Consumer Credit Act 1974 therefore require regulated agreements to be signed offline even if they have been initiated online. The Consumer Credit Act 1974 is just one example of a legal requirement for a contract to be evidenced in writing. Another obvious example is agreements relating to the sale or transfer of interests in land.

Electronic Communications Act 2000

Clearly, statutes such as the Consumer Credit Act 1974 and the Interpretation Act 1978 were drafted long before the widespread use of the Internet as a commercial tool. The government therefore recognised that it would be necessary to allow certain contracts that are currently required to be in writing to be entered into online.

The much heralded Electronic Communications Act 2000 which came into force on 25 July 2000 is commonly misconstrued as being a blanket authority to allow all forms of contract to be entered into online. In fact the Electronic Communications Act is merely an enabling Act which gives government ministers the power to amend, by means of Statutory Instruments, existing legislation for the purpose of authorising the use of electronic communications or electronic storage. A list of purposes for which the Electronic Communications Act may be used is given in the Act and one of these purposes is "the doing of anything which under any such provision is required to be or may be done or evidenced in writing or otherwise using a document, notice or instrument" (section 8(2)). Therefore, the Electronic Communications Act opens the door to electronic communications where traditionally the transaction or communication was required to be done in paper format.

However, only one set of regulations implementing the Electronic Communications Act (the Electronic Communications Act 2000: the Companies Act 1985 (Electronic Communications) Order 2000) have been made so far and these regulations provide for the use of electronic communications in company secretarial matters. At the time of writing, no order has been made which will allow contracts, such as Consumer Credit Act contracts, which are required to be in writing, to be made online. However, it is probably only a matter of time before the requirements for certain contracts to be evidenced in writing which were imposed long before the Internet existed or became commercially significant are removed using the powers granted by the Electronic Communications Act 2000.

3.   Offer and acceptance

Assuming then that the transaction the e-tailer wishes to conduct over the Internet is one which is not required to be in writing we need to look at the components of a valid contract in the eyes of the law.

Two of the necessary components to the formation of a valid contract under English law are the existence of an offer, which is then followed by an unequivocal acceptance of that offer. The question therefore is: what is the status of the details on a website? Can they be construed as an offer so that when a customer selects a product or service to purchase this constitutes an acceptance of the offer thus creating a binding contract?

Applying the established rules of English contract law, the answer to the second question would be: no. Analogies can be drawn with the way English contract law has been applied to goods displayed in shops. It is an established principle that the display of goods in a shop is merely an "invitation to treat", which is not binding on the seller. An invitation to treat is an invitation to another person to make an offer which can then be accepted in order to form a binding contract. To use the analogy of an ordinary shop further, the offer is made when the customer takes the goods to a till and this offer is accepted by the shop keeper accepting payment and handing over the goods.

Taking this example into the online world, the display of goods on a website should constitute an invitation to treat. The customer then makes an offer to purchase those goods by placing them in the virtual shopping basket and proceeding to the checkout. The offer can then be accepted in a variety of ways such as the performance of the contract through the delivery of the goods or by using an e-mail to the customer confirming their order.

Of course, the online scenario set out above may not always apply and the presumption that mere display of the goods on the website is an invitation to treat rather than an offer may be rebutted by the words or conduct of the e-tailer. Care must therefore be taken in the design of the website and the descriptions placed on the site to ensure that the display of the goods cannot be construed as an offer. It may also be wise to reinforce the idea that it is the customer making the offer which is then open to acceptance or rejection by the e-tailer on the terms and conditions which govern the transaction or on the terms of use of the website.

Getting the process by which the contract is formed right may, at first, seem simple but the Argos example discussed below demonstrates how important it is to get the offer and acceptance procedure right through taking care to construct the technical process properly.

The Argos example

Argos advertised televisions for sale on its website. For some reason the prices attached to the goods were displayed incorrectly and the televisions were shown as being priced at £2.99 instead of £299. Of itself this would not necessarily constitute an offer to the customer to purchase the televisions at that price – it was an invitation to treat. The customers then placed the goods in a virtual basket at which point they made an offer to buy the televisions at £2.99.

At this stage, Argos was not bound to sell the televisions to its customers at the price displayed (although there could be some liability for displaying a misleading price indication under the Consumer Protection Act 1987) since the offers could still have been rejected by Argos. However, Argos' systems were set up so that the customer received an automatic e-mail confirmation of the order, which could arguably have been seen as an acceptance of the customer's offer.

Nearly one million orders were placed before Argos corrected the error and one purchaser alone had ordered 1,700 televisions. Proceedings against Argos for breach of contract were issued by at least one purchaser but the matter was settled out of court so, unfortunately, there is no legal precedent on the formation of online contracts generated by the incident. It is likely that Argos' lawyers would have argued that there was a clear mistake made as to the contractual terms (*i.e.* the price) and in such circumstances the courts will allow a party to escape performance of the contract.

It is very difficult to assess now whether the facts would objectively support a claim that there was a clear mistake as to the terms of the contract since the web page was understandably removed very quickly after the discovery of the error. Perhaps Argos would have succeeded in its claim that there was a clear mistake and such a claim would certainly be easier to support if, for example, the television in question appeared amongst other televisions all priced at more realistic levels. On the other hand, if the television had appeared within a "special offers" section then perhaps Argos would have found it more difficult to claim that it was clearly a case of a mistake as to the price.

What is clear is that the problem could probably have been avoided had Argos stated in its terms and conditions on the website or in the e-mail confirmation that the e-mail confirmation did not constitute an acceptance of the customer's offer. It would probably also have been a good idea to include a degree of flexibility in the terms and conditions allowing Argos to vary the price in the event of a mistake being made.

4. Standard terms

Assuming that an offer has been made and that offer has been accepted, a contract will be formed provided that "consideration" (*i.e.* a benefit) flows from each party to the other and also subject to the parties intending to be legally bound to each other. These last two requirements are generally easily found in any commercial arrangement. The crucial question then tends to be: on what terms has that contract been formed?

An e-tailer will, of course, want the contract of sale or supply to be governed by its own standard terms and conditions. In order for this to be the case, those terms and conditions must be "incorporated" into the contract and to achieve this the standard terms must be brought to the attention of the customer before, or at the same time as, the contract is formed.

If the standard terms and conditions are not properly incorporated then, in the event of a dispute, a court would look at what terms could be implied as governing the contract and these could be implied terms imposed by statute, general contract law or through the course of conduct that the parties have adopted. Implied terms will not provide the e-tailer with anything like the same level of protection as its own standard terms and therefore it is important that the website is designed so as to ensure that the e-tailer's terms are adequately brought to the attention of the customer before a contract is formed.

Typically there are three main ways in which terms and conditions are commonly presented to users of a website:

- Option 1 – as a hyperlink displayed at the bottom of the web page;
- Option 2 – as a hyperlink within a sentence which reads something like: "by clicking on the "I Accept" button you acknowledge that you have read and accept the terms and conditions"; and
- Option 3 – as part of a "click-wrap" agreement which the agreement must scroll through before being able to click "I Accept" and proceed with the transaction.

Case law

There is a great deal of case law in England on the incorporation of standard terms but the cases all pre-date the advent of the Internet as a commercial tool. Many of the decisions are based on the incorporation (or otherwise) of standard terms and conditions via their inclusion on receipts or tickets. However, the principle laid down by these cases can still be sensibly applied to the Internet and consequently we can apply the established principle that the parties will be bound by those terms that are brought to the attention of the parties before or at the same time as the contract is concluded. It is therefore likely that an English court would find that by using the second and third options, the terms and conditions have been clearly brought to the attention of the customer before the contract is formed and would be binding on the customer. In addition, the following case regarding incorporation of terms in a scratch card competition might indicate a relatively flexible approach by the courts which should benefit Internet traders.

Lee O'Brien v MGN Limited (2000)

Mr O'Brien entered a scratch card game included in a newspaper and his card revealed that he had won £50,000. However, there had been an error in printing the scratch cards which resulted in too many winning cards being produced. The newspaper running the scratch card competition claimed that certain provisions within the competition rules prevented Mr O'Brien from winning his prize. The rules were not printed in the newspaper on the day it was purchased by Mr O'Brien but reference was made to them every time the competition was announced. The court ruled that O'Brien would have seen the terms and conditions in full in earlier editions of the newspaper and that the scratch card referred to the terms. Moreover, the court decided that Mr O'Brien would have appreciated that there were rules that applied to the competition and therefore it was fair to hold him to those rules.

There has also been some case law in the United States which may be instructive. These decisions would not be considered by an English court and have no binding effect on an English court but they provide an interesting insight into how the issue has been resolved in the United States.

Hotmail Corporation v Van Money Pie Inc

Hotmail provide free e-mail services. Users agree to the terms of service via a click-wrap agreement in which the customer, after being given the opportunity to view Hotmail's terms, clicks a box indicating his assent to be bound. The defendants used a third party Internet service provider to send spam e-mails which advertised pornographic materials. The defendants had altered the return addresses so that the e-mail received by the recipient would appear as if sent from a Hotmail account. Given the nature of the e-mails being sent by the defendants there were understandably a large number of complaints which were sent to e-mail accounts which the defendants had set up with Hotmail thus using up a relatively large proportion of the capacity available on Hotmail's systems.

Hotmail sued the defendants citing several causes of action, one of which was that the defendants' actions constituted a breach of Hotmail's terms of service. The US court held that "the evidence supports a finding that the plaintiff will likely prevail on its breach of contract claim". The contract was contained in Hotmail's terms of service which prohibited the defendant's activity. In order to come to this conclusion the US court had to hold that the plaintiff and defendant were party to an enforceable contract. In doing so the US court indicated the binding effect of a click-wrap agreement whereby a user indicates his or her assent by clicking on "I Agree" after being given an opportunity to view the terms and conditions.

However, another American case indicates that, as far as the US courts are concerned, mere reference to the terms and conditions as a hyperlink may not be enough to incorporate them into a binding agreement:

Ticketmaster v Tickets.com

The facts of this case were that Ticketmaster operates a website offering tickets to events for sale. Tickets.com also operates a website offering tickets for sale but it also listed other events for which Tickets.com did not have tickets for sale. In some of these instances Tickets.com linked through to Ticketmaster so that those users who were interested in those events could purchase tickets from Ticketmaster. Even though the links used by Tickets.com plainly told the user that he was being taken to another website, Ticketmaster sought to prevent Tickets.com from using the links to its site. One of the causes of action which Ticketmaster relied on was that such linking was a breach of its terms of use of its website.

The US court, in dismissing Ticketmaster's breach of contract claim, stated that a contract is not created simply by use of a hyperlink posted at the bottom of the site's home page which links to terms and conditions even if those terms and conditions provide that use of the website constitutes the user's assent to be bound by the site's terms and conditions. The court left open the possibility that use of a website coupled with knowledge of the terms and conditions which declare such use evidence of assent to be bound could thereby create a binding contract.

Summary

The most cast iron way of incorporating standard terms into a contract with the user of a website is to use the third option referred to above and include them as a clickwrap agreement. An English court would be likely to decide that terms displayed in this way would be incorporated into the contract and would therefore bind a customer. The second option is also likely to result in the standard terms being incorporated into the contract with a customer. The first option presents the most risky way of displaying the standard terms and conditions, and that system is far more likely to result in an English court deciding that the terms have not been clearly brought to the attention of the customer at or before the time the contract was made.

Clearly, a balance has to be struck between the aesthetics and functionality of the site and the contractual process that must be implemented. In assessing which method should be used factors such as the value of goods or services provided, the jurisdictions targeted and the financial risk of non-performance by either the e-tailer or the customer must be balanced against the look and feel of the website.

5. Standard terms – reasonable terms

An e-tailer's concerns should not end at merely ensuring that its standard terms are incorporated into the contract with the customer. The fact that the relevant terms and conditions are presented to the customer means that there is no opportunity for the customer to negotiate these terms and conditions. Whether the customer is an individual or a company, the fact that the contract is governed by the e-tailer's standard terms means that the Unfair Contract Terms Act 1977 will apply. One of the important provisions of the Unfair Contract Terms Act 1977 states that the e-tailer cannot exclude or restrict any liability in respect of a breach of contract except in so far as the contract term is reasonable (section 3).

There has been recent case law on the reasonableness of exclusion clauses and the two most recent cases centre around the supply of software or computer systems. In *St Albans City & District Council* v *International Computers Limited* [1996] ICL provided a computer system to the Council and were subsequently sued for over £1 million for breach of contract. ICL sought to rely on a clause in its standard terms which restricted liability to £100,000. The court held that this limitation was unreasonable since ICL was a large company with substantial assets and insurance cover of up to £50 million and was therefore in a better position to bear the losses than the Council. In addition, the court found that ICL was in a stronger bargaining position than the Council, the Council had no opportunity to get the service from elsewhere and ICL had not offered any inducement (such as a reduction in price) to the Council to accept the limitation of liability imposed.

In the more recent case of *Watford Electronics Ltd* v *Sanderson CFL Ltd* [2001] the Court of Appeal had to consider an exclusion of liability clause in a contract for the supply of software that excluded consequential and indirect loss and limited the amount of damages recoverable to the amount paid by the customer (approximately £104,000). When the software failed to perform properly Watford claimed £5.5 million for loss of profits and their increased operational costs. In this instance, however, the court held that the supplier was entitled to rely on the limitation of liability clause since the purchaser was experienced in this type of transaction and was well aware of the limitation clause since they had sought substantial amendments to it which to some degree had been incorporated.

Each set of terms and conditions and the types of transactions contemplated will have to be looked at on its facts but given that it is extremely unlikely that there will be any negotiation of a contract conducted entirely online, an e-tailer would be well advised to take a reasonable line on any limitations or exclusions of liability. This is especially advisable where the contract is with a consumer since a harsh limitation of liability clause will be considered even less reasonable as against a consumer than as against a company.

6. **Evidence of the contract**

Whilst a contract formed over the Internet is capable of being just as binding as a written contract signed by both parties it is much easier to prove that a written contract has been entered into and also what the terms of that written contract are. E-tailers must therefore bear in mind that the existence of a binding contract is no use without the necessary evidence which will enable the e-tailer to enforce that contract. It is important that an e-tailer's computer systems enable the generation of an audit trail so that it can prove that the user accepted the terms and conditions and is bound by those terms and conditions. E-mail correspondence with the customer confirming the order can also be useful evidence of the existence of the contract. Finally, it is wise to keep records of all previous versions of the website and in particular any changes to the terms and conditions that have been made. This would enable the supplier to show the wording on the website and also the precise terms and conditions which the customer accepted at the time he entered into the transation. Again, there is a balancing exercise to be conducted here since it will be technically and administratively difficult to store all previous versions of all pages of the website for long periods of time. It would, however, be unwise to discard previous versions of important pages of the website (such as those displaying product descriptions or prices) immediately and certainly previous versions of terms and conditions displayed on the site should be kept for longer.

7. Dealing with consumers – special considerations

Consumers are afforded a special degree of protection by English law which therefore impacts on the e-tailers' dealings with them and the terms and conditions that may be imposed on them. E-tailers therefore have to carefully consider their target market and the implications this may have not only on the terms and conditions but also on the design of the site and the e-tailer's contracting process.

Consumer law is a large and sometimes complex topic but it is hoped this section will provide a useful starting point when considering the impact of UK consumer protection law on the online contracting process.

Implied terms

The Sale of Goods Act 1979 and the Supply of Goods and Services Act 1982 both have the effect of implying certain terms into the contract for the supply of goods or services between a business and a consumer. By virtue of these Acts there is an implied term that any goods sold will be of "satisfactory quality" which is to be interpreted as being of the sort of quality that a reasonable person would regard as satisfactory taking into account the description of the goods, the price and all other relevant circumstances. In addition, the quality of the goods focuses not only on their state or condition but also on their fitness for the purposes for which goods of the kind in question are commonly supplied, that safety and their durability. There are exceptions to the application of the implied term as to satisfactory quality which does not apply, for example, if any defect is drawn to the attention of the consumer prior to purchase.

In a contract for the supply of services it is implied into the contract that the supplier will carry out the service with reasonable skill and care, that the services will be supplied within a reasonable time (unless the contract specifies otherwise) and that where the contract does not determine a price to be paid for a services a reasonable charge will be payable.

Unfair terms

The Unfair Contract Terms Act 1977 ("UCTA") and the Unfair Contract Terms in Consumer Contracts Regulations 1999 (the "UCTT

Regulations") impact on the sort of terms and conditions that can be used by e-tailers in contracts with consumers. Under UCTA an e-tailer operating on its standard terms of business cannot exclude or restrict its liability for breach of the contract or perform the contract in a substantially different manner unless (in both cases) to do so would be reasonable in the circumstances (section 3). Consequently, an e-tailer must ensure that it supplies a product which corresponds to that advertised on the website and cannot by reference to the contract with the customer provide a substantially different product.

The UCTT Regulations state that a consumer is not bound by a standard term in a contract with a seller or supplier if that term is unfair (reg 8). The UCTT Regulations also grant the Director General of Fair Trading (and certain other named authorities, including, for example, the Information Commissioner) powers to stop businesses using unfair standard terms. A standard term is unfair if, contrary to the requirement of good faith it creates a significant imbalance in the parties' rights and obligations under the contract, to the detriment of the consumer (reg 5). Finally, the UCTT Regulations also require that plain and intelligible language is used in consumer contracts and that the writing is clear and legible (reg 7).

Distance selling

The **Consumer Protection (Distance Selling) Regulations 2000** impose a number of important obligations on businesses entering into "distance contracts" and have important provisions which affect the contracting process adopted by e-tailers selling to consumers via the Internet. The obligations imposed by the Distance Selling Regulations are mandatory and any term in a contract with a consumer which is inconsistent with a provision for the protection of the consumer contained in these Regulations is void (regulation 25).

The Distance Selling Regulations (in regulation 3) define a distance contract as a contract for the supply of goods or services concluded between a supplier and a consumer where the supplier makes exclusive use of one or more means of "distance communication" up to and including the moment at which the contract is concluded. A means of "distance communication" is defined as any means which, without the simultaneous physical presence of the supplier and consumer, may be used for the conclusion of a contract. Clearly, a website is a means of distance communication since the supplier and consumer are physically separated and therefore contracts concluded via a website must conform with the Distance Selling Regulations unless the contracts concluded are within one of the exceptions which are set out in regulation 5. For the sake of completeness all of the exempt contracts are set out below although not all of them are necessarily applicable to the world of e-commerce.

The exempt contracts are:

- contracts for the sale of an interest in land but not rental agreements;
- contracts concerning the construction of a building where the contract also provides for the sale of an interest in land, (again other than rental agreements);
- agreements relating to financial services (a non-exhaustive list of the type of financial services that are excluded from the ambit of the Distance Selling Regulations is included in Schedule 2 of the Regulations and includes banking services, insurance and investment services);
- contracts concluded by means of an automated vending machine such as a chocolate machine in a train station;
- contracts concluded with a telecommunications operator through the use of a public telephone; and
- contracts concluded at an auction, by a telephone bidder, for example.

In addition, parts of the Distance Selling Regulations do not apply to certain other contracts which are listed in regulation 6. Again all of the exceptions are listed even though some are not directly applicable to the world of e-commerce. The contracts to which only parts of the Distance Selling Regulations apply are:

- timeshare agreements (regulations 7 to 20 do not apply);
- contracts for the supply of food, drink and other goods intended for everyday consumption supplied to the consumer's home or workplace by what the Regulations call "regular roundsmen" (regulations 7 to 19(1) do not apply);
- contracts for the provision of accommodation, transport, catering or leisure services where the supplier undertakes, when the contract is concluded, to provide these services on a specific date or within a specific period (regulations 7 to 19(1) do not apply); and
- contracts for package holidays (regulations 19(2) to (8) and 20 do not apply).

Supply of information

If a contract made over the Internet does not fall within one of the exceptions listed above, then under the Distance Selling Regulations (regulation 7), in good time before the contract is made the e-tailer must tell the consumer the following things:

- the identity of the e-tailer and, where the contract requires payment in advance, the e-tailer's address;
- a description of the main characteristics of the goods or services;
- the price of the goods or services, including all taxes;
- delivery costs (where appropriate);
- arrangements for payment, delivery or performance;
- the existence of a right of cancellation (except where one of the exceptions to the right to cancel applies);
- the cost of using the means of distance communication where it is calculated other than at the basic rate;
- the period for which the offer or the price remains valid;
- the minimum duration of the contract (where appropriate);
- whether in the event of the goods requested being unavailable the e-tailer proposes to provide substitute goods or services of equivalent quality and price; and
- the cost of returning any such substitute goods in the event of cancellation of the contract.

Regulation 7 states that the information listed above must be provided in a clear and comprehensive manner appropriate to the means of distance communication used, with due regard to the principles of good faith in commercial transactions and the principles governing protection of those, legally speaking, unable to give their consent (such as children). In practice, what that means is that the means by which the information is delivered must be assessed in the light of the likely customers and the goods being sold or services being provided. The information will commonly be provided via the website which is appropriate given that the sale is made on the website and in the context of a website commonly used by adults, such as an online electrical store, the information may be provided in a fairly unobtrusive manner without greatly impacting the design of the website.

However, the more complex the contract being entered into or the less sophisticated the consumer, the more prominent the information must be and this may impact on the design of the website.

The Distance Selling Regulations also contain a further separate obligation (in regulation 8) to the effect that further information must be provided to the consumer prior to the conclusion of a contract or, if later, while the services are being provided or on delivery of the goods. The information to be supplied by the e-tailer at this stage is all that included in the first six items of information listed above, the geographical place of business to which the consumer may address complaints, any after-sales service and further information regarding the right to cancel (see further below). The Distance Selling Regulations state that this information must be given to the consumer in writing or another durable medium (and this is where there is scope for confusion). The Regulations do not deal with whether an e-mail or display on a website is sufficient to discharge this obligation since, in regulation 8, "writing or another durable medium" is not defined. However, regulation 10, which sets out the consumer's right to cancel, states that the notice to cancel must be given in writing or another durable medium (*i.e.* the same wording as regulation 8) and then goes on to say that the notice is properly given if sent by: hand delivery, post, fax, or e-mail.

It seems logical therefore to suggest that the information to be given under regulation 8 is likely to be validly delivered if sent by one of these listed methods whilst delivery via display on a website is notable by its omission from the list. Here then is the problem. The information given under regulation 7 is not restricted to being given in writing or another durable medium and can therefore be given via a website (or even via a mobile telephone screen or via an interactive television service). However, the information required by regulation 8 (which repeats much of the regulation 7 information) must be given by hand delivery, post, fax or e-mail. Of course, in the case of an e-tailer, e-mail is likely to be the most viable option and the information could be built in to the order confirmation process.

It may be harder to comply with regulation 8 in the case of mobile or interactive television services where it is not necessarily guaranteed that the consumer will have an e-mail account. Consequently those businesses selling goods and services to consumers via mobile or interactive television programmes may have to rely on the more traditional methods of delivering the regulation 8 information.

Right to cancel

One of the most important aspects of the Distance Selling Regulations is that they give the consumer a statutory right to cancel the contract they have entered into with the e-tailer. Accordingly, as mentioned above and pursuant to regulation 8, the e-tailer must give the consumer information regarding the cancellation procedure including whether the consumer will be required to return the goods and who shall pay for the return of the goods. In addition, in the case of the supply of services, prior to the conclusion of the contract the e-tailer must inform the consumer that the consumer will not be able to cancel the contract once performance of the services has begun (regulation 8(3)).

The length of the cancellation period depends on the extent to which the e-tailer has complied with his obligations under regulations 7 and 8. The diagram below should help in understanding the cancellation period.

If the e-tailer has complied with regulations 7 and 8 the cancellation period starts on the day the contract is concluded and ends seven working days beginning with the day after the day on which the consumer receives the goods.

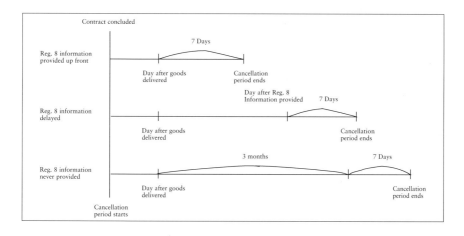

If the e-tailer fails to give the information required by regulation 8 but does so within three months of the day after the day on which the goods are delivered the cancellation period starts on the day the contract is concluded and ends seven working days beginning with the day after the day on which the consumer gets the information.

If the supplier fails to give the information at all the cancellation period starts on the day the contract is concluded and ends three months and seven working days after the day on which the consumer receives the goods.

A consumer can similarly cancel a contract for the supply of services and the cancellation period is again fixed by reference to the supply of the regulation 8 information. However, in the case of the supply of services there is no "delivery of goods stage" and so the cancellation periods start running from conclusion of the contract. The diagram below illustrates the cancellation periods in respect of contracts for the supply of services.

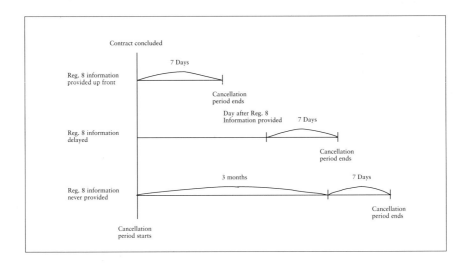

Exceptions to the right to cancel

There are certain exceptions to the mandatory cancellation right which are set out in regulation 13. These are:

- contracts for the supply of services if the supplier has complied with regulation 8(3) and performance of the contract has begun with the customer's agreement before the end of the cancellation period;
- contracts for the supply of goods/services whose price is dependent on fluctuations in the financial market;
- contracts for the supply of goods made to the consumer's specifications or clearly personalised or which are liable to deteriorate or expire rapidly;
- contracts for the supply of audio/video recordings or computer software if they are unsealed by the customer;
- supply of newspapers or magazines; and
- contracts for gaming, betting or lottery services.

Effect of the cancellation

The effect of a notice of cancellation is that the contract is treated as if it had never been made (regulation 10). In addition, if the goods are properly returned the e-tailer must refund the payments received relating to the contract. This refund should be made free of charge but the supplier may deduct from that sum the direct costs of recovering the goods if the contract states that the customer must return the goods but the customer does not do so or does so at the expense of the e-tailer (regulation 14).

Regulation 14(3) requires the e-tailer to refund the money as soon as possible and in any event within 30 days of the consumer's cancellation. Therefore, the refund must be made irrespective of whether the customer has returned the goods and e-tailers could therefore find themselves in a situation where they are forced to return the money without there necessarily being the prospect of having the goods returned.

There is some comfort for the e-tailer in regulation 17 which requires the consumer to retain possession of the goods and take reasonable care of the goods. The regulation also imposes a duty on the customer to return the goods to the e-tailer but in doing that need do no more than make them available at his or her own premises following a request in writing from the e-tailer.

As the contract is treated as never having been made the e-tailer can have no contractual right to the return of his goods but breach of these obligations is actionable as a breach of statutory duty. The e-tailer does at least then have a right of action against the consumer who fails to return the goods following cancellation of the contract. However, whether an e-tailer would ever consider taking such action in view of the time, expense and hassle involved is doubtful especially where the goods in question are of low value.

Credit agreements

One interesting aspect of the Distance Selling Regulations is that where a contract for the supply of goods is financed by a related credit agreement (for instance, where a sofa is bought on credit terms) and the contract for the goods is cancelled under the mandatory cancellation right the credit agreement is also automatically cancelled (regulation 15). This is the case even if the credit agreement is with a third party and there is a duty on the e-tailer to inform the provider of the credit that the underlying contract for the supply of the goods has been cancelled.

8. Terms of use of a website

Most websites include some form of wording which the operators of the website hope will govern the use of the website by the visitors to the site. Of course, as we have already pointed out, there is some difficulty in incorporating those terms into the contract with the user of the website and thereby making them binding on the user. Unless the user is forced through some form of registration process during which he or she must accept the terms of use in order to register then the likelihood is that a set of terms of use which are merely included as a hyperlink on the website will not bind the user. However, most designers of websites and e-tailers will resist including a registration process where it is not necessary for commercial purposes since it will discourage a proportion of users from going beyond the registration process.

Despite this there are still very valid reasons for including terms of use even if only as a hyperlink. For instance, the terms of use can be used to deliver certain elements of the information required by the Distance Selling Regulations. The terms of use can also be used to deliver certain information required by the Data Protection Act 1998 such as the identity or the person processing any personal data (namely the e-tailer) and also the types of data processing that will be undertaken.

Terms of use are also commonly used to assert the e-tailer's copyright in the design and content of the website and can also set limits on the licence that is granted to the user of the website in respect of the use that may be made of the website. For instance, an e-tailer may choose to restrict the user to viewing the site, printing pages for personal use and storing a copy of the site's pages in the user's cache on their hard drive. Another use of the website which e-tailers may restrict is any linking to the site or framing of its content. Linking and framing is discussed in more detail in Chapter 11 but briefly the commercial reason for an e-tailer restricting linking and particularly deep-linking, to its website is that such linking may serve to bypass some of the advertising on the e-tailer's website. If the linking of the website bypasses the homepage this may well mean that the most valuable advertising on the e-tailer's website is also bypassed resulting in a loss of revenue for the e-tailer. If such activity is prohibited by the terms of use of the website an e-tailer wishing to stop the linking to its site may have an option to claim breach of contract.

If the website gives the user the ability to interact with other users, for instance, through chat rooms or bulletin boards, the terms of use should set out the ground rules of the use of these facilities. The difficulty for e-tailers including chat rooms on their site is that the messages submitted may be obscene or defamatory which may leave the e-tailer open to civil or possibly even criminal liability. Consequently, the e-tailer should monitor chat rooms and bulletin boards and the terms of use must give the e-tailer absolute freedom to restrict access to the facility or remove messages for any reason. The liability of Internet sites for defamatory content is discussed further in Chapter 6 on the E-Commerce Directive.

9. **Summary**

-   Binding contracts can be entered into online but there are still certain contracts, such as Consumer Credit Act agreements and transfers of interest in land, which have to be in writing and signed.

-   The details on a website, of themselves, are unlikely to constitute an offer. The offer is more likely to be made when the customer places the goods in the "shopping cart" and proceeds to the checkout. The process of acceptance needs to be carefully thought out so that acceptance takes place at the time when the e-tailer has verified the order.

-   Standard terms and conditions must be clearly brought to the attention of the customer before or at the same time as the contract is made with the customer in order for them to be validly incorporated within the contract.

-   Contracts made online are "distance contracts" which must therefore comply with the terms of the Consumer Protection (Distance Selling) Regulations 2000. One important provision of these Regulations is the statutory cancellation right given to consumers in respect of distance contracts.

Chapter 3

Electronic Signature & Encryption

1. Introduction

One of the main obstacles to the development of confidence in online transactions has been perception held by many people of a lack of security of information transferred across the Internet. As a result, many people remain reluctant to divulge personal information or make valuable purchases (if at all) over the Internet. In addition, it is not always easy to identify the person with whom one is transacting and this uncertainty has also prevented both consumers and business from readily participating in online transactions. For these reasons a standardised system of encryption and electronic signatures is necessary to promote confidence in online transactions and also develop the use of the Internet for high value transactions.

In this chapter we will look at the use of these encryption techniques in the development of digital signatures and will go on to examine the legal regime surrounding them, both within the United Kingdom and internationally.

2. What Is an electronic signature?

The phrase "electronic signature" is essentially a generic term used to describe a variety of different ways in which a communication can be signed electronically and consequently the term encompasses the following:

- typing one's name at the end of e-mail/internet order form;
- the display of one's e-mail address at the top of a communication;
- the use of a "cookie" left by a computer when the user visits a website;
- a copy of one's signature which has been scanned into a computer;

- digital signatures which involve a form of encryption and increasingly a form of certification;
- the transformation of a written signature into a format which can be electronically stored on a magnetic strip; and
- "biometric" signatures - these are still in development but in basic terms they involve using a computer to record and then recognise an individual aspect of the user, such as their retina pattern, fingerprint or even their DNA.

In other words, an "electronic" signature could be anything that is electronic and which is intended to fulfil the same function as a person's signature in the "physical" world, *i.e.* to provide evidence of that person's unique identity and, in legal terms, their agreement to abide by what they have signed.

Currently the majority of consumer contracts made over the Internet involve the customer completing an order form with their name and address, or ticking a box confirming that they wish the order to proceed. In practice, however, such actions cannot automatically be assumed to constitute the same evidence of the customer's unique identity and agreement as a signature would in the physical world. Just as in the physical world where a signature is open to forgery, so in the Internet world it is possible for a customer to "sign" an agreement using someone else's details. However, the forgery of the latter is much easier.

It is for this reason that e-tailers require an additional layer of assurance that the customer is who they say they are, just as their retail counterparts sometimes do. To a degree this can be achieved through requiring payment via a credit card, although obviously this is also open to abuse if an unscrupulous third party is able to obtain another person's credit card details. Some e-tailers develop their own security measures, *e.g.* requiring customers who subscribe to their website to provide a password. Increasingly, however, e-tailers are turning to the use of encryption technology as a means of securing their own certainty that a customer is who they say they are.

3.   **What is encryption?**

Encryption is a means of hiding information that you do not want made public (just as decryption is a means of revealing information which has been hidden). Encryption typically operates through the use of a cryptographic algorithm (a mathematical device which transforms the information into a highly complex series of letters and numbers). To decrypt the algorithm the user will need a key – this is another series of letters and numbers which operates with the algorithm to reveal the information. There are two forms of encryption relevant to the current discussion.

Symmetric key encryption (also known as private key encryption)

In this form of encryption, the person encrypting the information uses the *same* key as the person decrypting the information. This can give rise to security problems – for example, if there are four parties to a contract, each party will need to know the key and the more people who have access to the key, the harder it is to keep the key secure.

Accordingly, a second means of encryption has been developed which will permit multiple parties to sign a contract without forcing them to provide details of their key that they would rather keep confidential.

Asymmetric key encryption (also known as public key encryption)

With asymmetric key encryption, the person encrypting the information has a *different* key to the person decrypting the information. The process is best illustrated in the following example:

> Arnold operates a website that offers turnips for sale to the general public. Brenda wants to buy 10 turnips over the web. Arnold uses asymmetric key encryption to ensure the security of contracts formed over his website. When Brenda first contracts on the website she is allocated a *private* key that is known only to her. Brenda then uses this private key to encrypt her order details and transmit them to Arnold. Arnold's website uses a *public* key to decrypt Brenda's order (this public key usually being known by all users of the site). Because Arnold knows that only Brenda uses that particular private key, he can assume that the order has legitimately come from her and arrange for delivery of the turnips accordingly.

The obvious problem with this system is that there is a danger that another customer to the site may be able to use Arnold's public key to decrypt Brenda's order, thereby endangering the confidentiality of her details.

What do digital signatures have to do with encryption?

Digital signatures take the concept behind asymmetric encryption one step further so that not only can a recipient be certain of the identity of the sender, but also he can verify that the message received is the same as the message sent. In addition, it is possible to encode the time and date within the digital signature so that the digital signature not only records the unique identity of its user and his or her agreement to be bound but also records the time and date of that agreement - something which cannot be achieved with a traditional signature. To illustrate how a digital signature operates it is best to return to the above example.

> As before Brenda wishes to purchase 10 turnips and encrypts her order using her private key. At the same time she runs her order through a "hash function" algorithm to produce a "message digest" (basically a series of numbers). Essentially, her order is put together in a different way and freeze-framed so that although the message digest will have no obvious meaning to the casual observer it will mean that if her order is changed even slightly, when run through the hash function it will produce a different message digest. Brenda then uses her private key to encrypt the message digest – this is known as the digital signature. The digital signature will then be attached to the order and transmitted to Arnold.
>
> In order to decrypt her order, Arnold will need to obtain a public key from Brenda. He will then use this to decrypt Brenda's digital signature and reveal the message digest. Because the message digest was created using Brenda's private key he knows that this must have been created by her. Arnold then determines whether Brenda's order has been tampered with by running it through the same hash function as Brenda used in creating her message digest. Arnold will know that the order has not been tampered with if his message digest matches Brenda's.

If we look at our example it can be seen that there is a danger with digital signatures that a third party has been impersonating Brenda by using a randomly created private key and then sending a corresponding public key to Arnold. If Arnold wants to be certain that he is really contracting with Brenda and not an impostor, he can ask Brenda to attach a digital certificate to her digital signature.

What are digital certificates?

A digital certificate is a document provided by a third party (a certificate or certification authority) that verifies that a particular public key belongs to a particular person. The authority can do this through requiring the individual applying for the certificate to present their public key and proof of his or her identity (*e.g.* a copy of a birth certificate, passport or driver's licence for an individual or incorporation documents for a business entity). A public key that has been certified in this way will only work with the certificate holder's private key.

Of course the question arises as to whether you can trust the certificate authority – usually these will be licensed or registered in accordance with the laws of a given state or alternatively the authority may have its own digital certificate issued by another certificate authority (the potential unlimited nature of the cross-certification created by this is known as the public key infrastructure).

4.   What does English law say about digital signatures?

The position under English law with regard to digital signatures and electronic signatures in general is set out in the Electronic Communications Act 2000 (the "Act"). The Act basically does three things:

- it establishes a scheme for the licensing of cryptography service providers (although in practice the government has decided to allow the industry to regulate itself for the next few years);
- it provides for the legal recognition of electronic signatures and defines the process under which they are created, verified or communicated; and
- it allows ministers to issue specific orders in areas where previously there was an express stipulation that something could only be done in physical (*i.e.* not electronic) form.

What does the Act say about electronic signatures?

The Act states that where an electronic signature has been incorporated into or is logically associated with an electronic communication, it can be accepted as evidence of that electronic communication's authenticity and/or integrity (section 7), provided that it has been certified. In other words, where there is a valid and certified electronic signature attached to an electronic communication, it can be taken as evidence of that person's intention to be bound by it. For these purposes, an electronic signature is certified where a statement has been made saying that the signature; or a means of producing, communicating or verifying the signature; or a procedure applied in creating the signature, is a valid means of establishing its authenticity or integrity (section 7(3)).

A digital signature, as described in the above example, clearly falls within the scope of the Act. By attaching her digital signature to her order, Brenda has ensured that it is "logically associated" with the electronic communication and, by sending a digital certificate, she is attesting that it is genuine.

However, it is important to note that the Act is arguably not limited purely to covering digital signatures and digital certificates. For example, if Brenda did not have a digital certificate, she would still be able to certify her signature in other ways, *e.g.* she could send an e-mail, fax or letter to Arnold confirming her order or confirming her digital signature.

Similarly, supposing we return to the common situation outlined earlier on in this chapter whereby an Internet contract is entered into by ticking a box or typing a name. Under the Act, an "electronic signature" is defined as something that is incorporated or logically associated with the electronic communication for the purposes of establishing the authenticity and/or integrity of that electronic communication or data (section 7(2)). Again, by typing your name or ticking a box confirming your order, it is arguable that this is a means of authenticating your agreement to the terms. Of course, such agreement would also need to be certified, and as above this could be done through a separate e-mail, fax or letter.

Whilst this argument seems tenable, unfortunately it has not been tested before a court and as such until someone does decide to litigate under the Act there will be no further guidelines as to what forms of electronic signature are covered. This is something which could have been avoided had the Act chosen to implement directly the European Union's Electronic Communications Directive (99/93/EC) (on which the Act is based). This is because the Directive operates a distinction between what it terms an "advanced electronic signature" and an "ordinary" electronic signature. Under the Directive an "advanced electronic signature" is one that meets the following criteria:

- it is uniquely linked to the signatory (*i.e.* only the signatory can have sent it – *e.g.* Brenda sending an order encrypted with her private key);
- it is capable of identifying the signatory (*i.e.* Arnold uses Brenda's public key to decrypt the order, thus demonstrating that the order can only have come from her);

- the signature has been created using means that the signatory can maintain under his sole control *(i.e.* Brenda's public key as certified by a certificate authority); and
- the signature is linked to the document in such a way that any subsequent change of the data is detectable *(i.e.* where Brenda uses a hash function to create a message digest).

Where the signature meets the above criteria and where it is supported by a certificate which meets the requirements of the Directive (which broadly relate to the identification of the certification authority and which requires certain things to be stated in the certificate), then it will be regarded as automatically satisfying the legal requirements for the signature of documents. By contrast, where an electronic signature does not meet these requirements, it will not be regarded as automatically satisfying the legal requirements for the signature of documents. At the same time, however, it will not be regarded as something which is totally inadmissible – instead, it will have to meet the relevant Member State's national requirements governing admissibility of signatures as evidence for entering into an agreement.

The Directive has to be implemented by Member States by 19 July 2001. It will be interesting to see how the different Member States deal with the distinction and it remains to be seen to what degree the Directive will be invoked in UK disputes relating to electronic signatures.

What does the Act say about cryptography service providers?

Cryptography service providers or certification authorities are those bodies that provide registration or certification facilities, generate and allocate private and public keys or which offer ancillary services such as directories of such service providers. Although the Act states that such providers should be approved and registered (sections 1 and 2), in fact the government has effectively granted a five-year moratorium on these obligations so as to allow the industry to establish and, theoretically, regulate itself. At the time of writing, no scheme has yet been formalised.

The Act also does not expressly deal with the liability of the cryptography service providers as was envisaged by the Directive. Since the system of certification of the private and public keys is only as good as the integrity or capability of the cryptography service providers which certify the keys there is obviously scope for considerable loss in the event that the cryptography service provider incorrectly (whether innocently, negligently or fraudulently) certifies that an individual or entity holding a key is who they purport to be. For this reason the Directive requires Member States to ensure that a certification authority is liable for any damage caused to any entity or individual who reasonably relies on the certificate issued by the authority unless the authority can show that it has acted reasonably. However, the United Kingdom has chosen not to implement this element of the Directive. Instead the government considered that the liability of the cryptography service provider in such instances is better determined by the contractual arrangements in place between the cryptography service providers and their customers. If the person suffering loss is not a customer of the cryptography service provider he or she will have to look to the principles or tort and in particular negligent misstatement in order to recover loss.

Those suffering loss will regard the position of the UK government as somewhat harsh given that they will undoubtedly find it harder to recover loss under an action in contract or in tort than they would were they able to claim under a form of statutory liability. Where a claim is founded on breach of contract there are likely to be limitation of liability clauses which will either totally exclude liability or restrict liability for certain types of loss (particularly a loss of profit or goodwill) and possibly also restrict the total amount that may be claimed for breaches of the contract. Where the person suffering loss has no contract with the cryptography service provider an action in tort based on negligent misstatement will require the plaintiff to show that the cryptography service provider owes that person a duty of care in making that statement. Depending on the circumstances this may not be easy to do.

5. International legislation applicable to electronic signatures

The United Nations Commission on International Trade Law is currently in the process of drafting what it terms the Uniform Rules on Electronic Signatures (the "Rules") that it hopes to publish by the end of 2001. The majority of its provisions already appear to have been anticipated by the Act (for example, electronic signatures should not be regarded as inadmissible evidence in questions relating to a document's authenticity, the need for certification etc).

Where the Rules will be of significance is in relation to their requirement that each signatory to them will be required to recognise electronic signatures and digital certificates which are recognised as valid in the other signatory states. This is aimed at achieving conformity and consistency amongst the signatory states as regards their approach to electronic signatures and digital certificates and should ensure that signatories do not seek to impose additional requirements or obligations.

6. **Summary**

- Encryption comes in two formats: symmetric (or private) and asymmetric (or public) key encryption. Symmetric key encryption is typically used where only a small number of people need access to the key. Asymmetric key encryption is more likely to be used on a "one to many" basis.

- Electronic signatures can be anything which can be attached to an electronic communication and which is intended to verify the identity of the sender of a communication.

- The Electronic Communications Act 2000 states that an electronic signature (as defined in the Act) can be accepted as evidence of an electronic communication's authenticity.

- In order for an electronic signature to be an effective tool it must be possible to verify that the communication comes from the person who purportedly sends the electronic signature. Such certification can be obtained from a certification authority or cryptography service provider.

- The EU Electronic Communications Directive states that the certification authority should be liable for any loss suffered by those reasonably relying on the certification as a result of that reliance. The UK government has decided to leave the question of liability to be decided by the courts applying the normal principles of contract law and tort.

Chapter 4

Jurisdiction &
· Governing Law ·

1. Introduction

A website is available at anytime to anyone anywhere in the world with Internet access. This worldwide accessibility has meant that the question of jurisdictional exposure is a key concern of corporations everywhere hoping to do business online. Where can a consumer sue? What law applies if there is a dispute? Are there mandatory laws that apply regardless of what law is chosen by an e-tailer? How can an e-tailer avoid falling within the jurisdiction of a nation's courts?

There are three main issues which will need to be analysed: which courts will have jurisdiction if a dispute arises; which law will govern the resolution of the dispute; and whether a court will enforce a foreign judgment.

2. Jurisdiction

"Jurisdiction" is a technical term denoting the assertion by a court of the authority to adjudicate upon a dispute. When a court claims to have jurisdiction over a dispute, it is asserting the authority to adjudicate on a particular issue. It is important for e-tailers to have an understanding of jurisdictional rules when setting up websites for the purpose of carrying on business internationally, so that e-tailers can anticipate which courts they can sue in or are liable to be sued in. By inserting a jurisdiction clause in a contract the parties agree that the courts of a particular country will have the right to determine a dispute which arises out of or in connection with the contract. Depending on its wording, the clause may also prevent the dispute from being decided by the courts of other countries. A jurisdiction clause therefore generally gives the parties some certainty as to where any disputes arising out of the contract will be resolved.

If a contract states that the courts of New York have jurisdiction, for example, then (in the absence of a contrary applicable rule, of which more later) the New York courts will generally have jurisdiction to hear any dispute which arises under the contract. Where that jurisdiction clause is stated to be "exclusive", most other courts will generally decline jurisdiction in favour of the New York courts (although some mandatory laws prevent this, particularly where consumers are involved).

Where there is no contractual jurisdiction clause, international conventions as well as national laws will determine whether a particular court can take jurisdiction if a dispute arises. In many cases more than one court may potentially assert jurisdiction. For instance, suppose an Australian company through its website sells clothes manufactured in India to a company based in England, and no jurisdiction clause is stated in the contract of sale. If the clothes turn out to be defective and the English company cannot sell them to their customers, the courts of all three countries may have jurisdiction to hear claims brought by the buyer against the seller and the manufacturer. The English courts could potentially take jurisdiction as the contract may have been made in England, the buyer is based in England and suffered harm there; the Australian courts could potentially have jurisdiction as the Australian seller is based there and the Indian courts would probably also have jurisdiction over any claims against the Indian manufacturer. To avoid potential conflicts between courts (which will make any litigation extremely long and expensive) it is therefore sensible to include a jurisdiction clause in which the parties agree, in advance of any dispute, which country's court will have jurisdiction.

In practice, where there are several courts which may have jurisdiction, it is for the claimant to choose where he wants to bring his claim. However, in some countries the defendant may have the option of persuading the court chosen by the claimant that it would be more appropriate for the action to be tried in the other country. However, where the choice is between different courts within most of Europe, once the action has been validly commenced in one jurisdiction, the defendant cannot argue that the action should have been brought in a different European court and the action will therefore proceed in that jurisdiction.

In relation to jurisdiction as between EU states the 1968 Brussels Convention on Jurisdiction and the Enforcement of Judgments in Civil and Commercial Matters, which has been ratified by all the EU Member States, determines which EU courts have jurisdiction as between each other. The Brussels Convention has effectively been extended to the EFTA countries (Iceland, Norway, Switzerland) and Poland by the Lugano Convention which regulates, amongst other things, jurisdiction as between Brussels and Lugano Convention contracting states. As from 1 March 2002, however, the Brussels Convention will be replaced in all Member States, except Denmark by

Council Regulation 44/2001 (known as the "Brussels Regulation") and from that date all three regimes will be running in parallel; the Brussels Regulation in all Member States except Denmark; the Brussels Convention in Denmark; and the Lugano Convention in Iceland, Norway, Switzerland and Poland. The Brussels Convention and the Brussels Regulation are deal with in more detail below.

3.   Governing law

The law that a court applies to decide a dispute is generally referred to as the "governing law" or the "applicable law". It is not always the case that a court will apply its own national or state laws. Parties can specify in their contracts which law they wish to be the governing law, and that choice will generally be upheld by the courts of most countries. For example, an English court may decide that it has jurisdiction to hear a dispute, but that the parties have stipulated that the governing law of their contract is French law. In such a case, the parties would have to produce evidence (supported by appropriate experts or otherwise agreed) as to the applicable French law, which would then be applied by the English court in reaching its decision. Each country has particular rules, called "choice of law rules", for determining the applicable law in any particular case if not agreed between the parties.

Within the EU Member States, the rules for determining the governing law in relation to contracts are set out in the 1980 Rome Convention on the Law Applicable to Contractual Obligations. The Rome Convention is dealt with in more detail below.

4.   Enforcement of a judgment

The third important element is the enforcement of judgments. In most cases, the losing party will comply with the court's judgment, but if he refuses to do so the winning party will need to take measures to enforce the judgment, such as seizing the loser's assets. If the loser has no assets in the country where the judgment was given, the winner will need to get the judgment enforced in the country where the loser does have assets. For example, a claimant may sue a US company in the English courts and may even win. However, if the US company has no assets in England, the successful claimant may then need to have the judgment enforced in the United States by asking the relevant US court to recognise and enforce the English court's decision. Whether the US court will do so is a matter to be determined by the law of the US state in question. In many countries, the enforcement of foreign judgments will depend on whether the enforcing court and the original court are from countries which have signed a treaty.

The enforcement of judgments abroad takes time and expense, and where there is no applicable international convention (note: there is presently none between England and the US) there can be no certainty that the judgment will be enforceable abroad. It is, therefore, important for claimants to consider the issue of enforcement before deciding where to commence proceedings.

5. **Brussels and Lugano Conventions and Brussels Regulation**

The texts of the Brussels Convention, the Lugano Convention and the Brussels Regulation are in general terms very similar, but there are some important differences of detail the most important of which are discussed below.

The basic principle in all three regimes is that, a defendant who is domiciled in one of the countries to which these regimes apply must be sued in the courts of that country, regardless of the defendant's nationality. This is known as the "domicile rule". Each country applies its own law to determine whether an individual is domiciled in that country. In the United Kingdom, an individual will be regarded as being domiciled in the United Kingdom if he is resident in the United Kingdom and the nature and circumstances of his residence indicate that he has a substantial connection with the United Kingdom (*e.g.* has resided there for at least three months). A company will generally be deemed to be domiciled in the country in which it was incorporated and/or has its registered office or some other official address, or its central management and control. From 1 March 2002, a company will also be deemed to be domiciled at the place where it has its principal place of business.

By way of exception to the basic principle referred to above, the defendant may also be sued in the courts of other countries covered by these regimes if one of the exceptions applies. For example, the parties can agree that a particular court will have jurisdiction by entering into a jurisdiction clause, and that court will generally have exclusive jurisdiction unless the parties have agreed otherwise. There are also special rules for consumers and insurance matters, and for cases in which there is more than one defendant. Finally, there are mandatory rules of jurisdiction in certain cases – for instance, a dispute concerning land can generally only be heard by the court for the place where the land is situated.

There are four exceptions to the general domicile rule which may be relevant to the operation of a commercial website:

(1) where the parties agree (in a jurisdiction clause) that a court of an EU/EFTA country or Poland will have jurisdiction;

(2) in relation to business to business contracts (i) in contractual disputes, where the courts for the "place of performance of the obligation in question" will have jurisdiction; and (ii) in disputes in tort, where the courts for the "place where the harmful event occurred" will have jurisdiction; and

(3) in business to consumer contracts, where the courts for the place where the *consumer* is domiciled will have jurisdiction provided certain conditions apply.

Jurisdiction clauses

A jurisdiction clause, in the contract, enables the parties to agree that any disputes will be resolved by their chosen court. It is always sensible to include a contractual jurisdiction clause, specifying that the courts of a particular country will have jurisdiction. Unless the parties specify otherwise, such a clause will also operate to deny jurisdiction to other countries' courts governed by the Brussels/Lugano Convention or the Brussels Regulation, and this gives the parties certainty as to where any action arising out of the contract will be heard. An e-tailer should note, however, that jurisdiction clauses in the contract will not necessarily bind consumers.

Where there is no jurisdiction clause

Business-to-business contracts

What if there is no contractual jurisdiction clause?

In non-consumer, business-to-business contracts, a defendant who is domiciled in one state may be sued for breach of contract in a second state if that second state is the place of performance of the contractual obligation in question. Alternatively, the defendant may be sued in tort in the second state if he has caused harm to the claimant in that second state. So, for example, if a website operated by an English company transacts with a Spanish company via the Internet, the English courts would have jurisdiction to hear a claim against the English company since the English company is domiciled in England. However, the Spanish courts may also have jurisdiction to hear the claim if the English company agreed to deliver goods or services to the Spanish company in Spain and failed to do so, or if the goods were faulty and caused damage to the Spanish company and the harmful event in question occurred in Spain.

If, on the other hand, the English web trader sues the Spanish company for failing to pay for the goods, the English web trader can either sue the Spanish company in the Spanish courts, as the courts of the country where the defendant is domiciled, or alternatively the English web trader can bring the claim in the courts for the place where payment should have been made, which will probably give the English courts jurisdiction. However, it can often be unclear where a particular obligation is to be performed. If the parties fail to include a jurisdiction clause in their contract, they should at least state where the place of performance will be.

The Brussels Regulation has attempted to clarify the case law on this point by fixing the place of performance in relation to contracts for the sale of goods and the provision of services, unless the place of performance has otherwise been agreed by the parties. In the case of the former the place of performance is "the place in a Member State where, under the contract, the goods were delivered or should have been delivered". For the latter, it is "the place in a Member State where, under the contract, the services were provided or should have been provided". It will have to be seen whether these additional words simplify or complicate this rather difficult issue.

Business-to-consumer contracts

As regards consumer contracts, provided certain pre-conditions are met, the consumer has an option of bringing an action against the seller either in the country of his own domicile, or in the country of the seller's domicile. So, to go back to our example, if the English web trader had contracted with a Spanish consumer rather than a Spanish company and the pre-conditions had been met, the Spanish consumer would always have the option of bringing an action against the English web trader in the Spanish courts rather than in the England. Moreover, if the English web trader wished to sue the Spanish consumer for non-payment, he would have to do so in the Spanish courts, and no other courts within the European Union would have jurisdiction. It is important to note that a jurisdiction clause will generally be invalid if it seeks to prevent the consumer from suing or being sued in the courts of his own domicile.

As stated above, there are certain pre-conditions for the application of these consumer contract rules. Under the Brussels and Lugano Conventions, for the rules as to consumers to apply the contract must have been preceded by a specific invitation addressed to the consumer in his own country and the consumer must have taken, in that country, the steps necessary for the conclusion of the contract. However, the Brussels Regulation elaborates on the circumstances in which consumers may sue and must be sued in their country of domicile. Under the Brussels Regulation, these rules will apply wherever the other party "by any means, directs its activities to the country of the consumer's domicile and the contract falls within the scope of such activities".

It follows that, under the Brussels Convention rules, a passive consumer – one who takes no action until an invitation targets him – has the right to sue and be sued in his country of domicile. On the other hand, an active consumer, who seeks out the goods or services of the foreign trader, will not have the right to sue and be sued in his own courts because he will not have received a specific invitation addressed to him from the seller. Under the Brussels Regulation, however, which comes into effect on 1 March 2002, it would appear that any consumer in a particular Member State will be able to take advantage of the consumer rules if the foreign trader has "directed" its activities to that Member State.

E-commerce in goods or services accessible in a Member State is deemed to be "an activity directed to that state". Many websites, of course, could be said to be accessible in every country and the concern expressed by business organisations is that e-commerce will be hindered as e-tailers face the risk of being sued in any number of foreign jurisdictions where their potential customers live. In an explanatory note to the Brussels Regulation, the European Commission and Council have indicated that the simple fact that an Internet site is accessible is not sufficient for this section to apply and nor will the language and currency used alone be sufficient for determining whether the activity is "directed". Instead, a website will be deemed to be directed at a state if it solicits the conclusion of distance contracts from within that state.

The impact of the Brussels Regulation will largely depend on the courts' interpretation of the phrase "directing its activities", but it does appear likely that consumers will generally be able to sue European e-businesses from their home countries by taking advantage of the rules of the Brussels Regulation. E-tailers should try to minimise the risk of being sued in unexpected and unwanted jurisdictions by taking the practical steps listed later in this chapter.

6. **Rome Convention 1980**

The purpose of the Rome Convention was to harmonise the choice of law rules on the governing law of contracts within the Member States of the European Union. Unlike the Brussels Regulation and its related legislation, which (with some exceptions) apply only where the defendant is domiciled in one of the European states involved, the Rome Convention is to be applied by the courts of Member States in all circumstances, even if the parties to the dispute and the applicable law have no connection with Europe. All that is required for the Rome Convention to apply is for the dispute to be heard in the courts of a Member State.

Three main principles are enshrined in the Rome Convention.

(1) The Rome Convention gives the parties to a contract the freedom to choose the applicable law, either expressly or demonstrably. If the parties have expressly agreed upon a particular governing law in their contract, that choice will be binding. The choice may also be demonstrated with reasonable certainty by the terms of the contract or the circumstances of the case. The parties may demonstrate their choice of law without making an express choice in the following ways:

- a previous course of dealing between the same parties, using contracts containing an express choice of law clause;
- an express choice of law clause in related transactions between the same parties; or
- the choice of a particular forum if the circumstances suggest that they intended the contract to be governed by that forum's system of law.

(2) If the parties do not expressly choose the governing law, the contract will be governed by the law of the country with which it is "most closely connected". The Rome Convention states that this is presumed to be the country of habitual residence or central administration of the party which is to effect the performance

which is characteristic of the contract in question. For example, in a contract for the sale of goods, the characteristic performance is done by the seller who delivers the goods. The law of the seller's country of residence or administration will apply, in the absence of an express choice of law clause. This may have little or nothing to do with the country from which the goods were physically sent. It follows that if the seller (in common with some Internet businesses) sets up its business in a tax haven, the laws of the tax haven would apply. The presumption outlined above can be rebutted in certain circumstances.

(3) Having determined the governing law of the contract, however, the third principle under the Rome Convention is that there are some circumstances in which the first two principles will be displaced, in relation to mandatory rules and consumer contracts. If, for instance, all other elements relating to the contract are connected with England but the parties have chosen Latvian law to be the governing law, the parties' choice of Latvian law will be applied to interpret the contract, but the parties will not be permitted to avoid the application of any of the mandatory laws of English law which would otherwise apply. Mandatory laws continue to apply despite the choice of governing law.

Mandatory laws are particularly important in the area of consumer protection. Examples of such mandatory laws in the United Kingdom are the Unfair Contract Terms Act 1977 and the Consumer Protection (Distance Selling) Regulations 2000 which are discussed elsewhere in this book. Where a seller has approached a foreign consumer, the parties may not choose a governing law which would deprive the consumer of mandatory consumer protection laws in the country of his habitual residence in the following circumstances:

- where the conclusion of the contract was preceded by a specific invitation from the seller to the consumer;
- where the seller advertised in the country in which the consumer was habitually resident;
- where the seller received the consumer's order in the country in which the consumer was habitually resident; or
- where the contract is for a sale of goods and the buyer travelled from the country of his habitual residence to another country to make his order, and the seller arranged his journey with the intention of inducing him to enter into the contract.

Business conducted over the Internet is likely to fall within the first two circumstances. An online business would be wise to be aware of mandatory laws in the countries at which its goods or services are targeted. However, there are some ways to reduce the risk of foreign law or jurisdiction applying, which are listed at the end of this chapter.

7. **Outside the European Community**

Jurisdictional risk

If an e-tailer plans to target countries outside Europe, then it is essential to take legal advice in those countries.

Of particular interest and concern to many companies is the jurisdictional reach of the United States, given the size of their Internet consumer market. Courts in the United States tend to apply a "sliding scale" of activity in order to determine whether they can assert jurisdiction. At one end of the scale there is the passive website, akin to a newspaper or magazine advertisement published world-wide. There is nothing for a user to do but to read the information on the website. On the whole, websites such as these do not fall within the reach of the US courts' jurisdiction since no intention to contract is demonstrated in such websites. At the other end of the scale, there are websites which actively solicit and transact business with US residents over the Internet. Such sites have commonly become subject to the jurisdiction of the US courts.

There is then a middle area between the above two extremes, within which those websites that have some interactive elements fall. Whether a court will take jurisdiction in relation to such websites depends on the level of such interactivity. However, the threshold varies from court to court, state to state, with some courts asserting jurisdiction following a very low level of user interactivity and some only where there is a very high level. The question is generally whether there is a "website plus something more". That "something more" has included:

- offline marketing;
- toll free telephone numbers (accessible from any US state);
- a certain number of "hits" on the website from the plaintiff's state;
- a certain number of persons from the plaintiff's state on the defendant's mailing list;
- sales to persons in the plaintiff's state;

- the ability to send e-mails to the defendant's business; and
- a particular domain name.

E-tailers who operate business-to-consumer websites should assume that there is a high risk of becoming subject to non-EU jurisdictions unless they have taken measures to prevent advertising or sales from being directed to consumers in such countries. Only local law advice can determine how effective a jurisdiction clause or other measures can be to prevent foreign courts from asserting jurisdiction.

8. Practical considerations

The majority of transactions in business-to-consumer websites will be of a low value, and in many cases the value will be too low to justify the cost of litigation by the consumer. However, it is important to remember that consumer protection bodies often bring cases on behalf of consumers, and it is therefore important to consider these issues carefully, even in relation to small value transactions. Plans are afoot in the EU to try to address the expense of consumer litigation through the courts by the setting up of special "ADR" (alternative dispute resolution) units in the Member States which are specifically designed to deal with low value international consumer disputes. Purchasers will be more inclined to sue if the value of the goods or services purchased is high enough to make the cost of litigation worthwhile, and this is more likely to be the case in business-to-business transactions.

There are certain practical steps or considerations which may reduce the risk of an unwanted choice of law or jurisdiction being applied.

(1) An e-tailer should analyse its target markets and design its website accordingly. There is often no real commercial need for the majority of websites to be targeted to a generic worldwide audience. Careful website design so as to isolate certain target countries will reduce the possibility of unwanted choices of law and jurisdiction being applied. It is wise to take local law advice in all the target markets so as to check the application of local law to the goods and services being offered.

(2) E-tailers should include jurisdiction and choice of law clauses in their online contracts. It is important to ensure these terms are validly incorporated into the contract with the customer (see Chapter 2 on Online Contracts).

(3) It can be useful to specify in which country specific obligations in online contracts are to be performed, since the courts for the place where the obligation in question is performed will have jurisdiction in the event that a dispute arises in connection with that performance.

(4) E-tailers should be aware that advertising and marketing, both online and offline, may expose them to jurisdictional risk by eroding any claim that their website is not actively directed at a particular country. Offline activities, such as the provision of free telephone numbers or sending promotional material to persons in non-targeted countries, may provide grounds for a court to assert jurisdiction in those countries.

(5) Websites can be designed to include disclaimers or statements that indicate certain countries from which customers are permitted to make orders and send payments. Such statements are especially important in areas such as financial services. The Securities Exchange Commission (SEC) in the United States, for example, provides an opt-out option to foreign securities issuers, brokers and exchanges to prevent sales or services being offered to US citizens. In order to avoid the SEC's jurisdiction, non-US websites must clearly indicate that such sales and services are not available to US persons. In the United Kingdom, the Financial Services Authority has insisted on much the same provisions are regards US mutual fund company websites. Similar opt outs can also provide a solution for other regulated services, such as legal or pharmaceutical websites.

(6) Terms and conditions for use of the site may ask the user to select a choice of venue. Alternatively, when users register to use the website, they may be required to select their country of residence. If a non-target country is selected, or their country of residence is not included, then users can be prevented from going further.

(7) If the aim is to target a number of countries, one expensive option is to set up separate websites for each of those countries in the local language, complying with local laws and regulations. This can also be done at the stage when a consumer attempts to purchase goods online, by directing the consumer to his national website from the master website. A cheaper alternative would be to include different terms and conditions for a contract depending on the target market.

(8) In the event of a dispute, it may be appropriate to offer the customer some contractual alternative to litigation, such as a type of non-binding alternative dispute resolution or binding online arbitration. Alternative dispute resolution may take many forms such as mediation schemes, voluntary codes of practice, ombudsman schemes, consumer group schemes or early neutral evaluation mechanisms. Providing an efficient dispute resolution mechanism will help to minimise the risk of costly litigation. However, such arrangements need to be designed with care, and it is important to ensure that the mechanism in question does not breach any mandatory rules, for instance where consumers are involved. As noted above, such mechanisms may soon be mandated at the European level, in any event.

(9) It is important to check that the e-tailer's business insurance covers legal disputes in overseas jurisdictions.

(10) It is wise to monitor the users of a website from time to time, in order to make sure that people in non-target markets are not gaining access to the website inadvertently.

9. **The Yahoo! case**

The *Yahoo!* case (January 2001) is an example of the potential risk in the matters of governing law and jurisdiction for any business which operates online (and reminds us of the risk of liability for content distributed online). In this ruling in January 2001, a Paris court found against Yahoo! Inc (an American company) for breaching a French law banning the sale of Nazi memorabilia in France.

Yahoo! was fined for allowing access to an auction of Nazi memorabilia on its US website, Yahoo.com, even though Yahoo! had ensured that such access was barred on its French language site. The problem was that French citizens could access the auction website via a link on the French language site to the US site. This US site was legal in the United States, but it gave rise to a criminal offence under French law. Two French human rights groups, the Union of French Jewish Students and the League Against Racism and Anti-Semitism sued Yahoo! in the French courts.

Yahoo! argued that the French courts had no jurisdiction to hear the dispute, as the activities took place in the United States. However, the

French court ruled that it had jurisdiction because the display of such memorabilia contravened French law and damage was suffered in France. Yahoo! was found guilty of contravening the French law concerning the sale of Nazi memorabilia. It was ordered to set up a filtering system to prevent French users from entering the auction website, and to post a warning on the French language Yahoo! France website that it is a criminal offence under French law to access the US auction website.

At the date of writing, Yahoo! has filed a counter-suit in a California court on grounds that a French court should not be able to impose its national laws on a US company. Yahoo! contests the ruling on two grounds: first, that it is technically impossible to block access using filtering systems and, secondly, that the French court has overstepped its jurisdictional bounds.

This case has been a significant one for jurisdictional purposes. It shows how far national courts can be prepared to go to assert jurisdiction – in this case, the fact that there was a link to Yahoo.com was sufficient to constitute a breach of French law and give the French courts jurisdiction. Furthermore, if this approach is to be adopted by other countries' courts, it raises the question of whether a website's content must comply not only with the laws of the country of where its servers are held, but also with the laws of all countries from which its content can be accessed, even indirectly. If so, Internet content could in theory be determined by the laws of the most stringent countries. The result in practice, however, might simply be that websites would choose to boycott such countries because of their stringent laws.

10. **Summary**

- Several courts may potentially have jurisdiction if a dispute arises out of or in connection with a website. It is, therefore, important for e-tailers to include jurisdiction clauses in their online contracts.

- Unless otherwise stated, an online contract may well be governed by a unfamiliar foreign law. It is, therefore, also important for e-tailers to specify the governing law of their online contracts.

- E-tailers should be aware that, at least within Europe, consumers may have rights to sue and be sued in their home courts. E-tailers should design their websites to reduce the risk of having to conduct litigation in unfavourable jurisdictions.

- In the light of the *Yahoo!* case, it is important to remember that potential risk can be generated by the content of a website or its links.

- E-tailers should audit their websites in relation to jurisdiction and governing law issues, in order to ensure that they have no potential surprises when disputes arise!

Chapter 5

· Electronic Money ·

1. Introduction

The combination of advances in technology and e-commerce have given rise to a new type of payment system. "Digital cash", "electronic money", "e-cash" - these terms are often used to describe these innovative new forms. Although none of the forms of electronic money are legal tender as yet and therefore retailers and e-tailers are not obliged to accept them, the European Commission has enacted directives, which this chapter will discuss, to ensure that the creation of such electronic forms of money are regulated. This will help to inspire consumer confidence, which through market forces, will ensure more and more retailers and e-tailers consider accepting such forms of electronic money in their day-to-day business.

2. Electronic money and the Internet

With consumer fears of online fraud, there is certainly a market for e-tailers wishing to provide a safe and secure method of payment for goods and services purchased via the Internet. Fear of credit card fraud is one of the main reasons consumers are reluctant to shop online.

Traditional methods of payment such as credit and debit cards are also problematic given the nature of many popular Internet purchases. Many goods purchased over the Internet are of a small amount (for example, a book or a CD) and some consumers may not feel comfortable with the risk of fraud by placing their credit and debit card details with an e-tailer for such a small amount.

Increasing use of the Internet has also led to increasing spending of low value micropayments. A micropayment is payment of which the value exchanged is very small. In the real world, coins will suffice but in the virtual world, micropayments are small enough to have the effect of making it less worthwhile for an e-tailer to use a credit or debit card payment system.

The spending of low value micropayments is expected to increase, as the Internet and the potential for e-commerce crosses over into digital television and mobile telephony ("t-commerce" and "m-commerce"). Micropayments are particularly evident in pay-per-use products and services, online articles and songs, pay-per-play games, and "one day passes" for monthly subscription sites. For micropayments to become truly practical, innovative new methods for collecting payments through computers, digital television set top boxes and mobile phones will have to be developed.

From the consumer's perspective, fear of online fraud with credit cards and debit cards may dissuade them from shopping online. There are also certain e-commerce markets which are not adequately serviced by the traditional payment systems. For example, people under a certain age cannot hold credit cards or debit cards, and there are those who do not have bank accounts. Privacy issues are also a consideration for the consumer, who may not wish to input their personal details on a computer.

It is the e-tailers who take the risk in allowing consumers to use their credit cards online to purchase goods or services, as the e-tailer cannot confirm the transaction by a signed credit card receipt. Credit card issuers may also impose charge backs on the e-tailers in cases of fraud – recovering the money whilst the e-tailer loses both the money and the goods he has delivered. E-tailers also face a greater cost than their high street counterparts in using credit cards online – administration fees can be twice as high making small value transactions more and more expensive for an e-tailer to process. For this reason, many e-tailers impose minimum order terms on their customers. Electronic money systems may therefore provide an attractive alternative to both e-tailers and consumers.

3. **Terminology**

There are a large variety of terms to describe electronic-based payment systems. Essentially, they are all electronic substitutes for cash. Unlike credit or debit cards, there is not necessarily a third party intermediary. A consumer purchases goods from an e-tailer, paying via a particular new method, and the "cash" is transferred immediately to the e-tailer.

Today, cash, cheques, credit and debit cards are used in parallel. A similar development may occur in the area of electronic money, with different forms jostling to dominate the marketplace. At the moment, however, there are two main forms of the electronic money system.

Software-based virtual cash

The first form is purely software-based, a virtual form of cash. It is not card-based but rather created and spent exclusively online. Software from e-tailers offering this service is downloaded onto personal computers. Value is then added from credit cards registered at the e-tailer's website. The value is "stored" in the software, and spent when purchases are made online. Users will have an online account through which they can check the amounts collected.

A popular form of the software-based system is a "wallet" offered by an online issuer. The user downloads software from the website, opens an online "wallet" and adds value to it via their credit card. When purchases are made online, the amount is automatically deducted from the "wallet". Purchases can only be made at e-tailers associated with the online "wallet" issuer, and many of the products and services tend to be online music or content which is downloaded after the purchase is made. The value in the "wallet" can be topped up by the user, usually up to a maximum amount. Because only certain e-tailers are associated with the "wallet" issuer, use of the "wallet" is limited.

Another form of software-based virtual cash are tokens. These, in essence, are loyalty points earned online which can then be "spent" at participating online business. The "points" are earned when shopping online, taking part in surveys, even visiting a website. The "points" are added to an online account from which the subscriber may then spend on goods available at other websites displaying an icon or payment scheme logo to evidence their affiliation to the e-tailer providing the online points system. The e-tailer makes its profits from its affiliated businesses.

This type of token has no value in the real world, is not backed by any currency and is unlikely to raise any regulatory issues. Subscribers can include children and teenagers, who would normally not have credit cards and debit cards.

E-tailers providing this token loyalty points system may also branch into the real world with smartcards which store the amount of the "points" as the equivalent of cash. Such smartcards are not credit cards, and a subscriber with a smartcard cannot ask a bank or the originator e-tailer to redeem the "points" as cash. These smartcards are of low value and enable the subscriber to pay for small cash purchases (*e.g.* groceries, petrol, vending machines).

Smartcards

Another form commonly seen is the stored value smartcard. This is not the same type of system as a prepaid single purpose card, such as a phone card. The former can be used at a variety of businesses, whereas the latter pays for a particular service exclusively, normally the service of the card's issuer.

The vital part of the smartcard is its microchip. The value is stored on a chip embedded in the smartcard, the chip replacing the functionality of black magnetic card stripes of credit and debit cards. The chip contains a "purse", in which value is held electronically. This may even include a variety of different currencies at any one time.

Smartcards are "loaded" with the value of money in a variety of ways. Compatible telephones or cash machines download the value from bank accounts. There are mobile phones which do the same with smartcards in the mobile phones (SIM cards), and which are then spent on products ordered via the mobile phone. Some digital television set top boxes and personal computers are being designed with smartcard readers. This will allow the smartcard to be used online as well as in the real world.

The chip will also contain the security programs to protect the transaction. The benefits of using a microchip are already being seen more often with traditional credit and debit cards, as the chip provides a greater level of security and far more associated information about the user than the black strip.

The electronic money is transferred directly between the customer's smartcard and the merchant's smartcard reader in the real world, or through card readers already set up on personal computers and digital television set top boxes to enable shopping online.

In another method, the merchant's card reader deducts the relevant amount but then "sends" this information to the originating company for settlement, in a manner similar to a credit card or debit card.

4.   **European Union developments**

Before the enactment of the directives discussed below, there was no legislation in the United Kingdom to allow for non-bank and non-credit

institutions to establish and issue electronic money. Compliance with
banking legislation such as the Banking Act 1987 would have been
cumbersome. For a while, only banks and credit institutions already
compliant with financial regulations were issuing smartcards. The
establishment of a European regime will help to promote consumer
confidence in those electronic money institutions which are not
regulated as banks or credit institutions. Financial integrity and
stability of the electronic money institutions under a regulatory system
would help to promote e-commerce as well.

Two directives (Directive 2000/46/EC and Directive 2000/28/EC)
were adopted by the European Commission to regulate and supervise
electronic money institutions ("EMIs"). The directives were adopted on
18 September 2000 and Member States are obliged to enact national
laws to comply with the directives by 27 April 2002.

They are based on the existing supervisory regime applicable to
credit institutions, but with certain amendments to adapt to the new
form of electronic money. It is Directive 2000/46/EC (the text of which
is included as Appendix 2) on the taking up, pursuit of and supervision
of the business of electronic money institutions which is the primary
piece of European guidance on this subject (the "EMI Directive"). The
EMI Directive is "technologically neutral" which means that
irrespective of the technology used if an EMI issues electronic money it
will be subject to the provisions of the directive.

Electronic money institutions

Under the EMI Directive, an electronic money institution means an
undertaking or other legal person, other than a credit institution as
defined in Directive 2000/12/EC, which issues means of payment in the
form of electronic money. A credit institution is one whose business it is
to receive deposits or other repayable funds from the public and to
grant credits for its own account, *i.e.* banks and deposit-taking or
credit-offering financial institutions. Such institutions are already
supervised by existing legislation so, should they issue electronic money,
they will not be governed by either of the Electronic Money Directives.

An EMI will be treated in some ways like a credit institution. This
will allow EMIs to benefit from the "single passport principle", which
was established to facilitate a single market for financial services in
the European Community. This principle will allow EMIs, having
obtained a licence in their home Member States, to conduct business

in other Member States and they need only comply with the regulations of their home Member State. However, the single passport will not apply to issuers who are recipients of a waiver under the EMI Directive (see below). An EMI will also, like a credit institution, be subject to money laundering requirements such as the UK Money Laundering Regulations.

Apart from not being able to grant credit, another distinction between an EMI and a credit institution or bank is that an EMI does not receive deposits within the meaning of the laws regulating deposit-taking which, otherwise, would require the EMI to be licensed as an authorised institution. Article 2 of the EMI Directive makes clear that the receipt of funds by an EMI does not constitute a deposit for such purposes if such funds received are immediately exchanged for electronic money.

This is important clarification, as under existing UK legislation, there is an arguable case that the EMI would be accepting a deposit for the purposes of the Banking Act 1987. Deposit-taking is widely drafted in the existing UK legislation. The Banking Act 1987 in section 5 defines a deposit as a sum of money paid on terms under which it will be repaid, with or without interest or a premium and either on demand or at a time or in circumstances agreed. Under section 3 of the Banking Act an institution cannot accept deposits in the United Kingdom in the course of a deposit-taking business unless they are authorised to do so – a breach of this provision is a criminal offence. An exception to the definition of "deposit" are sums of money referable to the provision of property, services or given as security. So, the purchase of a smartcard may perhaps be viewed as purchase of a service, but this is not clear. Thankfully for potential EMIs, the EMI Directive makes clear that they will not be accepting deposits if the funds received are immediately exchanged for electronic money. Guidance will, however, be necessary in the future over what constitutes "immediately".

Electronic money

Electronic money is described by the European Parliament as an electronic surrogate for coins and banknotes, which is stored on an electronic device such as a chip card or computer memory and which is generally intended for the purpose of effecting electronic payments of limited amounts. It is defined by the EMI Directive as monetary value represented by a claim on the issuer which is:

- stored on an electronic device;
- issued on receipt of funds of an amount not less in value than the monetary value issued; and
- accepted as means of payment by undertakings other than the issuer.

Original drafts of the EMI Directive contained two examples of "electronic devices": a chip card or the computer memory. Subsequently, however, these examples were dropped in favour of technological neutrality enabling the EMI Directive to meet new technological developments. At the moment, however, it is software-based electronic money and smartcards which are most likely to be used by e-tailers who wish to become EMIs.

It is significant to note in the definition of electronic money that the electronic money must not be in an amount which is more in value than the funds actually received by the issuer. Furthermore, the electronic money must be accepted by third parties and not merely the issuer. In fact, the EMI Directive only applies where a third party is involved (*i.e.* someone other than the issuer). The issuer may often be the sole recipient - this may occur frequently – universities, theme parks or large corporations which may issue smartcards to their students, visitors or employees which can only be used on goods and services provided by those institutions.

Article 3 of the EMI Directive provides that a bearer of electronic money may, during the period of its validity, ask the issuing EMI to redeem it in coins and bank notes, or by a transfer to an account free of charges other than those strictly necessary to carry out that operation. Again, this is intended to incentivise consumers to use electronic money, as they would hesitate to do so where there were commission charges for processing electronic money. This lack of charges may result in electronic money becoming more popular than credit cards, where commissions can be charged.

Under Article 3, the contract between the issuing EMI and the bearer must state clearly the conditions of redemption, such as a minimum amount. Such contractual obligations must also meet requirements of consumer protection laws.

Regulatory regime

Like credit institutions and banks, EMIs will be required to obtain a licence in order to operate. In the United Kingdom, the national regulatory authority granting the licence and regulating the activities of EMIs will be the Financial Services Authority.

A number of restrictions have been placed on EMIs in the EMI Directive. First, they can provide closely related financial and non-financial services (such as administration), but cannot grant credit. They are also prevented from holding any interests in other undertakings, unless those undertakings perform operational or ancillary functions closely related to the business of issuing electronic money.

As an EMI cannot grant credit, what is the status of an electronic cheque under the EMI Directive – does it qualify as electronic money? An electronic cheque contains the same information in electronic format as a tangible paper cheque, but is digitally or electronically signed and transmitted to the payee. However, because an electronic cheque, like a paper cheque, can be drawn on credit (over someone's overdraft), it would seem that this is excluded from the EMI Directive.

Another restriction is on investments an EMI can make, as they can only invest in highly liquid, low risk assets. This is to ensure they have enough liquidity to meet their commitments. Again, this should help promote consumer confidence in the product.

Furthermore, the EMI must meet capital requirements of EUR 1 million, to ensure financial stability and consumer confidence. This is a far lesser amount than banks need to provide (EUR 5 million). In original drafts of the EMI Directive, the initial capital was only EUR 500,000 but as this was arguably not enough to ensure the financial standing of the EMI the amount was increased.

Ongoing capital requirements are more favourable to EMIs than to banks. EMIs must at all times hold own funds which are equal to or above 2% of the higher of the current amount or the average of the preceding six months' total amount of their financial liabilities related to outstanding electronic money. It is unclear what "financial liabilities related to outstanding electronic money" actually entails but it may be the amount not yet redeemed. No guidance is provided by the EMI Directive. If the EMI has not completed six months of business, it must hold own funds equal to or above 2% of the higher of the current amount or the six months' target total amount of its financial liabilities related to outstanding electronic money. The business plan will indicate the six months' target total and the national regulatory authority may well require amendments to that business plan. The 2% minimum is lower than that required of ordinary banks, and it is hoped that this will encourage and facilitate a larger number of participants in the electronic money business.

Sound and prudent operation of the EMI is essential to ensure consumer confidence. Under Article 7, EMIs must manage their business properly through administrative and accounting procedures and adequate internal control mechanisms. The wording in this particular article is widely drafted, as Member States will already have financial legislation ensuring companies and institutions abide by certain accounting and administrative procedures.

Compliance with the provisions of the EMI Directive (and later the national law once implemented) on initial capital, ongoing own funds and investment limitations is left to national regulatory authorities.

EMIs who are already established before the coming into force of national rules of a Member State will be treated as authorised (this is known as "grandfathering"). However, to avoid a potential problem of EMIs being established before national laws are harmonised in order to exploit the legislative vacuum in some way, such firms will have to submit relevant information to the relevant national regulatory authority to demonstrate compliance with the EMI Directive. These EMIs will have six months from the date national legislation is enacted to do so. The Financial Services Authority in the United Kingdom and national authorities in other Member States will then assess whether those EMIs have complied with the national law.

Exemptions

If a bank authorised to accept deposits under legislation implemented pursuant to Directive 2000/12/EC wished to become an electronic money issuer, it would be regulated by Directive 2000/12/EC. This is a different regulatory regime from the EMI regime described above, and may create an uneven playing field which may affect competition in the market. However, the EMI Directive argues the opposite, that the less cumbersome features of the EMI regulatory regime are balanced by the fact that their business activities are limited, and especially that the EMIs investments are limited as well. The limitation on the investments of an EMI (as set out in Article 5 of the EMI Directive) are required in order to ensure that all outstanding electronic money is backed at all times by sufficiently liquid, low risk, assets.

Under Article 8 Member States may waive some or all provisions of the EMI Directive in respect of certain EMIs who fall under certain exceptions, for example, if the scale of business is relatively small or if they are located in a limited local area. Once waived, the single passport principle will not apply to these particular EMIs. The financial threshold for small EMIs is set at a total of financial liabilities relating to outstanding electronic money (non-redeemed) which does not normally exceed EUR 5 million and never exceeds EUR 6 million.

5. **Summary**

- In practice, it is e-tailers who carry the risk of credit card fraud, through charge-backs imposed by credit card companies and higher costs for using credit card payment systems online.

- Electronic money is an electronic surrogate for cash, and is normally stored on a chip card or computer memory.

- The EMI Directive will be technologically neutral to allow for future advancements in electronic money to fall under its ambit.

- EMIs must be authorised and licensed by their national regulatory authorities. Once licensed by their Member State, the "single passport" principle will apply and EMIs can operate in other Member States.

- An EMI cannot grant credit and is deemed to not be accepting a deposit.

Chapter 6

· E-Commerce Directive ·

1. Introduction

The preamble to the E-Commerce Directive (Directive 2000/31/EC – the text of which is reproduced in Appendix 1) makes it clear that e-commerce, in the eyes of the European Parliament and Council of the European Union, will be at the forefront of future economic and social development in the EU. The very first recital states that "the development of information society services within the area without internal frontiers is vital to eliminating the barriers which divide the European peoples". This chapter will look at the main provisions of the E-Commerce Directive and its likely impact on the United Kingdom.

2. Background

The E-Commerce Directive was formally adopted by the European Parliament on 4 May 2000. The version of the Directive agreed by the Council of Ministers on 28 February 2000 as its common position was approved without amendment. The Directive will now be implemented by Member States as part of each state's national law. Implementation must take place within 18 months following the publication of the Directive in the *Official Journal of the European Communities* on 17 July 2000, *i.e.* by 16 January 2002. Its significance is possibly demonstrated by the rapidity with which it was passed. The fact that the E-Commerce Directive was quickly approved by the European Parliament without amendment (which is extremely rare) shows the importance attached to the development of e-commerce within the European Union.

The main objectives of the E-Commerce Directive are:

- to enable the growth of e-commerce throughout Europe through the removal of barriers to the development of e-commerce in the European Union;

■ and to ensure that e-tailers and consumers alike benefit from the fundamental EU principles of freedom of movement, freedom of services and freedom of establishment.

The E-Commerce Directive aims to establish a legal framework for electronic transactions within the EU to ensure legal certainty and regulation of the provision of electronic services. However, it is worth noting that the scope of the E-Commerce Directive is intentionally limited to distinct areas, excluding significant issues such as data protection and taxation which are dealt with elsewhere in EC legislation (and in this book).

As with all EU directives, the E-Commerce Directive will have to be implemented by each Member State through domestic legislation. Elements of the E-Commerce Directive have already been implemented in the United Kingdom through the Electronic Communications Act 2000. The remaining elements of the E-Commerce Directive are likely to be implemented in the United Kingdom by way of changes to existing legislation rather than by introducing new legislation. The government has just issued a consultation paper dealing with implemention of the directive.

An analysis of the E-Commerce Directive has to deal with five main areas of interest:

(1) home state regulation;

(2) electronic contracts;

(3) identification of commercial communications;

(4 status of intermediaries; and

(5) dispute resolution.

3.   Home state regulation (the "country of origin" principle) – Article 3

The E-Commerce Directive states that online traders may provide services as long as they comply with the existing regulations of the Member State in which they are "established". The intention behind this provision of the E-Commerce Directive is a welcome one, since it seeks to ensure that operators are unable to evade supervision, whilst at the same time imposing only those laws with which the e-tailer will be familiar thereby introducing a greater degree of certainty.

Problems arise, however, in finding a suitable definition of what is meant by the term "established". The most useful definition to date of "place of establishment" is found in the ninth recital (as amended) which states that the place of establishment of an e-tailer is the place where the e-tailer has "the centre of his (the operator's) activities relating to this particular service." Yet even this is inadequate: multi-national institutions with branches in several Member States would have to decide the place of their establishment and this decision could be based on a number of criteria. For instance, a multi-national corporation may consider that it is established in the area with its largest customer base, or the place from which a particular service is operated. This, if it remains uncertain, leaves open the possibility of larger more multi-national companies being over regulated by the laws of several Member States all acting independently over the same issue. This would inevitably result in unfair disparity in practice, which would surely be contrary to the fundamental aims of the E-Commerce Directive.

There are a number of derogations from the country of origin principle. They include, for example, certain provisions of the Third Insurance Directives. It is understood that the principal reason for this is likely to be that the Third Insurance Directives already contain provisions regulating cross-border insurance transactions. However, a Commission Communication (adopted 2 February 2000) on the Commission's interpretation of the concept to provide services and the general good as applied to the insurance industry, states that a Green Paper will be produced to examine whether the existing provisions of the Third Insurance Directives provide a regulatory framework that is appropriate to the development of e-commerce in financial services.

Further derogations from the country of origin principle include contractual obligations concerning consumer contracts (that is, the private rules governing the contract), copyright, and the formal validity of contracts transferring real estate (presumably because the Member State in which the land is situated will want jurisdiction over transactions which affect the ownership of land in that jurisdiction, as the rules for validly transferred land vary from country to country). Whilst all the derogations are essentially logical in nature, expressly setting them out may avoid the risk of conflicting regulatory requirements.

4. **Electronic contracts – Articles 9-11**

Article 5 of the E-Commerce Directive states that the e-tailer must provide the following information in a way which is easily, directly and permanently accessible to the users of the service:

- the name of the e-tailer;
- the geographic address of the e-tailer;
- particulars of the e-tailer, including an e-mail address;
- details of any trade register in which the e-tailer is entered;
- where the service offered by the e-tailer is subject to an authorisation scheme, the particulars of the relevant supervisory authority;
- where the e-tailer is a member of a regulated profession details of the relevant professional body and a reference to the applicable professional rules; and
- whether prices quoted are inclusive of tax and delivery costs.

This section of the E-Commerce Directive has little in it that will create onerous obligations for e-tailers. Indeed, many of these information requirements also form part of the information requirements imposed on consumer facing traders by Directive 97/7/EC (the Distance Selling Directive) which deals with the protection of consumers in respect of distance contracts (now implemented by the Consumer Protection (Distance Selling) Regulations 1999 in the UK).

The law of contract in England is almost certainly able to adapt existing rules to ensure the binding nature of contracts formed online (see Chapter 2 on Online Contracts). However, the position is not necessarily the same throughout Europe. The Commission, presumably recognising the need for harmonisation of the legal effect of contracts made online, has sought to achieve this by firstly obliging Member States to remove any prohibitions or restrictions on the use of electronic contracts. There are exceptions to this general rule and the following types of contracts fall outside this general requirement:

- contracts that create or transfer rights in real estate (except rental rights);
- contracts which require some involvement of the courts or a public authority;
- contracts of suretyship or security (where the suretyship or security is given by persons acting outside their trade or profession); and
- contracts governed by family law or the law of succession.

The rather more critical issue of the time and method of conclusion of electronic contracts clearly caused some late nights for the draftsmen. A previous draft of the E-Commerce Directive contained a robust formula which made it plain when, and how, an electronic contract was to be concluded. Under the previous Article 11, an online contract would be concluded when the recipient received from the e-tailer an electronic acknowledgement of receipt of the recipient's acceptance and he had confirmed receipt of the acknowledgement of the receipt. These processes would actually occur when the parties were able to access the acknowledgement of receipt and the related confirmation.

The re-drafted version of Article 11 of the E-Commerce Directive completely omits this requirement and in so doing does not confirm the point at which the online contract is concluded. The only requirement on the e-tailer under the revised version is to acknowledge receipt of the recipient's order expeditiously, and by electronic means. This requirement may be excluded by agreement in business-to-business transactions. At least one reason for this extraordinary volte-face is the difficulty of harmonising diverse sets of contract rules which exist in the European Community.

Another possible theory is that the original form of the E-Commerce Directive may, potentially, have thrown up a conflict with the Distance Selling Directive (Directive 97/7/EC), which is designed to protect consumers from risks involved in contracts negotiated at a distance. This will include sales concluded via the Internet. The reformulation of recital 14 in the E-Commerce Directive provides:

> "Whereas this Directive complements ... Directive 97/7/EC on the protection of consumers in respect of distance contracts."

The Distance Selling Directive contains a right of withdrawal which could have been hard to square with a standard contracting process. Article 6 provides:

> "For any distance contract, the consumer shall have a period of at least seven working days in which to withdraw from the contract without penalty and without giving any reason."

In any event, the dramatic change to Article 11 was at the expense of certainty and leaves the time and method of the conclusion of electronic contracts open to the interpretation of the law of each Member State.

Article 10 of the E-Commerce Directive lists the information which online traders are obliged to furnish to the customers, although the requirement to give such information may be waived by agreement between the e-tailer and the customer in business-to-business transactions. The information to be furnished is:

- the necessary technical steps to conclude the contract;
- information on how the contract will be filed and its accessibility;
- the means of detection and correction of errors in the order; and
- the languages available for the conclusion of the contract.

Article 10 also states that contract terms and provisions provided to the customer must be made available in a way which allows the customer to store and reproduce them.

5.   Identification of commercial communications – Articles 6-7

The E-Commerce Directive also attempts to bring clarity with regard to commercial communications. The provisions of Article 6 are concerned with making clear the nature of commercial communications, particularly with regards to unsolicited e-mail. Obviously, the main aim of this is to ensure fair-trading and protection of the consumer from intrusion. An electronic commercial communication must be clearly identified as a commercial communication and it must be obvious who, or on whose behalf, the commercial communication is sent. Promotions, and their terms, must also be presented clearly and unambiguously.

Senders of unsolicited communications are singled out to respect the opt-out registers which may be used by consumers to indicate that they do not wish to receive unsolicited commercial communications.

For further information on unsolicited communications, please see Chapter 9.

6.   Status of intermediaries – Article 12

Internet Service Providers (ISPs) are referred to as "intermediaries" in the E-Commerce Directive. The E-Commerce Directive attempts to define their status, a large part of which includes determining the limits of their liability. Under the E-Commerce Directive where the ISP can be shown to have acted as a mere a conduit, it can receive exemption from liability. It is, however, necessary first to establish this status as a mere conduit. The E-Commerce Directive also limits the liability of ISPs for other "intermediary" activities such as transient storage of information for the purposes of transmission.

The liability of ISPs has already been considered in the English courts in *Godfrey* v *Demon Internet* [1999], a case concerning the posting of defamatory material on a Demon News Group. The court held that Demon Internet, in its role as distributor of the news group, was effectively a publisher and knew, or ought to have known, the content of the defamatory material. In any event, the plaintiff, Mr Godfrey, had advised Demon Internet of the material and they failed to remove it for some time. However, to regard an ISP as a publisher, and therefore subject to the same laws, is a rather strained analogy: the Internet obviously moves at a much faster pace than traditional publishing, so the traditional laws cannot be easily transferred. The sheer volume of transmissions makes monitoring a vast undertaking and the actual content evaluation is a legal process, therefore necessitating a potentially huge legal staff with the concomitant cost implications for both business and service recipient. Ultimately the test for liability for defamatory statements is whether the ISP had knowledge of the content or ought to have knowledge of the defamatory statement. In the *Godfrey* case, the judge, Mr Justice Morland, wholly rejected the suggestion that the defendants were not publishing the material but were rather merely an electronic conduit through which postings were transmitted.

Godfrey v *Demon Internet* is a useful case since in it the judge clearly laid out the necessary criteria to be met in order to qualify for exemption from liability for defamatory statements. These were:

- the ISP was not the author, editor or publisher of the statement;
- the ISP took reasonable care in relation to its publication; and
- the ISP did not know, and had no reason to believe, that what it did caused or contributed to the publication of a defamatory statement.

The E-Commerce Directive contains similar principles since it states that an ISP can receive exemption from liability when it can effectively demonstrate that it had no knowledge or control over the content of the transmissions. The only practical course that can be taken by ISPs, or indeed any website which allows users of the site to post content on its site, is that if they receive notice that anything on their site is or may be defamatory or otherwise illegal, offensive or obscene, the offending content should be suspended immediately. For this reason it is advisable to include provisions in the terms of use of the website or ISP service which set out the standards to which any contributor should adhere and the sanctions that will result following any failure to follow those standards.

Recent legal developments

A recent development arising out of the release of Jon Venables and Robert Thompson (the killers of James Bulger) gives more guidance on the approach of the Courts to the activities of ISPs. In January 2001 the High Court in England granted an injunction restraining the publication of information concerning Robert Thompson and Jon Venables. The injunction was extensive since not only was it indefinite but also covered, amongst other things, the following actions:

> "Publishing or causing to be published in any newspaper or broadcasting in any sound or television broadcast or by means of any cable or satellite programme service or public computer network:

- any depiction, image in any form, photograph, film or voice recording made or taken on or after the 18 February 1993 of Jon Venables or Robert Thompson;

- any information likely to lead to the identification of Jon Venables or Robert Thompson; and

- any information likely to lead to the identification of the past, present or future whereabouts of Jon Venables or Robert Thompson."

One of the provisos to the injunction is that any person may publish any information already in the public domain at the date of the original order in January 2001. However, the injunction states that this proviso does not include any material that has at any time been published on the Internet and/or outside England and Wales. In these provisions and the fact that the injunction extends to publication via a public computer network (which would seem to include the Internet) the High Court has appreciated the ability of the Internet to act as a very efficient information distribution tool.

The original injunction did give rise to concern for ISPs who are, following the decision in *Godfrey* v *Demon Internet*, already on their guard with regard to information posted on their newsgroups. Whereas a defamation action, which was the foundation of the *Godfrey* case, could give rise to damages, a breach of an injunction could lead to the infringing party being held in contempt of court and therefore liable for imprisonment or sequestration of its assets.

It is not surprising then that Demon Internet sought a variation of the terms of the January 2001 injunction to protect the position of ISPs. The variation was granted on 10 July 2001 so that an ISP shall not be in breach of the injunction unless it, or any of its employees or agents:

- knew that the material had been placed on its servers or could be accessed via its service; or
- knew that the material was likely to be placed on its servers, or was likely to be placed on its servers, or was likely to be accessed via its service; and in either case
- failed to take all reasonable steps to prevent the publication;

An employee or agent of the ISP will be liable in the two circumstances set out above if he or she failed to take all reasonable steps to prevent the publication and also failed to take reasonable steps to induce the ISP to prevent the publication.

The variation to the injunction goes on to say that the ISP, its employees or agents will be considered to know anything which he, she or it would have known if he, she or it had taken reasonable steps to find out. Moreover, "taking all reasonable steps to prevent the publication" includes the taking of all reasonable steps to remove the material from the ISP's servers or to block access to the material.

The variation to the injunction would appear to be consistent with the results of the *Godfrey* case. The variation also indicates that the High Court would regard that the ISP in taking "reasonable steps" must remove the offending material from its servers and block access to the material. These are therefore actions which ISPs must be able to take within the terms of its contract with its customers and ISPs must have in place procedures which enable complaints or notice of offending material to be processed swiftly and effectively.

The variation of the injunction by the High Court also fits in with the approach towards ISP liability adopted by the E-Commerce Directive.

7. Dispute resolution – Article 17

The new Brussels Regulation which may open the doors for consumers to sue e-tailers in the consumer's home courts has been met with some dismay from the Internet business community. The perception is that e-commerce may not develop as freely as it might be hoped if e-tailers are faced with the prospect of being sued in foreign courts. Article 17 of the E-Commerce Directive, it has been suggested, goes some way to addressing this potential problem, as it states that out of court schemes for dispute settlement (including electronic dispute resolution mechanisms) ought not to be hampered by the national laws of Member States. But difficulties still remain likely as there is a potential conflict with paragraph 1(q) of the Annex to the Directive of 5 April 1993 on Unfair Terms in Consumer Contracts which establishes the presumption that arbitration clauses in consumer contracts are unenforceable. In *Zealander & Zealander* v *Laing Homes Ltd* [1999], the judge, decided not to give effect to an arbitration clause which conflicted with paragraph 1(q).

However, recital 14 of the E-Commerce Directive states that the E-Commerce Directive is without prejudice to the protection afforded by the Unfair Contract Terms Directive. It is therefore possible that Article 17 is directed at mediation and other forms of alternative dispute resolution (excluding arbitration). In addition, Article 17 specifically refers to out of court *settlements*. This would, on the face of it, appear to exclude arbitration, which is not a settlement procedure. Whether this was actually the intention, or whether it is particularly helpful or not, is a different matter. It may be that to ensure that arbitration provisions in electronic contracts are valid, an amendment to the Unfair Contract Terms Directive will be required.

8. **Summary**

- Although elements of the E-Commerce Directive have already been implemented in the United Kingdom by the Electronic Communications Act 2000, remaining elements are likely to be implemented in the United Kingdom by way of changes to existing legislation.

- An e-tailer should ensure it complies with the regulations of the Member State in which it is established – where the centre of its activities are.

- An e-tailer should ensure it provides the correct information to customers as set out in the Directive.

- If the e-tailer is an ISP or allows users to post information on its site, it should ensure its terms of use set out the standards to which users should adhere and sanctions that may result if the user does not do so.

- The E-Commerce Directive is a significant progression in monitoring trading over the Internet. It begins to address some important questions with patchy success. There remains significant potential for conflict in some areas, perhaps most of all with the conclusion of electronic contracts. If anything this directive is a starting point, and it remains of course in the hands of Member States to implement, support and enforce the directive into their national law. Ultimately, it is positive symbol of the EU's commitment to e-commerce and its continued, controlled success.

Chapter 7

· Domain Names ·

1. Introduction

One of the first things considered by any company contemplating an Internet venture is its domain name. The domain name may form a crucial factor in the venture's success and it is therefore not surprising that certain domain names have become valuable commodities. It is also not surprising that there has been a large number of disputes regarding the use of domain names. This chapter deals with the resolution of domain name disputes, covering the dispute resolution service currently offered by Nominet UK, its proposed new dispute resolution policy and the current state of the law in England on domain name disputes. Also included are some practical tips for dealing with such disputes.

2. Domain name registration in UK

The domain name system is divided into generic top level domains (GTLDs) and country code top level domains (CCTLDs). The GTLDs which are available for registration on a first-come-first served basis are .com, .net and.org. Unlike the CCTLDs, the GTLDs are not country specific. The CCTLD for the United Kingdom is the .UK domain.

Nominet UK Limited is the company that administers the .UK top level domain. It is a non-profit organisation and the UK domains that can be registered are .co.uk (which is intended for commercial organisations), .org.uk (which is for non-commercial organisations), .plc.uk and .ltd.uk which are intended for registration by registered companies only (and who need to produce their company registration certificate to obtain the domain name registration), .net.uk (which is intended for Internet service providers) and .sch.uk which is intended for schools. The most commonly registered are the .co.uk and the .org.uk domains. In practice, anyone can register the .co.uk, .org.uk and .net.uk domains and they are awarded on a first-come-first served basis. This distinguishes the United Kingdom from various other jurisdictions where the registration requirements are far more stringent. For example, a number of countries require the registrant to be domiciled in that country. There are over 70 registries that offer domains on a first-come-first served basis which, in addition to the United Kingdom include, for example, South Africa, Switzerland, Turkey, Mexico and more obscure ones, such as the Cook Islands, Western Samoa, the Turks and Caicos islands and Tuvalu. Some of these have become popular for serendipitous reasons, such as Tuvalu's '.tv'.

The table below sets out a comparison of total registrations of various CCTLDs as of March 2001. With over 2.5 million registrations to date, the .co.uk domain is the most popular and .co.uk domain names have been known to change hands for vast sums of money; for example, the ask.co.uk domain name which is said to have changed hands for $100,000 and the bbc.co.uk domain name which the BBC allegedly purchased for £80,000.

Top 10 CCTLD Jurisdictions			
1.	United Kingdom	.co.uk	2,500,000
2.	Germany	.de	1,050,000
3.	Netherlands	.nl	613,000
4.	Italy	.it	469,000
5.	Coco Islands	.cc	440,000
6.	South Korea	.co.kr	350,000
7.	Argentina	.com.ar	327,000
8.	Canada	.ca	195,000
9.	United Kingdom	.org.uk	172,000
10.	Austria	.at	168,000

3. Resolution of disputes over generic top level domains: UDRP

The Universal Domain Name Dispute Resolution Policy (the UDRP) is a policy set up in January 2000 by ICANN (the Internet Corporation for Assigned Names and Numbers) and administered by various bodies, including WIPO (the World Intellectual Property Organisation). However, since the UDRP applies only to disputes over the registration of GTLDs and only a handful of CCTLDs (such as the CCTLDs of Tuvalu, Mexico and Niue), this chapter will not cover the UDRP in depth.

The UDRP is a relatively cheap administrative procedure for resolving disputes and has proved to be extremely popular, with over 2500 decisions rendered in the first 12 months since the procedure was launched. The UDRP entitles anyone who owns a trade mark and who is aggrieved by the existence of an "abusive" domain name which is identical or similar to the trade mark, to apply to have the dispute resolved by an independent panel for a modest fee. UDRP complaints are filed electronically and there is no right to a hearing. Also, the Policy sets out strict time limits for the filing of responses and for the panel to give its decision.

A copy of the UDRP can be found at www.icann.org.

4. Resolution of disputes over UK domain name registrations

The fact that the .uk domain is available on a first-come-first served basis has inevitably led to a large number of disputes over domain names allegedly registered by people or companies not entitled to those registrations. Nominet has not adopted the UDRP, but instead provides its own dispute resolution service. The current service encourages parties to come to an agreement with the help of the impartial intervention of Nominet staff.

Nominet's current dispute resolution service

Nominet boasts that approximately one-third of the cases reported to it have been successfully mediated but, putting this in context, only 0.05% of .uk registrations result in mediation. Nominet has no power to impose a solution and so most disputes tend to result in settlement between the parties or High Court proceedings. In particular, Nominet cannot transfer a domain name under its current terms and conditions without the consent of the current owner or a court order for it to make such a transfer. Nominet does, however, have the power to suspend the domain name, but usually will only do so if legal proceedings have been commenced.

Nominet's proposed new dispute resolution policy

At the time of writing, Nominet is redrafting its dispute resolution policy which it hopes to launch in Autumn 2001. This will be accompanied by a launch of new Nominet terms and conditions of registration. Importantly, the new terms and conditions will allow Nominet unilaterally to transfer domain name registrations without the consent of the current owner. The new policy will be aimed at resolving disputes over abusive registrations only and, interestingly, Nominet has chosen not to adopt the UDRP despite the success of the UDRP system. The reasons for this are that the UDRP does not provide any mediation service, that there is inconsistency in published decisions of arbitrators under the UDRP, and Nominet perceives the UDRP to favour trade mark holders whereas Nominet claims to operate a principle of "neutrality and equality".

For each complaint there will be a two-stage test where the complainant must show that it has rights in a mark that is identical or similar to the domain name in question and must show that the respondent has registered and/or is using the domain name in bad faith. The onus will therefore fall on the complainant to demonstrate bad faith and to prove that the existence of bad faith is "beyond reasonable doubt". Nominet sees this as an improvement to the current test under the UDRP where the complainant has to show that the domain name was not registered in good faith. Examples that Nominet has provided of bad faith include the registrant offering the domain name for sale at a premium to the rightful owner or registering the domain name as a blocking registration to prevent the trade mark owner from registering it – a tactic sometimes employed by competitors. Alternatively, that the registration was aimed solely at disrupting the complainant's business or that the registration has caused actual confusion.

The draft proposals set out various defences. A complaint will not succeed if the respondent can show that before being informed of the dispute, it was genuinely offering goods or services for sale under the domain name, that it is commonly known by or legitimately connected to that name or that it is making a legitimate non-commercial or fair use of the domain name. Interestingly, Nominet has said that fair use could include protest or tribute sites.

Each complaint will be dealt with according to a strict timetable that will include an opportunity for mediation, but if this is unsuccessful after 10 days then the complaint will be referred to an expert for a decision. It seems likely that the experts will be appointed in much the same way as arbitrators are appointed to act as panellists under the UDRP, albeit UK-based. The complainant will not have an opportunity to select the expert as the experts will be allocated to hear the disputes, on a "cab rank" basis. There will be a £750 fee per case. The proposals include a provision relating to "reverse domain name hi-jacking" which essentially means that if a complainant brings three unsuccessful complaints then no further complaints filed by that complainant will be considered by Nominet. Any decision of the expert may be appealed to a panel of three experts.

It is difficult at this stage to assess how effective the dispute resolution service will be, although the current indications would suggest that it will be more difficult for trade mark owners to succeed in a complaint to Nominet than under the UDRP as there will be a higher burden of proof for showing bad faith. Nevertheless, the complainant could ultimately issue proceedings in the High Court if the complaint was unsuccessful and a Nominet complaint will of course be far cheaper in the first instance than issuing proceedings.

UK High Court litigation

Why litigate?

Why spend the time and money on litigation in the United Kingdom instead of using alternatives such as the UDRP to resolve the domain name dispute?

The main reason will be that the domain name in question is not subject to the UDRP and this applies in respect of the .uk domains and various other country code top level domains. High Court proceedings may also be appropriate where there is no obvious bad faith involved. For example, a .com registration may have been taken by a German company which already trades legitimately in Germany using a name similar to a UK registered trade mark, but whose website is targeting the UK market. In these circumstances, a UDRP complaint will not succeed and the merits of bringing proceedings in the United Kingdom for trade mark infringement and/or passing-off must be considered.

Unlike the United States (which has the Anti-Cybersquatting Consumer Protection Act), the United Kingdom has not enacted any specific legislation to deal with cyber-squatting and so to succeed in a High Court action it is necessary to show that the domain name registration in question amounts to trade mark infringement or passing-off. Various cases have also included other, more obscure, claims such as for conspiracy, wrongful interference with contract and abuse of process, but such claims rarely succeed. Of course, the problem with an action for trade mark infringement is that the domain name in question is not always in use - it may simply have been registered - whereas the Trade Marks Act 1994 requires a claimant to show that a similar or identical mark is being "used" by the defendant in the course of trade. Lack of use also makes it difficult to argue that the registration amounts to passing-off since, for a passing-off action to succeed, the claimant must show that use of the domain name has damaged the claimant's goodwill in the name due to confusion. Without use, how can confusion be demonstrated?

Another particularly difficult problem is that of the new brand which is about to be launched by the claimant, but the launch plans have been leaked before the claimant has put in place its trade mark and domain name registration strategy for the new brand. The claimant then finds out that someone else has coincidentally registered the new brand name as a domain name. In this instance the claimant has no trade mark registration that it can rely on and since the brand has not yet been launched there will be little, if any, reputation or goodwill in the new brand name to rely on in an action for passing-off.

Finally, there is the problem of the registrant who is using the complainant's trade mark as a domain name but is providing services or goods under the domain name that are completely different from those covered by the complainant's trade mark registration and whose business is completely different. In the circumstances it will be difficult, if not impossible, to show that use of the domain name will give rise to confusion.

How have the courts handled these issues?

Where the claimant was successful

The first cyber-squatting case decided by the UK courts was the case of *Harrods Limited* v *UK Network Services Ltd* in 1997. Harrods, the internationally famous department store, had trade marks registered in the United Kingdom and elsewhere in a number of classes, including class 9 in respect of computers and computer programs. In August 1995 the defendant registered www.harrods.com with the US-based service provider, NSI. The defendant did not use the name itself but offered it for sale to others. Harrods complained to NSI which suspended use of the domain name and awaited the outcome of the decision of the English courts. Harrods sued the defendant alleging trade mark infringement under section 10(1)-(3) of the Trade Marks Act 1994 as well as passing-off. Whilst the defendant did not appear and did not file any evidence, Mr Justice Lightman granted Harrods an injunction requiring the assignment of the domain name to Harrods, stating that this was a wrongful registration of the domain name under section 10 of the Trade Marks Act, but he left unanswered what use (*i.e.* "use in a trade mark sense") the defendant had made of the claimant's trade marks.

Perhaps the best known case on cyber-squatting in the United Kingdom is the case of *British Telecommunications & Ors* v *One in a Million Limited* [1998]. One in a Million Limited was a company that had registered famous names of well known brands. The domain names in question included, for example, Virgin, Sainsbury, Ladbroke and Marks & Spencer. No websites had been activated at any of the domain names. In this case, the defendants had offered to sell the names at a premium to their rightful owners; for example, they offered to sell burgerking.co.uk for £25,000 plus VAT and bt.org for £4,700 plus VAT. At first instance, the judge granted an injunction preventing the defendants' use and made an order for the defendants to assign the names to their rightful owners. He held that the defendants had threatened passing-off and trade mark infringement even though no damage had yet occurred. The case went to the Court of Appeal which decided that passing-off was made out, and stated that the act of mere domain name registration by the defendants in these circumstances amounted to the creation of an "instrument of fraud". The question was whether there was an intention to use the registrations or to provide the registrations to third parties for their use where such use would amount to passing-off. The Court of Appeal found that mere registration of the domains amounted to a false representation that the registrants were associated or connected with the claimants and constituted passing-off. This case is therefore an authority for the proposition that if a brand name has been registered as a trade mark or is well known in the United Kingdom and the registrant offers to sell it for a price which goes well beyond his costs of registration, then the brand name owner is likely to succeed in an action for passing-off.

The *One in a Million* case follows a line of cases on company names. For example, Mr Justice Laddie in the *Direct Line* case stated that the court would consider "with displeasure" attempts by companies to register names for purposes of a business which uses the reputation of another or where the purpose of the business is to make illegitimate use of another's trade mark. Also, in the *Glaxo Wellcome* case in 1996, the defendant registered the Glaxo Wellcome company name in anticipation of those two companies merging, hoping that he could charge £100,000 to the new company for the name. Mr Justice Lightman in that case referred to this as a dishonest plan to appropriate the goodwill of the claimant.

The *One in a Million* decision was followed in the case of *Britannia Building Society* v *Prangley & Ors* [2000]. In this case, the defendant had registered the domain name britanniabuildingsociety.com. The claimant was the well known UK building society with a number of trade mark registrations for the name Britannia. The court granted an injunction and ordered the immediate transfer of the domain name in an action for summary judgment. The basis for the judge's decision was that the defendant had "clearly" registered the name with a view to commercial gain knowing that it represented the name of the claimant, but it is interesting to note that no offer for sale of the name was made by the defendant and the defendant had not actually set up a website under the name britanniabuildingsociety.com.

In his defence, Mr Prangley said that he was aware of the existence of the Britannia Building Society but that he did not intend to use the mark for the provision of building society services. Instead, he had considered setting up a new business in Iran under this name, being the business of acting as a broker to provide the services of British builders to Iranians. Accordingly, his use of the mark would not amount to trade mark infringement as it was to be used in respect of different goods and services from those for which the Britannia trade mark was registered. He said that his intention in registering the domain name was not in any sense to make use of it in any fraudulent way or to use it as a means of passing himself off as connected with the claimant, nor for extorting money from the claimant. The judge described his evidence as "wholly incredible" and said that he had no doubt that the defendant registered the name having regard to the fact that it represented the name of the claimant and that it was plain that any use of the domain name would lead to a serious risk if not certainty of confusion in the mind of anybody who sees its use as to whether or not the user was connected with the claimant. The judge asked what other purpose there could possibly have been for having a domain name incorporating the name of the claimant if it was not to be used for the purpose of indicating that it was somehow connected with the claimant. The registration was therefore an instrument of fraud in the same way that Lord Justice Aldous described the domain names in the *One in a Million* case.

It would seem that, provided a mark is registered and well known in the United Kingdom and the defendant has no apparent good faith reason for registering the domain name, it is likely that the courts will find in favour of the owner of the mark, even if no offer for sale has been made.

Where the claimant was unsuccessful

Following on from the *One in a Million* and *Britannia* cases was the action brought by French Connection Limited against Sutton in 1999. This was an application for summary judgment claiming passing-off, trade mark infringement and breach of contract regarding the defendant's registration of fcuk.com. The claimant had registered fcuk as a trade mark. The defendant argued that the letters were already in use on the Internet and did not refer only to the claimant and that he intended to use the registration for his own business as an Internet consultant. The defendant had also offered the registration for sale to the claimant.

Mr Justice Rattee held that there was an arguable defence to the passing-off claim because of the two motives the defendant claimed for prompting him to file fcuk as a domain name, namely:

(1) his intention to use it as the domain name for his own business; and

(2) that the value of the fcuk letters to him were derived from the confusion which would arise between those seeking pornography on the web and thus attracted to his future business website by that association.

On the evidence presented on the application, the claimant had not proved that the letters fcuk were necessarily to be taken as a reference to French Connection because they were in use on the Internet before the defendant started using them as a domain name. The judge also considered that the defendant's excuse for the domain name registration (*i.e.* that he registered the domain name for his own purposes), could not be dismissed without a full trial and that the registration was not obviously therefore an instrument of fraud within the meaning given to that term in the *One in a Million* case. French Connection had also failed to show that it had sufficient goodwill in the fcuk letters to support a passing-off action, nor had it established a real likelihood of confusion between the claimant's business and the defendant's. This case adds little to the *One in a Million* decision because of its unique facts (which the judge found "unpalatable in the extreme"). It is important to bear in mind that this was an action for summary judgment in which case a claimant would have to show that there was no real prospect of a defence succeeding. The case never went to full trial.

In the *French Connection* case the defendant's website consisted of nothing that was remotely similar to the claimant's business. Their business concerned clothes, whereas the defendant's business concerned Internet and e-mail consultancy. Also, the claimant had failed to establish any real likelihood of confusion.

A more recent Internet domain name case where the defendant claimed to have a genuine intention to use the name for his business was the case of *MBNA v Stephen Freeman* [2000]. This was an action brought by MBNA Bank for an interim injunction. MBNA has offered credit card financial services and online shopping via the mbna.com website since 1996. It also has a Community trade mark registration for the letters MBNA in respect of various classes of business including banking and computer services. In 1999 MBNA discovered that the defendant had registered mbna.co.uk. In March 2000 MBNA contacted the defendant who said that he was entitled to the domain name and intended to use it for his "Marketing Banners for Net Advertising" business. MBNA claimed that he had deliberately chosen those letters to take advantage of MBNA's goodwill in that acronym and to increase hits to his website.

The claimants cited the *One in a Million* case in their arguments and said that if this was the defendant's intention then the court should conclude that there had been misappropriation of goodwill and that users may well believe his service was licensed or owned by them. Further, the increased traffic to the site would increase the value of the domain name if he decided to sell. They also alleged that his use of the domain name was trade mark infringement under section 10(3) of the Trade Marks Act which relates to use of the name in respect of different services to those for which the mark is registered. The defendant claimed that his intended use was for a dissimilar business to that of the claimants and that there was no risk of confusion.

In this case the claimant lost at the interim stage and the case subsequently settled, so it did not go to full trial. At the interim stage, the court held that the claimant had failed to prove loss of business due to users searching against the letters MBNA and coming across Mr Freeman's website. Also, MBNA failed to show that it could not be compensated in damages if the court ruled in favour of the claimant at a full trial of the action. The court in particular was influenced by the fact that Mr Freeman appeared to be a competent business person and was unlikely to damage MBNA's reputation by providing a poor service. The court made an interim order for the defendant not to sell the domain name prior to trial.

In this case there was no threat to sell the domain name and it was not clear that the name had been registered in bad faith. If this case had gone to full trial then there is of course the possibility that MBNA would have succeeded under section 10(3) of the Trade Marks Act 1994 although it is notoriously difficult to succeed under this section of the Act.

There have been a number of other domain name disputes where the claimant has been unsuccessful either at the interim stage or at full trial.

In the case of *Pitman Training Limited and PTC Oxford Limited* v *Nominet UK and Pearson Professional Limited* [1997], both the claimant and the defendant believed that they owned the name PITMAN. The defendant had registered the pitman.co.uk domain name and started to construct its website. In the meantime, the name was re-delegated by Nominet to the claimant and then back again to the defendant. The question was whether the defendant should be restrained from using the domain name. The claims for passing-off, tortious interference with contract and abuse of process were all dismissed. The court said that the claimant had insufficient goodwill in the PITMAN name. There was a prior co-existence agreement between the claimant and defendant whereby the parties had agreed upon their respective uses of the PITMAN name and the claimant had agreed always to use the name in conjunction with the word "training". The defendant had already traded under the PITMAN name for 150 years. So the fact that the claimant had a trade mark registration did not mean that it was automatically going to succeed in obtaining an order for transfer of the domain name.

Avnet Inc v *Isoact Ltd* [1998] was also a case of two legitimate traders fighting over the right to use the same name - in this case, the name Avnet. The claimant had registered the Avnet trade mark for advertising and promotional services whereas the defendant used Avnet on its website and as the domain name www.avnet.co.uk. There was no conflict between their respective businesses. The claimant sold technical goods through its catalogues whereas the defendant was an Internet service provider which advertised the services it provided. Mr Justice Jacob found that the public was not likely to be confused by the defendant's use of the Avnet domain name and, because the defendant was not providing the ability for its customers to advertise, its use did not amount to trade mark infringement (*i.e.* it did not amount to use in respect of advertising services which was what the claimant's registration covered). The specification of the claimant's trade mark registration was therefore narrowly construed.

5. **Practical points**

The first thing to consider when faced with a potential domain name dispute is whether or not there are any alternatives to High Court litigation. If the domain name is a generic top level domain and there is evidence of bad faith, then the UDRP procedure is probably the e-tailer's cheapest option. Once Nominet's new dispute resolution procedure is in place then this might be worth considering where relevant. If there is any doubt as to whether or not the domain name has been registered in bad faith then it may be worthwhile for an e-tailer to instruct agents to approach the registrant on a no-names basis to see whether they would be willing to sell the domain name. This may lead to a resolution or may provide evidence of bad faith. Obtaining evidence of bad faith can be tricky and an e-tailer should also run a search to see what other names might have been registered by that same registrant. If other "famous" names have been registered, this may indicate bad faith.

There may be a choice of forum, based on the residence of the defendant and any country code top level domains registered. The registrant may have registered the same name with a variety of suffixes. One jurisdiction might be more cost effective than another, or provide speedier or more stringent remedies.

An e-tailer should also consider joining the Internet service provider in the proceedings and checking the ISP's terms and conditions of registration and hosting since these may well include a provision for the ISP unilaterally to de-activate the website at that domain name while the dispute is in progress. Nominet is not keen to be joined as a party to proceedings but, at the same time, is not in a position to undertake to comply with any court order against a defendant to assign a name by assigning the name itself, since this is not in keeping with its terms and conditions which require the registrant's consent for any transfer. Accordingly, a court order which names Nominet as a party will be needed. If an e-tailer is seeking an interim injunction then it will need to act swiftly and at the same time it is always worth writing to Nominet asking it specifically to suspend the domain name registration pending trial.

Where a domain name is not yet in use, the claimant may benefit from filing a trade mark application in order to bolster its rights, particularly if the claimant itself has little or no trading history. Since confusion and evidence of confusion is important in both trade mark infringement and passing-off actions, then a claimant should monitor all hits to its website and collect any evidence of confusion, particularly if a reduction in hits to its website may indicate that customers are confusing the defendant's website with that of the claimant.

Of course, the best way to avoid domain name disputes is by obtaining a comprehensive domain name and trade mark portfolio in the first instance to avoid any possibility of third parties registering your names without the authority of the e-tailer. Also, an e-tailer should choose distinctive names for new brands (abbreviations are less likely to be granted protection by the courts) and pay close attention to the drafting of specifications for new trade mark applications.

It is also worth noting that only 88 out of the 244 country code top level domain registries currently provide on-line "whois" services, so it can be difficult to track down the defendant in the first place. Agents can be used to conduct investigations.

An e-tailer should be cautious when writing to registrants to complain about their registration bearing in mind the threats provisions under section 21 of the Trade Marks Act 1994.

The US company, Prince Sports Group Inc, came unstuck under this provision when they wrote to a UK company, Prince PLC, in respect of their registration of prince.com. The UK company brought an action claiming unjustified threats under section 21 of the Trade Marks Act and the court upheld the claim. The court said that although the letter appeared innocuous on its face, it could be regarded as a threat of proceedings when placed in context. Section 21 provides that:

> "where a person threatens another with proceedings for infringement of a registered trade mark, other than (a) the application of the mark to goods or their packaging; (b) the importation of goods to which or to the packaging of which, the mark has been applied, or (c) the supply of services under the mark, any person aggrieved may bring proceedings for relief under this section".

The US company argued that it was implicit in the letter that their complaint related to the use of the word Prince in the prince.com domain name for the supply of services. This argument was rejected by the judge because the letter was not explicit and would be read by the ordinary reader in Prince PLC's position as constituting a threat of proceedings generally. The court also alluded to the purpose of section 21 which is to protect business people against threats based on unjustifiable allegations that they were infringing trade marks registered in the United Kingdom by third parties.

6. Conclusion

This is a changing area, so it is important that an e-tailer makes sure it knows what developments are taking place, particularly with regards to the introduction of new top level domains (such as .biz and .info), but also as regards the Nominet dispute resolution procedure and any developments in the ICANN UDRP procedure. Given that the Internet is an international tool it is also becoming more important to monitor developments abroad so that an e-tailer can make the appropriate decisions regarding choice of forum. If the e-tailer itself is registering and using domain names then it is worth bearing in mind that, whilst use in the United Kingdom may not be infringing any rights of third parties in the United Kingdom, it may nevertheless find itself party to proceedings outside the United Kingdom. Whilst the law in this area is not yet fully developed, the e-tailer should bear in mind that it may find itself party to proceedings in any country if its website is targeted at customers in that country, regardless of the fact that it is using a .uk website address.

7. Summary

An e-tailer should:

- Monitor developments in this area, particularly with regard to the introduction of new GTLDs.

- Take advice on both trade mark and domain name registration measures that it should be taking to protect its brands portfolio.

- If someone has registered the e-tailer's brand as a domain name, consider whether or not a UDRP complaint would be appropriate. This depends upon the nature of the domain name suffix in question and whether or not the name appears to have been registered in bad faith. Investigations into the registrant may need to be undertaken.

- Consider other dispute resolution options, for example, if the disputed domain name is a .uk registration, consider whether it would be worth making a complaint under the Nominet Dispute Resolution Policy.

- If an e-tailer does decide to bring UK High Court proceedings in respect of a .uk domain, it should ask Nominet to suspend the registration in the first instance and consider asking the ISP to deactivate any website at that domain name, pending resolution of the dispute.

Chapter 8

· **Data Protection** ·

1. **Introduction**

The use of customer data is often an essential part of any business but those involved in e-commerce in particular make regular use of customer and user data for a variety of reasons. This data can range from the names and addresses of the customers to the usage statistics recorded by the e-tailer as a customer uses the website. Whatever data concerning individuals is collected and however it is to be used, the laws governing data protection must be considered.

Current data protection law in the United Kingdom is based on the Data Protection Act 1998 (the "Act") which came into force in March 2000 aiming to broaden the scope of existing legislation and implement an EU Data Protection Directive (Directive 95/46/EC) which brought all the Member States of the European Community up to the same standard of data protection. The Act completely replaces, and is broader than, the previous 1984 legislation. As well as the Act, there is further legislation in place dealing with the use of data in the telecommunications field. This legislation is discussed in Chapter 9 where the legal implications of direct marketing campaigns are discussed.

In this chapter, we shall explain in some depth the practical effect of the Act on the way in which data can be handled, as well as the rights of the individual whose data is collected and enforcement of the Act. Whilst we do not aim to cover every aspect of data protection we intend to deal with those aspects of data protection law most applicable to e-commerce.

2. **Data Protection Act 1998**

This statute is the cornerstone of legislation governing the treatment of personal data in the United Kingdom. It covers how such information can be handled and maintained, and the obligations of those who process it, as well as penalties for non-compliance and enforcement procedures.

The Act is extensively promoted and to an extent policed by the Information Commissioner, an independent officer who reports to Parliament. The Commissioner maintains a register of bodies and individuals which process personal data (these terms are defined below). She is also responsible for spreading awareness of the Act, and developing codes of practice to assist data controllers. These are distributed via the data protection website (www.dataprotection.gov.uk).The guidance notes issued by the Information Commissioner are a very useful source of information on current data protection law and also provide a useful insight into how the legislation will be interpreted by the Information Commissioner.

The Information Commissioner has a duty to assess any complaints made by individuals that the provisions of the Act are being flouted, and is empowered to serve enforcement notices on data controllers (see definitions below) who do not comply with the Act. Failure to comply with an enforcement notice is an offence unless a diligent attempt by the body concerned was made to do so, and bodies can appeal against enforcement notices in some circumstances to the Data Protection Tribunal.

Important definitions

The Act contains a number of definitions peculiar to the field of data protection and this "data protection speak" is one of the reasons why the United Kingdom's data protection law can, at first, appear quite confusing.Broadly speaking the Act governs the *processing of personal data* by *data controllers*. It would be helpful therefore at this stage to explain these terms, which are all defined in detail in sections 1 and 2 of the Act.

"Data"

There are several different aspects to the definition of "data", which is defined in the Act as meaning information which:

- is being processed by means of equipment operating automatically in response to instructions given for that purpose; or
- is recorded with the intention that it should be processed by means of such equipment; or
- is recorded as part of a relevant filing system or with the intention that it should form part of a relevant filing system; or

- comprises other records referred to under the Act as "accessible records", which are health records (information relating to a patient's physical or mental state recorded by health professionals in connection with the care of the individual concerned); educational records (of local education authority schools and special schools only) and certain public records such as local authority housing records or local authority social services records; or
- comprises recorded information not falling within the above categories which is held by any public authority.

Therefore, information collected via a website constitutes data for the purposes of the Act since it is collected and recorded on equipment operating automatically in response to instructions and additionally it is recorded with the intention that it should be processed by means of such equipment.

Relevant filing systems would include any system not operating automatically in response to instructions but which records information systematically by reference to individuals (for example, their names or their personal identification numbers) or by reference to criteria relating to individuals, (absence record, address, membership of organisations, credit history, profession etc) in such a way that specific information relating to a particular individual is readily accessible. Such systems would include letters filed according to who has sent them, or manuscript details of individuals living within a certain postal area, and the data concerned does not need to be recorded on a computer, or made with the intention of doing so. It is not necessary for the information to be physically collected together either: it could be dispersed over departments or branch offices of an organisation, as long as it is still structured as described and, as a result of this, specific information relating to an individual can be readily accessed. Information which is likely to be used by the data controller is likely to be the sort of data which would be seen as "specific", for example, this might be employees' absence records, customers' addresses, or individuals' credit history.

Since the Act covers information collected and dealt with non-automatically, file notes and letters, rolodex, non-automated microfiche and faxes would all need to be considered when reviewing the processing of personal data that is undertaken by a company. It is important therefore that people handling data relating to individuals conduct an audit of all non-automated data under their control, considering if it is organised in such a way that it may be caught by the Act, and if so ensuring compliance. It will not always be clear which individual methods of storing information will amount to a "relevant filing system". The position will become clearer as and when any disputes in relation to this issue are settled by the courts and in the meantime, the Information Commissioner has suggested that if a decision not to treat the information as being covered by the Act will prejudice the individual concerned then compliance with the Act is recommended. If manual data is identified, it should be borne in mind that the provisions of the Act relating to notification and the rights of data subjects (see below) will not be enforced until 24 October 2001. Further transitional relief is available until 23 October 2007.

In this chapter we will concentrate on data held electronically as this is clearly of more relevance to those engaged in e-commerce. However e-tailers must always bear in mind that the Act is equally capable of applying to the hard copy records and notes which it holds regarding its customers and employees.

"Personal data"

Personal data means data which relate to a living individual who can be identified:

- from those data; or
- from those data and other information which is in the possession of or is likely to come into the possession of, the data controller.

Data does not have to relate solely to one individual and the same data may relate to two or more people and still be personal data about each of them. Personal data would include a person's name, address, information held by credit agencies, or even expressions of opinion about a person.

It is important to realise that the information does not necessarily need to relate to an individual's personal life - it can relate to a person in their business capacity, for example. In addition information about a sole trader will amount to personal data as the sole trader conducts business as an individual. (It is important to note that in some countries outside the United Kingdom, data protection rights protect companies as well and for this reason e-tailers conducting business with consumers or businesses abroad should take local law advice on the issue of date protection.)

The second part of the definition expands the scope of personal data significantly since it captures data which of itself cannot identify an individual but which in combination with other data can identify the individual. Importantly, the second part of the definition also covers combination with data which is *likely* to come into the possession of the data controller.

As a result of the wide scope of the definition of personal data, a wide range of information is likely to be covered. An e-mail address which has the format "firstname.lastname@domain" is certainly personal data since it explicitly identifies the individual. However, what may not be so obvious to e-tailers is that any e-mail address, no matter what the format, is likely to be considered personal data as it effectively identifies the individual and allows messages to be specifically directed at the individual. The Information Commissioner in fact interprets "personal data" very widely and has given the following example:

> "A business collects information about the usage of a website by users over a period of time with the intention that it will be combined with each person's name later. That information is therefore personal data and its processing is governed by the Act. In fact there may be no intention to combine the data at all – there might merely be an intention to target that particular user with advertising focused by reference to the data related to the user's use of the website."

In this example there is no way that the website owner could locate the user in the physical world since (without having more information) all the e-tailer has is an IP address for the user's computer, it does not necessarily know the individual's name, address, sex or age amongst other things. However, the Information Commissioner takes the view that such information is nevertheless personal data since it allows the e-tailer to identify an individual in the virtual world if not in the physical world. If the e-tailer is able to identify the individual in the virtual world then the e-tailer is able to target advertising or offers specifically at that individual and the Information Commissioner is likely to view this activity as being much the same as being able to send such advertising or offers to the individual's postal address.

It is commonly thought that the simple way around having to comply with the Act is by "anonymising" the data, that is to say, by removing all personal identifiers. On the face of it this would seem to take the data outside the definition of "personal data" since it no longer explicitly refers to living individuals. However, the Information Commissioner has indicated that anonymising personal data is not necessarily an easy process and therefore does not always provide an antidote to the provisions of the Act.

The process of anonymising the data by removal of people's names from a list of data will constitute processing of personal data and therefore such processing will have to comply with the Act.

The Information Commissioner regards true anonymisation as hard to achieve since the data controller may retain the original set of data. In that case the anonymised data is *capable* of being linked to the list containing the personal identifiers and therefore the anonymised list remains personal data in the hands of that data controller.

"Processing"

The definition of "processing" within the Act is so wide that it is safe to assume that if one has any personal data in one's possession then it is being processed. Specifically, the following actions are covered: collecting, recording, holding, organisation, adaptation, alteration, retrieval, consultation, use, disclosure (by transmission, dissemination or otherwise making available), alignment, combination, blocking, erasure or destruction.

"Data controllers"

The obligations of compliance under the Act are principally imposed on "data controllers", that is:

> "persons who (either alone or jointly or in common with other persons) determine the purposes for which and the manner in which any personal data are, or are to be, processed."

"Persons" here is used in the legal sense, *i.e.* it refers to individuals as well as organisations. Where data are processed for the purposes of the business of a company, the company is the data controller. This should not be confused with the role of individual members of staff who may be given duties as "data protection officers" or the like – such duties are not prescribed by the Act and are purely a matter for the company to organise as (and if) it sees fit. Hence, anyone who decides how data are dealt with will be a data controller, and therefore responsible for compliance under the Act. This will be so whether or not the person makes such decisions jointly with another person, or whether or not the person is the only one making such decisions with regard to the data.

Section 5 states that the Act only applies to:

- data controllers established in the United Kingdom where the data are processed in the context of that establishment (note, this includes individuals normally resident in the United Kingdom and persons or organisations which maintain in the United Kingdom an office, branch or a regular practice); or
- data controllers who are established outside of the European Economic Area ("EEA") but who use equipment in the United Kingdom for processing data other than for the purposes of transit through the United Kingdom.

The EEA, at the time of writing, comprises the EU states plus Iceland, Liechtenstein and Norway. The Channel Islands and the Isle of Man are not part of the EEA.

Therefore, if a company sites computer equipment (such as a server) within the United Kingdom and that equipment actively undertakes some processing of personal data, then that company will have to comply with the provisions of the Act. However, the company is not a data controller where such data is merely transmitted via such equipment. This may well be the case where data is transmitted across the Internet and therefore is routed via telecoms systems in many countries possibly including the United Kingdom. In such circumstances companies will not be bound by the provisions of the Act. In cases where a website is aimed at users in more than one country, or represents the activities or branches of an organisation in more than one country, several countries' data protection laws may apply.

Data controllers established outside the EEA who fall under the ambit of the Act are required to nominate for the purposes of the Act a representative established in the United Kingdom.

"Data processors"

Processing of personal data may be carried out by an outside person or organisation on behalf of the data controller, in accordance with his instructions. The Act refers to such persons as "data processors". This may be in a formal business sense, for example, where data storage or back office functions are outsourced or it may arise less formally in individual circumstances. Whilst a data processor is not required directly to comply with the Act, compliance with certain aspects of the legislation will inevitably be required in practice.

A person cannot be both a data controller and a data processor in respect of the *same data*. If a person has any discretion to determine the manner in which or the purposes for which he processes data on behalf of another person, he is likely to be regarded as controlling that data *jointly or in common* with that other person and not as a mere data processor. In that regard, it is important to consider the wide definition of "processing" under the Act.

Special rules apply to the appointment of data processors, with which data controllers must comply (see Section 7 below).

"Sensitive data"

Section 2 of the Act describes "sensitive and personal data" as any personal data about any of the following:

- racial or ethnic origin;
- political opinions;
- religion (this would include philosophies such as atheism);
- trade union activity;
- health;
- sexual life (this includes marital status as well as sexual orientation);
- offences (actual or alleged) and associated proceedings.

"Data subject"

This means anybody to whom the personal data relates. In the case of an e-tailer the most likely data subjects will be its customers and users of the website but employees are also likely to constitute data subjects with the e-tailer as employer processing their personal data.

3.   Notification

In order to process personal data, data controllers are (subject to a few exceptions) required, under section 17 of the Act, to register their non-exempt data processing activities with the Information Commissioner, giving the following details:

- the name and address of the controller;
- any nominated representative (in cases where the data controller is based outside the EEA);
- the description of the purpose(s) for which the data are being or are to be processed;

- the description of the recipient(s) or intended recipient(s) of the data;
- the name of any territories outside the EEA to which the data controller is transferring or intends to transfer the data; and
- measures to be taken to comply with the seventh data protection principle (the obligation to prevent unlawful processing of and damage to personal data – discussed below).

An annual notification fee is also payable, and data controllers are required to notify the Information Commissioner of any changes to their registrable particulars within 28 days if any inaccuracy or incompleteness arises. This requirement, however, is modified in the case of existing registrations (*i.e.* under the previous legislation) where certain transitional provisions apply.

Certain processing operations are exempt from the need to notify. These include a range of processing operations involving staff administration, advertising, marketing and public relations, accounts and record-keeping and certain processing operations carried out by non-profit-making organisations. The requirement to notify also does not apply in relation to processing done whose sole purpose is the maintenance of a public register (such as the Electoral Roll).

Under section 19 of the Act the Information Commissioner is required to maintain a list of all data controllers who have notified their processing activities to the Information Commissioner (the list is open to the public, on the Information Commissioner's website), and section 21 of the Act states that it is an offence to process personal data without having notified the Information Commissioner. This offence is a strict liability offence – that is to say that all that needs to be shown is that personal data has been processed and that the person processing the data has not notified the Information Commissioner. It is, however, a defence for the person charged to show that all due diligence had been exercised in attempting to comply with the duty.

There is guidance on the notification procedure on the Information Commissioner's website and the relevant forms can also be obtained from the website.

4. Obligations imposed under the Act – Eight Data Protection Principles

The Act aims to protect the interests of private individuals by imposing restrictions on the way in which individuals or bodies can process personal data. Rights are also granted to data subjects in relation to their personal data. These obligations are summarised in the Eight Data Protection Principles, with which the Act, in section 4, requires that the data controllers must comply. The Principles are set out in Schedule 1 of the Act and are broadly as follows:

(1) Personal data shall be processed fairly and lawfully.

(2) Personal data shall be obtained only for one or more specified and lawful purposes, and shall not be further processed in any manner incompatible with that purpose or purposes.

(3) Personal data shall be adequate, relevant and not excessive in relation to the purpose(s) for which they are processed.

(4) Personal data shall be accurate and, where necessary, kept up-to-date.

(5) Personal data processed for any purpose or purposes shall not be kept for longer than is necessary for that purpose or those purposes.

(6) Personal data shall be processed in accordance with the rights of data subjects under the Act.

(7) Appropriate technical and organisational measures shall be taken against unauthorised or unlawful processing of personal data and against accidental loss or destruction of, or damage to, personal data.

(8) Personal data shall not be transferred to a country or territory outside the European Economic Area unless that country or territory ensures an adequate level of protection for the rights and freedoms of data subjects in relation to the processing of personal data.

All of these principles impact on the business processes of companies processing data but we will focus on those principles of particular concern to e-commerce: the first, sixth, seventh and eighth principles.

5. Fair and lawful processing (1st Principle)

Data controllers must make sure that personal data is not only obtained in a fair and lawful manner but also that it is subsequently dealt with fairly and lawfully. In order for personal data to be processed in a fair and lawful manner certain conditions set out in the Act must be met and the relevant requirements for fair and lawful processing depend on whether or not the personal data concerned is classed as sensitive.

General conditions for processing all types of data

In order for processing of any data to be carried out fairly and lawfully one of the conditions set out in Schedule 2 must be met unless an exemption applies (these are further explained at the end of this section) and these are:

- the data subject has given his consent to the processing;
- the processing is necessary for the performance of a contract to which the data subject is a party or for taking steps, at the request of the data subject, with a view to entering into a contract;
- the processing is necessary to comply with any legal obligation to which the data controller is subject;
- the processing is necessary in order to protect the vital interests of the subject;
- the processing is necessary for the administration of justice or for the exercise of public functions exercised in the public interest; or
- the processing is necessary for the purposes of legitimate interests pursued by the data controller or by the third party to whom the data is disclosed, except where the processing is unwarranted in any particular case because of prejudice to the rights and freedoms or legitimate interests of the data subject.

The "consent" justification is the one most commonly relied on but first some thoughts on the other conditions.

The second justification is also widely used and can be used, for example, where there is only one simple transaction to be entered into with the customer and where, without another form of justification, no other processing of the data will take place. The scope within which data can be processed under this condition is therefore fairly narrow since data can only be processed for the purposes of the contract in hand.

Data controllers may process data where required by law. Most commonly this is going to be where data controllers are required to disclose information in order to cooperate with police or similar investigations. For instance, the Regulation of Investigatory Powers Act 2000 can be used to compel Internet service providers to hand over details of communications sent across their systems.

The condition which centres around the "vital interests" of the data subject is very narrow in its application and only applies where the processing is necessary for matters of life and death, for example, the disclosure of a data subject's medical history to a hospital casualty department treating the data subject.

The final criterion listed above may seemingly provide a catch-all justification for a business looking to justify the processing of its customers' data. However, it is not always clear what might constitute "legitimate interests". It is safe to assume that non-obvious marketing activity (such as sending marketing e-mails) will not be legitimised by this "catch-all" since it is not "necessary".

Consent

What constitutes consent by the data subject is, rather unhelpfully, not defined in the Act. However, it is defined in the European Directive on which the Act is based as being:

> "any freely given specific and informed indication of his wishes by which the data subject signifies his agreement to personal data relating to him being processed."

The fact that the data subject must signify his agreement means that there must be some active communication between the parties. The Information Commissioner therefore takes the view that data controllers cannot infer consent from non-response to a communication. The Information Commissioner's approach is that consent should be obtained on an "opt-in" basis rather than an "opt-out" basis. The consent must be indicated by a *positive act* on the part of the data subject which must be *communicated* to the data controller.

The requirement for active consent does not necessarily require a process where a data subject must communicate consent in a separate communication or statement outside of the transaction or registration process with the e-tailer. For example, provided that the fact that data will be processed and the purposes for which it will be processed are brought clearly to the attention of the data subject as part of the transaction or registration process, then the data subject can be said to have actively consented to such processing by proceeding with the transaction or registration. However, the cast iron method of obtaining consent is to include, in the design of the website, a method by which a user can positively indicate consent to processing by, for example, checking a box or clicking an "I accept" button. Indeed, the latter example could be built into the contracting process as outlined earlier. In any event, the data subject must always be able to request that data are not used for marketing purposes.

So, the customer must communicate consent to the processing of data, but what does that consent have to cover?

The Information Commissioner takes the view that the consent must be specific, that is, the consent obtained must refer to a specific type of processing. A blanket consent to the processing of data for all purposes is not sufficient. Also, the less foreseeable the processing that is to take place, the more information should be given to the data subject.

Other conditions for fair and lawful processing

In addition to the requirement to comply with a condition in Schedule 2, processing will not be considered "fair" unless further requirements (set out in Schedule 1, Part II) are fulfilled (known as the "Fair Processing Code"). As part of the Fair Processing Code, the data controller must provide certain information to the data subject at the time the data is collected. This information is:

- the identity of the data controller;
- the purpose for which the data are intended to be processed; and
- any further information which is necessary, taking into account the specific circumstances in which the data are to be processed, to enable the processing in respect of the data subject to be fair.

In determining what information is "necessary" one has to consider what processing of data is going to be undertaken and also whether or not the data subject is likely to understand:

- the purposes for which their personal data are going to be processed;
- the likely consequences of such processing; and
- whether any disclosures to third parties would be envisaged.

Where the personal data is obtained from someone other than the data subject the fair processing information should also be given to the data subject unless the provision of that information would involve "disproportionate effort".

When assessing whether the provision of the information would involve a disproportionate effort the factors to be considered are:

- the cost of providing the information v the benefit of processing;
- the time it will take to provide the information v the benefit of processing; and
- how easy/difficult it is to provide the information v the benefit of processing.

For example, having bought in a computerised mailing list of potential customers an e-tailer might carry out a screening process of the data to identify suitable targets for a marketing e-mail or mailshot. Certain individuals would then be selected as appropriate targets for marketing whilst others might be rejected as unsuitable and deleted from the mailing database. The obtaining of the data, the screening and sorting by computer and the deletion of records all constitute "processing" of the data as defined in the Act.

The cost to the data subject of writing to each individual whose data has been filtered out and deleted to inform them of that fact would be considerable, weighed against the negligible benefit which the data controller obtains from the processing of that data; indeed, once the data are deleted the data subject will not process the data further and will derive no further benefit. In addition, the risk of the data subject being prejudiced as a result of the data controller's failure to inform him of the processing is likely to be minimal. It is therefore arguable that informing the data subject would represent a disproportionate effort on the part of the data controller in such circumstances.

Processing sensitive personal data

When processing sensitive personal data one of the conditions set out in Schedule 3 must be met as we well as one of the Schedule 2 conditions. Typically this means that the individual's explicit *consent* will be required. This means a specific reference to the nature of the data concerned and the purposes for which such data are to be processed. There are other conditions set out in Schedule 3, for example, where the processing is necessary for the purposes of or in connection with any legal proceedings, for the administration of justice or for the exercise of statutory functions by any person. Additionally, there are 10 exemptions provided for in secondary legislation which relate specifically to the processing of sensitive personal data. These include circumstances where processing sensitive data is necessary for the purposes of making certain disclosures for journalistic, artistic or literary purposes, for the administration of certain insurance or occupational pension schemes, for monitoring equality between persons with different religious beliefs or between persons of differing physical or mental conditions or for research purposes, but are subject to a number of conditions – in many cases, for example, the processing must be in the substantial public interest.

6. Data subjects' rights under the Act (6th Principle)

Right of access to data

Under the Act the data subject has various rights in relation to personal data held by data controllers. These include firstly the right to be informed promptly if the personal data about the individual concerned is being processed by (or on behalf of) that data controller (section 7(1)(a)). If such processing is taking place under section 7(1)(b), the data controller must provide the data subject with the following information, should the data subject make a written request to that effect:

- a description of the personal data concerned and any disclosure of it;
- a description of the purposes for which the data are being or are to be processed;
- who is to receive the data; and
- any information as to the source of the data (where available).

The data controller may charge a fee for the provision of this information up to a maximum of £10. In addition, the data controller may require such information as is necessary in order to satisfy himself as to the identity of the person making the request, before he provides any information regarding the personal data of the data subject (section 7(3)). The data controller may also refuse to give the data subject access to records to the extent that, in doing so, data relating to another individual will be disclosed without that other individual consenting and where it would be unreasonable to carry out the request without the consent of the other individual (section 7(4)).

There are a limited number of exemptions from the data subjects' rights of access provided for in the Act. For example, a data controller could refuse to allow data subjects access to:

- confidential references given by the data controller;
- data processed in the course of management forecasts;
- data processed in order to provide certain corporate finance services (such as underwriting or placing issues, advice as to capital structure, industrial strategy or mergers); and
- any personal data which consists of a record made by a data controller in relation to any negotiations with the person concerned (if showing the data subject such records would prejudice the negotiations).

There are further exemptions set out in secondary legislation which exempt from the data subjects' rights of access in certain circumstances personal data relating to the physical or mental health of the data subject, the education records of the data subject and social work/welfare records of the data subject, for example. Personal data which is the subject of legal professional privilege need not be revealed to data subjects. In addition, a data controller need not reveal that they are processing data and which data is being processed if, in doing so, they would incriminate themselves.

Totalise plc v Motley Fool Ltd & Anr

This case centred on the fact that the defendants (Motley Fool) run a website on which users can make anonymous postings. In one instance the complainant (Totalise) were the subject of defamatory remarks and attempted, after the comments had been taken down following a complaint, to ascertain the identity of the user. Motley Fool rejected the request, and consequently Totalise brought an action to force disclosure of the identity of the user who had posted the defamatory comment. The court held that Motley Fool, despite running the service, had no control over content and could not be considered "responsible" for it, but that clearly Totalise had been defamed, potentially on a huge scale, and that there was really no way for them to come about the identity of the contributor other than through disclosure by Motley Fool.

Motley Fool tried to rely on section 35 of the Act which states that the provisions of the Act restricting disclosure of data do not apply where the disclosure is necessary for the purpose of legal proceedings or the obtaining of legal advice. The court rejected Motley Fool's argument that such use is limited to use of the data by the data controller and therefore section 35 did enable disclosure of the data to Totalise in order that it may take legal advice and possibly commence proceedings. Following this decision, perhaps the best option is for the website to include in the terms of use, which have to be accepted by the user prior to use of the service, the acceptance of disclosure of details by the operator if it believes a user's activities to have been unlawful, notwithstanding anything agreed to in privacy policies.

Rights concerning automated decision making

Many organisations use personal data as the basis for making decisions concerning the data subject. For example, an Internet-based credit card company may use information on a person's financial status and credit history in deciding whether or not to accept a customer's application for a credit card. Data subjects have special rights concerning this type of processing.

Where data are processed automatically and that is likely to form the sole basis for a decision significantly affecting the data subject, then, under section 12, he is entitled to know the logic involved in that decision-making.

Section 12 also states that the data subject will also have the right not to have a decision made solely on the basis of automated processing of data. There are, however, certain "exempt decisions" to which the data subject's right does not apply. These exempt decisions must satisfy two conditions:

- the decision must be taken by the data controller for the purpose of considering whether or not to enter into a contract with the data subject, or with a view to entering into or performing such a contract or in the course of performing the contract; and
- the effect of the decision must be to grant a request of the data subject or steps must have been taken to safeguard the legitimate interests of the data subject (for example, by allowing him to make representations).

Right to prevent processing likely to cause damage or distress

Section 10 states that data subjects have the right by giving written notice to the data controller to require the data controller not to commence, or to cease, processing of their personal data where the processing is causing or is likely to cause unwarranted substantial damage or distress to them or to another. This right is unavailable where certain of the general conditions for processing data have been complied with, for example, where the processing is necessary to comply with any of the legal obligations of the data controller.

Right to claim compensation for damage

Quite separately from the enforcement procedures in place to ensure compliance with the Act data subjects have the right (granted by section 13) to claim compensation for damage caused by any breach of the provisions of the Act and distress where it accompanies such damage.

Rectification, blocking, erasure and destruction of data

Data subjects may apply to the court for an order under section 14 requiring the data controller to rectify, block, erase or destroy inaccurate data about them (including any expression of opinion found to be based on inaccurate data).

7. Special rules on the use of data processors (7th Principle)

It is not uncommon for data controllers to outsource their data processing to a data processor. The Act contains special rules on such arrangements which the data controller must observe in order to comply with the Seventh Principle (concerned with security of data). The data controller must:

- choose a data processor providing sufficient guarantees in respect of the security measures they take;
- take reasonable steps to ensure compliance with those measures; and
- ensure that the processing by the data processor is carried out under a contract which is made or evidenced in writing, under which the data processor is obliged to act only on the instructions of the data controller and in accordance with the Seventh Principle.

Such contracts are useful tools to ensure that data processors comply with all relevant provisions of the Act (in order that the data controller can itself comply with the Act) and with certain regulatory requirements. Data processors can use such contracts to cover the following points:

- compliance with the Eighth Principle where the data processor is physically located outside the EEA;
- observance of other regulatory regimes (such as banking or financial services) which require certain standards of data protection; and
- assisting the data controller to respond to subject access requests and correct or delete inaccurate data;

8. **Special rules on the transfer of personal data outside the EEA (8th Principle)**

In today's international markets, frequent cross-border transactions means that many data controllers will need to transfer data abroad and the global nature of the Internet means that international transfers of data will become increasingly more common. In addition, many multinational organisations may also wish to share personal data between their various branches or affiliates in different countries. Wherever personal data are transferred outside the EEA, the data controller must ensure compliance with the Eighth Principle, which states:

> "Personal data shall not be transferred to a country or territory outside the European Economic Area unless that country or territory ensures an adequate level of protection for the rights and freedoms of data subjects in relation to the processing of personal data".

One common misconception is that the Eighth Principle prohibits transfers of data outside the EEA. This is not the case. Data may be transferred outside the EEA provided that an adequate level of protection exists in relation to the processing of the data. In addition, there tends to be a misconception that in all cases of international transfer the data controller should obtain the data subject's consent. It is true that the consent of the data subject is a derogation from the Eighth Principle but it is not always necessary or desirable.

The Information Commissioner recommends that data controllers approach the issue of transfers outside the EEA in the following order:

- is there an EU finding, or presumption, of adequacy?
- considering the type of transfer in question, can any presumptions of adequacy or inadequacy be made?

- consider and apply the "adequacy test" which is a test designed to determine whether there is an adequate level of protection in the recipient country; and
- finally, where there is any doubt, look at the derogations, such as consent.

EC findings of adequacy

The European Commission is in the process of considering the data protection laws of several non-EU countries with a view to adopting decisions indicating if they are likely generally to offer adequate protection. As at the time of writing, Switzerland and Hungary have been found to provide adequate protection.

Given that many companies either have a group company presence in the United States or otherwise transfer data to the United States it is important to note that the United States has no comprehensive data protection law in the way that the European states understand data protection. Discussions between the European Commission and the US government have led to the establishment of a system where there is a presumption of an adequate level of security if data are transferred to US businesses which have signed up to "safe harbour" arrangements which ensure an adequate level of protection for personal data. The safe harbour arrangements require the US Department of Commerce to maintain a list of organisations which agree to comply with a list of "safe harbour privacy principles" and which will therefore provide an adequate level of protection for personal data. It will still be possible to transfer data to organisations who do not sign up to this safe harbour list, but the data controller will have to consider the points further down the Information Commissioner's check list. Organisations which have signed up to the safe harbour list can be viewed at www.export.gov/safeharbor/.

Presumptions of adequacy and the "adequacy test"

In deciding what constitutes an "adequate level of protection", the Information Commissioner considers the following factors as being relevant:
- the *nature* of the personal data being transferred – the more sensitive the data, the higher the level of protection required;

- the *origin* of the data – if the personal data originated in Bahrain and were sent to the United Kingdom for processing before being transferred back to Bahrain, it might be that this transfer will be permitted more readily than if the data originated from the United Kingdom and were sent to Bahrain for processing, although this is not certain;
- the *final destination* of the personal data being transferred;
- the *purpose* for which and *period* during which the data are intended to be processed;
- *legal protections* and *codes of conduct* in force in the country in question (*e.g.* Bahrain); and
- any *security or legal measures* taken in respect of the data in that country.

A general consideration when determining adequacy is the extent of the "risk" involved in a particular transfer. If the personal data are particularly sensitive and any unlawful disclosure of such data would have particularly undesirable results, it is likely that any transfer of such data would be regarded as high risk and would be prohibited unless the destination country has adequate levels of protection in place.

It can also be possible to create a climate of adequate protection through the use of contractual clauses or codes of conduct which put in place certain safeguards regarding the treatment of the data following transfer of the data outside the EEA. However, there are problems with the use of such contracts such as:

- the need for a detailed, enforceable contract governing the recipient's handling of the data and which as a consequence may reduce the utility of the data to the recipient;
- the need for data subjects to have a legal remedy for breach of contract, despite not being party to it;
- the lack of any real incentive for the recipient to comply with the terms of the contract unless there is some supervisory authority which has the power to monitor, investigate and enforce the terms of such contracts;
- the possible existence of laws, such as state rights to seize data, which could override contractual provisions.

On 18 June 2001 the European Commission announced that it had adopted a decision concerning standard contractual clauses which may be used by a data controller established in the EU in order to adduce sufficient safeguards for a transfer of data to a person outside the EEA. Indeed, the decision obliges Member States to recognise that companies or organisations using such standard clauses in contracts concerning personal data transfers to countries outside the EEA are offering adequate protection to the data subject's personal information. The decision regarding standard contractual clauses does not cover the scenario where data is transferred by data controllers established in the EU to data processors outside the EEA since those transfers do not require the same safeguards since the processor acts exclusively on behalf of the data controller. Consequently, that type of transfer has formed the subject matter of a subsequent draft decision by the European Commission. The text of the decision and the draft decision are reproduced as Appendices 4 and 5.

Cases where 8th Principle does not apply

Finally, if none of the three previous steps demonstrate that there will be adequate protection for the data subjects following an international transfer, the data controller must turn to the derogations in the Act. Fortunately, for data controllers, there are a number of exceptions (set out in Schedule 4 to the Act) where the Eighth Principle does not apply. These operate so that transfers to countries where the general level of protection is inadequate may still be permitted provided certain other conditions are met. These conditions are as follows:

- the data subject has given his consent to the transfer;
  To obtain valid consent here, data controllers must explain the reasons for the transfer, any country to which the information will be sent (as far as possible) and any risks the data controller knows of. Consent must also be freely given. The Information Commissioner has suggested that the words "By signing below you accept that we can transfer any of the information we keep about you to any country when a business need arises" would not produce valid consent. As an alternative, the words: "By signing below you accept that we may pass details of your mortgage application to X Ltd in Singapore who we have chosen to arrange mortgages on our behalf. You should be aware that Singapore does not have a data protection law" would be acceptable in appropriate circumstances. This is consistent with the Information Commissioner's guidance on the first principle where we have seen that she requires the active communication of specific and informed consent.

- the transfer is necessary for the performance of a contract with the data subject or for the taking of steps at his request with a view to his entering into a contract with the data controller;
- the transfer is necessary for the conclusion or performance of a contract between the data controller and a third party entered into at the request of the data subject or which is in his interests;

    When considering what is "necessary" for the purposes of the two contract exemptions set out above, data controllers must consider what is necessary for the conclusion of the contract rather than needs arising from the organisational structure of their business. For example, it may be necessary for a UK-based Internet company selling goods manufactured in the United States to transfer UK customer details to the manufacturer in order that the goods can be delivered. However, if that Internet company chose to locate its accounts department on the Isle of Man, the transfer of personal data to the accounts department would not be necessary for the performance of the contract since the contract could have been concluded without the need to transfer the data outside the EEA. In order to effect the transfer to the accounts department it would be necessary to run it through the Information Commissioner's four point test.

- the transfer is necessary for reasons of substantial public interest. The Secretary of State may make Orders which set out what does and does not constitute "substantial public interest";
- the transfer is necessary in connection with legal proceedings or obtaining legal advice;
- the transfer is necessary in order to protect the vital interests of the data subject (again, this would mean a matter of life and death);
- the transfer is part of the personal data on a public register, provided that any conditions to which the register is subject are honoured after the transfer;
- the transfer is made on terms which adequately protect data subjects' rights (*e.g.* under a contract made between the data controller and the organisation receiving the data where that contract contains terms which will ensure the privacy of the data subjects); and
- the transfer has been authorised by the Information Commissioner as being made in such a manner as to ensure adequate safeguards for the rights and freedoms of data subjects.

9. **Enforcement**

The Information Commissioner is keen to encourage those with a valid complaint to pursue the issue themselves with the data controller insofar as it is possible to do so. The Information Commissioner believes a significant number of complaints which she investigates could be settled sooner without official involvement.

Moreover, data controllers would be well advised to establish a clear mechanism for dealing with data subject complaints since many problems could be resolved before the data subject feels the need to involve the Information Commissioner. Once official involvement is undertaken, there begins a process of investigation. One of the Information Commissioner's tools in the investigation process is the issue of an "Information Notice" (section 43) which can be used to compel the recipient to answer the questions posed by the Information Commissioner and to provide details about its data processing activities. Once the evidence is assembled and reported, it is for the Information Commissioner to decide if she believes there to have been an offence committed. If yes, it is possible for a prosecution to be mounted, and fines can be imposed. It is possible for the Information Commissioner, if she harbours serious suspicion that a criminal offence has been committed, to apply to a judge for a search warrant to investigate the premises of the accused.

However it is more common for the Information Commissioner, upon establishing that there has been an infringement, to serve an Enforcement Notice under section 40 detailing the infringement and the necessary steps to correct it. The prohibition of information transfer overseas can be effected through a Transfer Prohibition Notice. Any recipient of notices issued by the Information Commissioner is entitled to appeal to the Data Protection Tribunal, an independent body, who can replace the Information Commissioner's decision with a binding one of its own. It is important to note that under Section 47 failure to comply with a notice issued by the Information Commissioner is a criminal offence.

Fast track enforcement procedure

The Information Commissioner's 13th annual report set out plans for the fast track enforcement procedure. The procedure for dealing with complaints which qualify for fast track enforcement is slightly different since supervisory powers are assumed straight away without attempts at negotiation. The circumstances in which this could be expected to occur are, for example, where

- when one or more of the principles of the Act has been breached; and
- the complainant has informed the data controller, providing them with sufficient information to identify and tackle the infringement, but they failed to do so after a reasonable amount of time had lapsed.

Immediately a preliminary notice will be issued by the Information Commissioner, without any prior discussion. The Information Commissioner has also indicated that this prompt action will be taken where a breach exists in an area where a decision or announcement has already been made, and the person committing the infringement can reasonably have been expected to be aware of the established position.

10. **Privacy policies**

There is no strict requirement in the Act to use privacy policy wording on a website. Wide-ranging privacy policies on websites are common now but not because the Act requires websites to have one. Instead, a privacy policy can be a useful way to ensure compliance with some aspects of the Act.

As has been stated, in order for a data controller to obtain and process the data in a fair manner, the data controller must be able to show that there is a valid justification for the processing of the data. The most commonly used justification is that the data subject has consented to the processing and a privacy policy can be used to obtain that consent. Again to recap, the Information Commissioner requires there to be "active communication" of the consent and therefore the registration process or product buying process should require the user to acknowledge acceptance of the privacy policy (or a set of terms and conditions which incorporate the privacy policy). In addition, the Commissioner requires the consent obtained to be specific and a privacy policy enables the data controller to state clearly what will be done with the data. Broadly speaking, processing purposes which one might expect to see in a privacy policy would be: marketing, disclosure to third parties and disclosure or transfer overseas.

These purposes are typically the sort of non-obvious processing which ought to be brought to the data subject's attention and for which the data controller will require consent. However, the processing purposes which need to be included will have to be determined on a case-by-case basis looking at all the surrounding facts.

A privacy policy also enables the data controller to comply with elements of the Fair Processing Code by delivering to the data subject certain information such as the data controller's identity as well as the purpose of processing, quite separately from any need for consent. The e-tailor can also use the privacy policy to inform his customers that the website makes use of cookies. The Information Commissioner has issued a guidance note to Internet companies informing them that users should always be informed that the website makes use of cookies or other covert software to collect data about the user. The best place to deliver this information is probably in the privacy policy. In addition, privacy policies can be used to inform data subjects of their right to access personal data held by the data controller and how the data subject might go about changing that data if necessary. However, this last function of a privacy policy is not a legal requirement imposed by the Act.

Example

It may be helpful if we set up an example of how a privacy policy might be formulated in accordance with the business practices of an imaginary Internet trader.

Example.com is an online electrical retailer which supplies UK customers with white goods such as fridges and dishwashers. Example.com is part of a wider corporate group and its parent company is located in the United States. Some of the goods supplied to customers may have to be sourced from the United States. In addition, example.com would like to give certain details of its customers to its sister company examplecd.com which sells music and videos, so that its sister company can send customers details of its special offers. Finally, example.com makes use of cookies so that it can customise the site to the individual user and ensure that each individual user receives a personal greeting.

A privacy policy for example.com based on the limited facts set out above might look like this:

> "Example.com is a website operated by Example.com Limited and we may collect certain information about you in the course of your use of this website or through transactions with you. We take privacy and

security of customer information seriously and will only use your personal data as set out in this privacy policy. By using the example.com site you agree to us collecting and using your personal information in accordance with the details below.

What information will we collect about you?

We will collect information about you when you register with example.com, when you purchase goods from us and when you contact us either by e-mail or through our call centre. We will also collect data regarding your usage of the example.com site.

How will we use the information we collect about you?

We will do the following with your personal information:

- store and use it to provide you with any goods which you order from us;
- disclose it to third parties who supply us with the goods – this may require disclosure of your information to companies within the example.com group which are located in the United States. Please note that not all countries have the same level of legal protection for personal information as exists in the United Kingdom;
- improve and develop the products we offer by analysing your information including information related to your usage of the example.com site; and
- send you information about products and services which may be of interest to you.

Will we share your information with anyone else?

We will share your information with other members of the example.com group who may e-mail you with information about products and services which may interest you. If at any time you no longer wish to receive such e-mails please follow the instructions set out in the e-mails and you will be removed from the mailing list. We may also need to pass your personal information to anyone to whom we transfer our rights and duties and we may also disclose your information to any applicable regulatory body or if the law requires or allows us to.

Can you update your information?

You may update your information by contacting us by e-mail or phone as set out below.

Can you ask for a copy of the information we hold?

You have a right under the Data Protection Act 1998 to access the information we hold about you, subject to certain conditions. Please contact us as set out below for further information.

Cookies

Cookies are files we transfer to your computer's hard disk. Cookies can store information about your preferences and other information which you need when you visit a website, helping to avoid the need to type the same information on each visit. We can also use cookies to show us how you are using our website. Example.com uses cookies in order to personalise our service and to help you to use the example.com website more easily. Most web browsers automatically accept cookies. However, you do not necessarily have to accept them, since your browser may allow you to turn off this feature.

Contacting us

If you:

- do not wish to receive marketing material; or
- wish to update your personal information or request access to it; or
- have any other queries or requests about our processing of your personal information.

please telephone us on ******* or send us an e-mail at contact@example.com. "

This is of course, only an example of how a privacy policy for inclusion within a website might look. It is not necessarily appropriate, in its entirety, for use by all Internet traders, as a privacy policy must be tailored in particular to cover all aspects of the processing that will be undertaken by the Internet trader.

The information padlock

In order to alert the public in situations where they are being asked to disclose personal information which will then be processed, the Information Commissioner and the National Consumer Council have launched an information signpost scheme featuring the above padlock symbol. This will be used by data controllers and placed at any point where information is requested in the media used.

It is intended that customers will then be able to tell at a glance that their personal information is being collected, and they will be directed to sources which will clearly explain how their information is to be used. Bodies wishing to make use of the padlock symbol can download copies of it from www.dataprotection.gov.uk

11. **Summary**

- If any personal data is being collected or used in any way the e-tailer must notify the Information Commissioner and that notification should aim to cover all likely present and future uses of personal data.

- Personal data includes information which is obviously personal data such as names and addresses but also includes less obvious data such as usage statistics and patterns showing an individual user's use of a website.

- A data controller must have one of the statutory justifications for processing data. If in doubt the data subject's consent to the processing should be obtained. This can be done effectively by use of a privacy policy.

- Data subjects have the right to access the data that is held regarding them and have the right to prevent processing that is likely to cause damage or distress.

- Where data is to be transferred outside the EEA, the data controller should apply the Information Commissioner's four point test.

Chapter 9

Advertising &
· Direct Marketing ·

1. Introduction

E-tailers can generate useful revenue streams from advertising placed on their site. Also, if an e-tailer does not itself advertise elsewhere (both online and offline) and implement direct marketing campaigns it will be less likely to continue to see an increase in user numbers on its website. An increase in user numbers on its website is likely to trigger an increased demand for advertising space on its website and increased revenue from existing advertising. However, advertising and direct marketing are regulated activities and therefore it is important to consider the legal implications of any advertising or direct marketing campaign before its implementation.

This chapter will look at how advertising is regulated in the United Kingdom as well as how UK data protection law places limits around what can be done by companies wishing to undertake direct marketing campaigns.

Much of the regulation of direct marketing focuses on more traditional forms of communication such as mail, telephone and fax. This regulation will concern those companies wishing to undertake more traditional direct marketing campaigns but can also impact on those undertaking e-mail marketing campaigns. In any event the law in this area is in the process of being changed and this chapter will look at possible future developments. Finally, this chapter will deal with the more intrusive side of electronic marketing – spamming.

2. Advertising

Advertising on a website

A website is a non-broadcast media since, whilst the content is available for viewing on a one-to-many basis, the transmission of that content does not happen simultaneously but rather when the website is accessed by each individual user.

The British Codes of Advertising (the "Codes") apply, amongst other things, to "advertisements in non-broadcast electronic media" which therefore encompasses advertising on a website. Although the provisions of the Codes are not legally binding, in respect of all advertising on a website (and arguably a website could be construed as advertising itself) an e-tailer should comply with the following major principles (although there are others):

- all advertising should be legal, decent, honest and truthful;
- all claims, whether direct or implied, must be capable of objective substantiation;
- the advertisements must not contain anything which may cause serious or widespread offence (for instance, on the grounds of race, religion, sex, sexual orientation or disability);
- advertisers must not exploit the credulity, lack of knowledge or inexperience of consumers;
- any stated price must be clear and relate to the product advertised and prices quoted should include VAT and other non-optional taxes; and
- no offer should be described as being free unless consumers pay only the current public rates of postage, the actual cost of delivery or the cost of travel if the customer has to collect the offer.

The Codes are issued and administered by the Advertising Standards Authority (the "ASA") and although the Codes are voluntary it is wise to abide by them. Non-compliance with the Codes is likely to lead to a request from the ASA to remove the advertising from view and complaints are published in the ASA's monthly report which could result in bad publicity for the e-tailer and any advertising agency used. In some cases the ASA may report breaches of the Codes to the Director General of Fair Trading who may take more severe action under the Control of Misleading Advertisements Regulations 1988. Under these regulations the Director General can seek an undertaking from anyone responsible for commissioning, preparing or disseminating the advertisement that it will be discontinued. If this undertaking is not honoured the Director General can seek an injunction from the court to prevent the dissemination of the advertisement. Anyone in default of an injunction is in contempt of court which could lead to a fine or even imprisonment.

It is worth remembering that there is a risk that advertising which could be considered as perfectly reasonable in the United Kingdom may not be considered acceptable in other countries. For example, content which includes scantily clad women or alcohol may well be considered offensive and even illegal in certain Middle Eastern countries. This issue can be dealt with, to an extent, by choosing advertisements and content carefully and ensuring that it is clear that the website is targeted at the United Kingdom and/or other countries where the goods advertised are actually intended to be sold. The issue of dealing with the laws of foreign countries is dealt with in Chapter 4 on Jurisdiction.

Advertising on other websites

When placing advertisements on other websites it is just as important to ensure adherence to the codes and when employing an advertising agency to design and place advertisements on the e-tailer's behalf it is important that they also adhere to all relevant laws and regulations. It may also be wise for the e-tailer to place restrictions on the sort of websites on which the agency can place advertisements or even require them to be approved before they can be placed on the other site. By an e-tailer placing its brand on a disreputable website that e-tailer is running the risk of damaging that brand by association and it is therefore wise that some degree of control over placement of advertisement is maintained.

3. **Direct marketing**

In recent years there has been increasing legislative activity intended to restrict and monitor the practices adopted by businesses wishing to market services or products to individuals directly, whether by telephone, fax, e-mail or other methods. Existing legal restrictions in the United Kingdom are largely focused on marketing by use of the more conventional communications technologies, namely, telephone and fax. However, it appears that existing restrictions may to some extent be applied to marketing by e-mail. In any case, new legislation designed explicitly to extend existing regulations to marketing by e-mail (and probably any other existing or future communications technology) is likely to come into force in the near future. Whilst the remainder of this section will deal with laws affecting marketing by phone and fax, such information is not only a useful source of reference for a wide range of businesses (including those conducting business online who may wish to undertake offline marketing activities) but also a taster for the form that the new legislation might take.

Data Protection Act 1998

Before looking at the legislation specifically dealing with direct marketing it is worth remembering that the Data Protection Act 1998 itself impacts on a company's direct marketing activities. Direct marketing will involve processing personal data and therefore the company undertaking such marketing must ensure that it has one of the statutory justifications in place before undertaking such processing.

In the case of direct marketing the only two applicable justifications will be either that the individual has consented to the processing of his data for the purposes of direct marketing or that the processing is necessary for the legitimate interests of the company wishing to undertake the marketing and such activity will not interfere with the rights and freedoms of the individual. The latter justification is rather more risky than the first, given that direct marketing is not necessarily an obvious use of an individual's data (for example, where an individual has purchased something from a website the natural conclusion might be that data provided by the individual would be used for little more than delivering the product to the customer and billing the customer for the product) and, in addition, such activity is more likely to provoke complaints from individuals than other less invasive forms of processing. For these reasons it is advisable, quite outside the obligations set out in the specific legislation concerning direct marketing, to obtain the data subject's consent to direct marketing activity. The consent obtained from the individual should be obtained on an opt-in basis. Non-response to a communication or statement is not enough.

The Data Protection Act 1998 also states, in section 11, that data subjects have the right, by notice in writing to the data controller, to bring an end to the processing of his personal data for marketing purposes. Consequently, e-tailers should establish processes which will enable individuals to convey their wish not to receive further marketing materials from the e-tailer. For example, when sending marketing e-mails the e-tailer would be well advised to provide a method for the recipient to unsubscribe from the marketing list. This could be done by, for example, allowing the recipient to respond with the words "remove" or "unsubscribe" in the title or providing a URL linking to a web page which enables the recipient to register the fact that he does not want to receive more marketing messages. Of course, the crucial element to any system like this is that the requests received from individuals to be removed from marketing lists must be acted upon.

Telecommunications (Data Protection and Privacy) Regulations 1999

The Telecommunications (Data Protection and Privacy) Regulations 1999 (the "Telecoms Regulations") came into force on 1 March 2001 and effectively supplement the Data Protection Act 1998.

The Telecoms Regulations, amongst other things, apply restrictions to all individuals or organisations who use "publicly available telecommunications services" to send any advertising or marketing material. The Telecoms Regulations therefore protect the privacy and other rights of those whose contact details and other personal data is held and used by direct marketers insofar as those marketers use telecommunications services to carry out their marketing. There is some debate as to whether the provisions of the Telecoms Regulations can be applied to the use of e-mail but first we will outline how the Telecoms Regulations apply to traditional marketing methods.

Obligations under the Telecoms Regulations

The Telecoms Regulations restrict the use of telecommunications networks for the purposes of advertising and marketing. The definition of these activities is so broad as to include sales promotion, communication of information, public announcements, customer care services and fund raising (*i.e.* whether or not such activities directly involve an attempt to sell products or services). The Information Commissioner refers in her guidance to a definition of direct marketing activities included in Recommendation no R85(20) of the Council of Europe on "the protection of personal data used for the purpose of direct marketing":

> "activities which make it possible to offer goods or services or to transmit other messages ... to a segment of the population by post, telephone or other direct means aimed at informing or soliciting a response".

Some of the rights contained in the Telecoms Regulations are allocated according to the status of the "subscriber" to a telecommunications service which they receive over the relevant telecommunications network. "Subscribers" can either be "individual subscribers" (living individuals or unincorporated bodies) or "corporate subscribers" (incorporated bodies) which have a contract with a telecommunications service provider for the supply of a publicly available telecommunications service. This would include, for example, an individual who holds a contract with a mobile telephone operator for the use of their mobile telephone.

The Telecoms Regulations contain the following specific restrictions:

Automated calling systems

Use of automated calling systems for direct marketing to individual subscribers or corporate subscribers is prohibited without having previously received their consent to receive calls via an automated calling system.

Unfortunately, the term "automated calling system" is not defined in the Telecoms Regulations but the Information Commissioner's view is that the term "automated calling system" refers to a system where the individual receiving the call does not speak to a live person, instead receiving a recorded message or some pre-determined voice activated response. The use of a system whereby telephone numbers are automatically dialled but a human being will talk to the person who answers the phone is not likely to be affected by this provision of the Telecoms Regulations.

Again, for subscribers to give effective consent to receiving marketing calls via automated calling systems, consent must involve a positive act of communication, such as the ticking of an opt-in box, and in addition such consent must be specific and informed meaning that the subscriber must appreciate what it is that he is consenting to. The Information Commissioner in her guidance notes gives the example of text messages being sent to a subscriber's mobile telephone and states that in this instance the subscriber must have previously consented to this activity as this would constitute an individual receiving marketing communications from an automated calling system.

Unsolicited communications

Under the Telecoms Regulations, cold calling an individual subscriber for marketing purposes is prohibited where that individual subscriber has notified the caller that he objects to receiving such calls or where he is listed in the "Telephone Preference Service".

Sending unsolicited faxes to individual subscribers or corporate subscribers for direct marketing purposes is also prohibited where a subscriber has previously notified the company sending the marketing material that such communications should not be sent to the subscriber's number or where the subscriber is listed in the "Fax Preference Service". Individual subscribers have additional protection, prohibiting the sending of faxes to them (whether solicited or unsolicited) unless they have previously consented to receive marketing faxes.

The references to the "Telephone Preference Service" and "Fax Preference Service" are references to the lists which the Telecoms Regulations require the Director General of Telecommunications to maintain. They record telephone and fax numbers of subscribers who have registered the fact that that they object to receiving unsolicited direct marketing via telephone and/or fax. The Director General of Telecommunications has appointed the Direct Marketing Association to maintain lists of registered individuals who do not want to receive unsolicited marketing calls (the Telephone Preference Service) and those individuals who do not want to receive unsolicited marketing faxes (the Fax Preference Service) and to make such lists available to subscribing organisations at a small fee. Subscribing organisations to each scheme undertake to ensure that the mailing lists they use do not contain the names of those who have registered under the scheme.

The Direct Marketing Association has set up two companies, the Telephone Preference Service Limited and the Fax Preference Service Limited, which are wholly owned subsidiaries of the Direct Marketing Association and which are responsible for maintaining the relevant list. The Fax Preference Service Limited is obliged to remove fax numbers where they have reason to believe that a fax number recorded on this list is no longer allocated to the objecting subscriber, on the request of marketers wishing to send marketing faxes or subscribers wishing to receive them. The companies also log complaints from individuals and report to the Information Commissioner any activities which they believe may infringe the Telecoms Regulations or the Data Protection Act.

Because direct marketers may have difficulty in distinguishing from a list of businesses those which are partnerships or sole traders (to whom, therefore, no marketing material can be sent without prior consent) it is also possible for these businesses as well as individuals to ensure they receive no such material by registering with the Fax Preference Service.

Whilst not all direct marketers are a member of the preference schemes, the preference schemes are strongly supported by the Information Commissioner, who can compel companies to join. In addition, quite apart from the Telecoms Regulations' requirements, several direct marketing industry codes of practice require members to subscribe. Non-membership of such schemes would be viewed dimly in any investigation into whether a data controller regularly sending marketing materials was processing personal data fairly.

All e-tailers planning to undertake a telephone or fax marketing campaign, for example, should therefore check their marketing list against the Telephone Preference Service and Fax Preference Service and any internal records listing subscribers who should not be called or sent marketing faxes.

It is important to note that the provisions relating to such cold calling or sending of faxes would not apply if the recipient of the fax or call indirectly invited contact by, for example, returning a request asking for information on a product, supplying their fax or telephone number for that purpose. In those circumstances the communication sent to the individual is not unsolicited and the provisions of the Telecoms Regulations do not apply.

For the sake of completeness it is worth mentioning that a scheme similar to the Telephone Preference Service and Fax Preference Service operates in respect of direct marketing mail. The Mail Preference Service records the names and address of those people who do not want to receive marketing materials by post. This is done free of charge and registration is effective for five years. Direct marketers are required by marketing industry codes of practice to refrain from sending marketing material to those who have registered. This will prevent "junk" mail being sent by those marketers who subscribe to the scheme to registered individuals personally, though there is little preventing such material being sent "to the occupier". Similarly, the scheme will not prevent mail received by individuals from organisations with whom they have done business. In these cases, individuals should write to those organisations and ask that such mail not be sent.

Membership of the Mail Preference Service scheme is not a specific requirement of the Data Protection Act 1998 but the Information Commissioner strongly supports the scheme and in some instances she can insist that direct marketers who do not currently subscribe to the scheme, do so in future. In addition, several direct marketing industry association codes of practice specify that members should "clean" their lists against the Mail Preference Service list.

Traffic and billing data

There are also provisions in the Telecoms Regulations designed to
regulate the way in which personal data is processed in the
telecommunications sector. Traffic data consist of data held, or
processed, by any telecommunications network or service provider in
respect of, or for the purposes of facilitating, calls by individual
subscribers and corporate subscribers. Where such traffic data contain
personal information which would allow a subscriber to be identified
and contacted, such data must be erased or dealt with in such a way
that they cease to include personal information on the termination of
the call in question.

Similar provisions in respect of billing data dictate that information
required for the purpose of calculating a subscriber's bill (for example,
a subscriber's name, address and consumption of the service) may only
be kept by any relevant telecommunications network or service
provider until the end of the time period during which the bill may be
challenged or payment pursued. In practice, this means that generally a
network or service provider may be able to keep such information for
periods of up to six years and more (by reference to statutory limitation
periods, *i.e.* the time limits on the ability of a party to initiate litigation
following the event giving rise to the relevant legal cause of action and
which, in the case of contractual disputes, are generally six years)
although the Information Commissioner has stipulated that data can
only be kept where circumstances require it; for example, where a
challenge is made to a bill whilst the individual concerned is still a
customer. In any case, under the Data Protection Act 1998 personal
data can only be kept for as long as is necessary for the purpose for
which they are processed.

The Telecoms Regulations impose a stricter control on the processing
of billing data than the control on processing of personal data generally
under the Data Protection Act 1998. Billing data must not be processed
for the purposes of marketing telecommunications services provided by
a telecommunications service provider unless the consent of a
subscriber has first been obtained. Further, each subscriber would on
giving such consent and for such consent to be valid need to have
appreciated how the data was going to be used and the consequences of
such use.

Telecoms Regulations and e-mail

On the basis that the Telecoms Regulations were drafted with reference
to public telecommunications networks and services, the Information
Commissioner has taken the view that the Telecoms Regulations apply
equally to e-mail marketing since e-mailing involves the use of a
telecommunications network. However, the Telecoms Regulations were
not drafted with the intention of applying to e-mail. The Telecoms
Regulations make no specific mention of e-mail, and records of debates
in Parliament whilst the Telecoms Regulations were being debated
indicate that the government was unwilling to include e-mail within the
ambit of the Telecoms Regulations.

It may, however, be wise to follow the Information Commissioner's
guidance, not least because the Information Commissioner is
responsible for the enforcement of the Telecoms Regulations. Further,
European legislation is in the pipeline which is designed specifically to
cover e-mail marketing. Such European legislation will probably
ensure that national laws furnish appropriate protections in respect of
marketing by e-mail and other newly developed communications
methods, regardless of changing communications technology. Further
information on the relevant draft EC Directive is included in the
next section.

If the Telecoms Regulations are to be applied to electronic forms of
marketing we can interpret "calling", as referred to in the Telecoms
Regulations, as including e-mails, text messaging and sending messages
via interactive TV. The Telecoms Regulations would then act so as to
prohibit any unsolicited marketing messages via these media if an
individual subscriber has previously notified the e-tailer that such
messages should not be sent, or has registered their e-mail address with
the list of those people who do not wish to receive any marketing e-
mails. The difficulty with this proposition is that it is only the
Telephone Preference Service and Fax Preference Service that have
"official" status under the Telecoms Regulations. There is no such
official list for e-mail or other forms of electronic marketing although
the Direct Marketing Association has created an E-mail Preference
Service which maintains a list of individuals who do not wish to receive
unsolicited marketing by e-mail. Given that it is not established by the
Telecoms Regulations the E-mail Preference Service currently does not
have the same status as the Fax and Telephone Preference Services
(there is no statutory obligation to clean data through it and there is no
obligation for the list to be maintained). However, members of the

Direct Marketing Association are required by the rules of the Association to run e-mail marketing lists through the E-mail Preference Service and the service is available for use by non-members.

A final reason why it would be prudent to treat the Telecoms Regulations as covering e-mail communications is that certain other laws imposed requirements which overlap with the requirements of the Telecoms Regulations. Both the Data Protection Act 1998 (for instance, the fundamental principle that all personal data must be processed in a fair and lawful manner and otherwise, as discussed above) and the Consumer Protection (Distance Selling) Regulations 2000 are relevant in this regard.

Enforcement

The Telecoms Regulations are enforceable by the Information Commissioner who may take enforcement action on her own initiative or at the request of the Director General for Telecommunications or of individuals who have suffered from contravention of the Telecoms Regulations. It is also worth noting that any person who suffers damage due to a breach by another person of the Telecoms Regulations will be able to claim compensation from that person, although it is a defence for the party allegedly in contravention to show that he has taken reasonable care to comply with the Telecoms Regulations.

The future

At the time of writing, a new Electronic Communications Directive currently entitled "Electronic Communications: processing of personal data, protection of privacy" is being drafted. It aims to replace the directive upon which the Telecoms Regulations are founded with new provisions governing how personal data may be processed so that privacy is protected. These provisions will largely reflect those of the Telecoms Regulations but an attempt has been made to ensure the new wording will include all forms of electronic messaging currently in use, such as e-mail, texting and interactive TV, as well as foreseeable developments in electronic communications services and technologies.

The idea behind the new Electronic Communications Directive is to ensure that privacy protection encompasses all forms of technology, and that the wording is flexible enough to continue to do so in the future. This is largely so that the public and the private sectors do not lose the protection of the directive upon which the

Telecoms Regulations are founded when new electronic messaging systems not covered by it become available to those engaged in direct marketing activities.

The Electronic Communications Directive (which must be implemented by 31 December 2001) will ultimately be reflected in changes to the current Telecoms Regulations. Provisions of the Electronic Communications Directive include replacing references to "establishing a call" with "the transmission of a communication", which substantially widens the kind of messaging which will be caught by the provisions. Hence, the current provisions relating to telephone calls will soon apply explicitly to e-mailing. In addition, spamming is also to be covered by the same type of protection as exists for faxes. This means that spamming will be prohibited unless subscribers have indicated that they are happy to receive unsolicited e-mails for direct marketing purposes (an "opt-in" system). This will help to harmonise the divergent laws which currently exist in EU Member States where some countries have banned spamming whilst others have not, so that direct marketers who are banned in their own country from sending unsolicited e-mails still continue to target consumers in other countries with more liberal legislation. Further information on spamming is set out below.

Another significant addition to the privacy protection laws so far discussed will be the addition of a section obliging data processors to inform subscribers of the personal data that are being collected. This is intended to empower the subscribers to control and object to ongoing data processing. Interestingly, the Electronic Communications Directive will also prohibit the use for marketing purposes of information giving the exact geographical location of individuals using mobile telephones (sometimes known as "cell of origin" information) and other mobile telecoms equipment which can now be gathered from satellite and cellular networks. Marketers will only be able to use such location information to carry out geography-specific marketing with the individual's prior consent. This will not, of course, prevent emergency services from using this information in emergencies, or the police force for purposes of public and national security or crime-fighting.

The proposed Electronic Communications Directive is part of a wider "telecoms package" agreed in principle by Member States of the European Union. Measures are designed to open up competition in the European telecommunications market and include ensuring a minimum set of high quality services for all users at an affordable price, ensuring users have access to the Internet and that disabled users and those with special needs can take advantage of the choice of companies and service providers available to the majority of users.

4. **Spamming**

Unsolicited e-mails sent in bulk (commonly known as "spam") become increasingly problematic as the Internet becomes more commercialised and more widely used. Such e-mails are used for advertising or promotional material, and are often sent to personal e-mail addresses with the sender's identity disguised. They are far cheaper than conventional forms of marketing, such as faxes and mailshots. As mobile Internet access becomes more widely used, the problem of spam may well continue in that medium as well.

Internet service providers face the burden of carrying the spam e-mails. Such large numbers of e-mails clog up their systems and the reduced storage space on the Internet service provider's servers have the effect of slowing down the traffic of e-mail transmissions. Furthermore, because many of the senders are unknown, if any mail is undelivered it cannot be returned to the sender's e-mail account. Indeed, some senders of spam e-mails alter the return path of the e-mail so that any replies (presumably including any complaints and requests to stop the sending of the e-mails) are sent to another e-mail account, making it even harder to identify the sender.

The reputation and image of the Internet service provider is also at stake. Subscribers may chose to go to another service provider if they find that their current one does not prevent spam from being sent to them. Internet service providers have tried to address this problem by including terms within their user terms and conditions which prohibit their customers sending spam with a threat of removing the service if they do so in breach of the terms and conditions. Unfortunately, in the event that an Internet service provider does deny a spammer service, spammers can then simply move to another Internet service provider, given that there are so many being offered.

E-mail users ultimately carry the cost of spam e-mails. They are effectively paying to download the e-mail, by paying the telephone and Internet service provider charges. Further annoyance is caused by the poor targeting and the time wasted dealing with spam. It may also be regarded as an invasion of privacy and in November 2000, the Data Protection Working Party of the European Union announced that sending of spam constituted a specific form of privacy violation.

Judicial action against spam

In the absence of specific legislation, any person wishing to take action against someone sending spam e-mail would have to rely on traditional causes of action and there are a number of such causes of action that may arise out of spamming. Spamming may consititute the commission of the tort of trespass, or (if the spamming caused damage) it may be actionable under the Torts (Interference with Goods) Act 1977. As has already been mentioned, the Internet service provider may be able to found an action in contract law based on a breach of the Internet service provider's terms and conditions.

In the United Kingdom there has been one successful anti-spamming court action which has been reported. In *Virgin Net Limited* v *Adrian Paris* the Internet service provider, Virgin Net, claimed that Adrian Paris, an individual spammer, sent over 250,000 messages from four accounts with Virgin Net. Following this, Virgin Net was placed briefly on an Internet e-mail boycotting tool known as the Realtime Blackhole List. This damage to Virgin Net's reputation led to Virgin Net bringing the court action based on breach of the terms and conditions of the Virgin Net user contract. On settlement of the case, Paris agreed not to open yet another Virgin Net account or to send unsolicited e-mails to subscribers of Virgin Net, and paid Virgin Net £5,000 in settlement of costs.

In the US case of *BiblioTech* v *Sam Khuri*, a UK Internet service provider (BiblioTech) took legal action against Sam Khuri and his company, Benchmark Print Supply. The case was brought in the United States as this was the place of Khuri's business. Khuri was a subscriber to BiblioTech's free "Postmaster" e-mail service and sent thousands of spam e-mails through their systems. BiblioTech requested that he stop doing so, as the vast number of e-mails were creating capacity problems on the servers as many e-mail addresses were out of date and were therefore bounced back to BiblioTech servers. Consequently, BiblioTech began a court action in the United States against Khuri, alleging that the spam was disrupting BiblioTech's service and causing BiblioTech loss.

Khuri tried to settle out of court, but BiblioTech, determined to put an end to Khuri's actions, was adamant that he must agree not to send any more spam using other Internet service providers as well as via BiblioTech. BiblioTech won and Khuri agreed to pay undisclosed damages. Furthermore, Khuri agreed to pay $1,000 to any person affected by his future spamming activity. This includes not just BiblioTech but all e-mail service providers, domain owners and e-mail users.

The *BiblioTech* case highlights how far the US courts appear to be prepared to go to stamp out the practice of spamming, by placing such a high financial disincentive on potential spammers.

Legislation against spam

Some European countries such as Austria, Germany, Italy, Denmark, and Finland and some US states prohibit the sending of spam without the prior permission of the recipient (which would then seem to remove such e-mails from the definition of "spam"). In the United Kingdom, however, there is no specific legislation prohibiting the sending of spam e-mails although as has been seen, the Information Commissioner may consider such activity to be a breach of the Telecoms Regulations if recipients have notified the sender to the effect that they do not want to receive such e-mails or are registered on the E-mail Preference Service list held by the Direct Marketing Association.

The E-Commerce Directive, however, does include provisions dealing with spam e-mails. Article 7 of the E-Commerce Directive provides that Member States should ensure in their national legislation that unsolicited commercial communication by e-mail must be clearly and unequivocally identified as such as soon as it is received. This may be in the form of the header to the e-mail, which would allow the e-mail user to delete without opening it. It is debatable whether this is enough to impress e-mail users, who may feel that simply receiving the spam in their in-box is a step too far. Article 7 also provides that service providers undertaking unsolicited commercial communications by e-mail should regularly consult and respect opt-out registers in which national persons not wanting to receive such commercial communications can register themselves.

The E-Commerce Directive specifically calls for opt-out registers. An opt-out system means that unsolicited e-mails can be sent to all e-mail users unless they have positively opted out. An opt-in system, on the other hand, would allow unsolicited e-mails to be sent only to those who have positively opted-in to such a system. The United Kingdom, when faced with a choice between the two systems at the time of consultation on the Distance Selling Directive 1997 (now the Consumer Protection (Distance Selling) Regulations 2000), chose to implement neither option. The Department of Trade and Industry is of the view that self-regulatory schemes (such as the Direct Marketing Association's E-mail Preference Service) provide necessary protection against spam.

Practical tips

Although it is legal to send unsolicited e-mails, e-tailers should be aware of the possible problems such an action could cause. Most importantly, the e-tailer's reputation may suffer as a result. Consequently, it is important that an e-tailer:

- ensures that its website has a privacy policy which contains details about future marketing and how such marketing shall be conducted;
- is cautious about use of "send this page to a friend!" or "e-mail this page to a friend!" features, as these may fall foul of anti-spam laws in foreign jurisdictions; and
- ensures that it seeks legal advice about specific anti-spam laws or decisions in each country which it targets, and if in the United States, each state.

5. **Summary**

- All advertising must be legal, decent, honest and truthful. It should also be capable of objective substantiation.

- E-tailers should obtain the consent of individuals (on an opt-in basis) prior to sending any marketing material to the individual.

- E-tailers should ensure that processes are put in place which enable individuals to register the fact that they do not want to receive marketing material. If such a request is received it must be acted upon.

- New European legislation will extend the existing legislation governing direct marketing to include marketing materials sent by other, less traditional, forms of communication such as e-mail. The new legislation is also likely to place restrictions on geographical location information.

- Sending of spam e-mails may constitute trespass or may be actionable under the Torts (Interference with Goods) Act 1977. It may also constitute a breach of the relevant Internet service provider's terms and conditions and is even illegal in certain countries.

Chapter 10

· Intellectual Property ·

1. Introduction

Intellectual property (IP) is intangible property resulting from a person's (or team's) mental efforts and labour. There are a variety of different rights that can arise in relation to IP. These intellectual property rights ("IPRs") enable the owner(s) of the rights to use and/or exploit the IP and to prevent others from using the IP without the owner's consent.

The scope of IP is broad, covering things such as written material, music, film and software programs (copyright), databases (copyright and database right), brands, product and company names and logos (trade marks) and inventions (patents). Ideas are not intellectual property per se. However, the physical embodiment of the idea may be protected by copyright or design right (although this only prevents others copying the physical embodiment, not the idea) or, if the idea is an invention, it may be patentable. An idea may be confidential information or know-how. A business may also possess confidential information or know-how that gives it a competitive edge over its competitors. Confidential information/know-how is not property in the same way as intellectual property. However, in certain circumstances it is possible to prevent another person making unauthorised use or an unauthorised disclosure of confidential information.

Intellectual property is likely to be relevant to almost every business, but may have particular significance for businesses operating online. Certain IP arise automatically without any further action being required by the owner of the IP (*e.g.* copyright). Other IP such as patents and registered trade marks are only protected once they are registered. This is described in more detail below.

The aim of this chapter is to give an overview of the various IP that may be encountered in relation to an e-commerce venture.

2. Copyright and associated rights

Copyright is likely to be the most commonly encountered and most useful IPR as far as an e-commerce venture is concerned as it protects many aspects of the content of a website.

What is copyright and what does it protect?

Copyright protects the expression of an idea rather than the idea itself (see "Confidential Information" below). This expression can take many forms and copyright can exist in any of the following: *original* literary, dramatic, musical and artistic works, published editions of works, sound recordings, films, videos and broadcasts. It is important to note that a work must be original (*i.e.* not copied) if it is to benefit from copyright protection.

When a person views a web page, there could be copyright in the text, the graphics and logos, any sound recordings, video clips or photographs shown on the web page and the coding behind the web page (*e.g.* the HTML coding). In addition, the Copyright, Designs and Patents Act 1988 ("CDPA") includes computer programs as literary works and, as such, there is likely to be copyright in the software incorporated in the website.

How does an e-commerce venture acquire copyright protection?

Copyright arises automatically when the work is created without the need for any further action on the part of the creator of the work (*e.g.* the payment of fees or registration). In the United Kingdom, it is not necessary to use the © symbol to demonstrate that material is protected by copyright. However, use of the © symbol indicates to other people that the owner of the work considers it to be protected by copyright. Also, certain foreign countries require the use of the © symbol on copyright works.

What can be done with copyright?

The owner of copyright has the right to control the way in which the copyright work is exploited. Broadly speaking, the owner of a copyright work can prevent its unauthorised use and copying. This unauthorised use can include issuing copies of the copyright work to the public, performing or broadcasting the copyright work. It does not, unlike certain other IPRs such as patents, grant the owner a "monopoly". Therefore a copyright owner cannot prevent the use of an identical work by another person where that identical work has been created by someone else independently (*i.e.* without any copying).

The United Kingdom is a member of several international conventions which mean that copyright works created by UK nationals or residents or created in the United Kingdom are likely to be protected in many other parts of the world.

Who owns copyright and for how long?

In the United Kingdom, copyright is governed by the CDPA which provides that, as a general rule, the first owner of copyright is the person who creates the copyright work. In relation to specific types of work, for example, a literary, dramatic, musical or artistic work which is computer generated the creator (the "author") is taken to be "the person by whom the arrangements necessary for the creation of the work are undertaken" (section 9(3) CDPA). It is important to note that this refers to works generated by computer rather than works generated on computers.

However, the copyright in a work created "by an employee in the course of his employment" will belong to the employer unless there is agreement to the contrary (section 11 CDPA). It is though important to note that this only applies to employer-employee relationships and not where a work is commissioned and undertaken by an agent or self-employed person, for example, in which case the author (creator) will own the copyright unless agreed otherwise. For this reason, it is very important to establish at the outset who is to own the copyright in any works that are to be created (for example, by website design agencies or contractors). It is likely that the commissioner will need to own the copyright in the commissioned work in order to exploit fully the copyright work in its business. The commissioner should, therefore, ensure that there is a written agreement that provides for the transfer of all intellectual property in a commissioned work from those who are creating it.

Copyright does not last indefinitely. The duration of copyright depends on the type of work it attaches to. As a general rule, copyright lasts for a period of 70 years from the end of the calendar year in which the author of the copyright work dies. However, if such works are computer-generated (*i.e.* the work is "created" by a computer) the copyright lasts for 50 years from the end of the calendar year in which the computer-generated copyright work was made.

How is copyright infringed?

As discussed above, the owner of copyright can prevent others doing certain things with the copyright work. The most obvious way of infringing copyright is by copying. Copying in relation to literary, dramatic, musical and artistic works is defined in section 17 of the CPDA as *reproduction* "in any material form", and this is stated to include storing electronically. There must be *reproduction* of a *substantial* part of the copyright work. It is often not easy to assess what will amount to a "substantial part". The courts interpret "substantial part" qualitatively rather than quantitatively. In other words, the courts look at what has been reproduced not just at how much has been reproduced.

Copying is not the only way of infringing copyright. Issuing copies to the public, which is described in section 18 of the CDPA as "the act of putting into circulation" will also be an infringement, as will showing or playing a work in public and broadcasting or including a work in a cable program service.

Copyright also protects literary, dramatic and musical works from unauthorised adaptation. An adaptation is stated to include a translation of a literary work, and, more specifically in relation to computer programs, "an arrangement or altered version of the program or a translation of it" (section 21(3) CDPA).

Copyright and the Internet

Due to the rapid rate of development of the Internet it sometimes appears that intellectual property laws, and in particular the law relating to copyright, is somewhat out of step with the practicalities of Internet use. This is not simply because of the ease with which material can be transmitted (*e.g.* by e-mail) and reproduced (*e.g.* both by downloading and printing out material from websites). The way the Internet and the technology used to access the Internet works involves the taking of electronic copies of website content which are stored on the computer's hard drive ("caching") in order to make it more easily accessible to the end user. Therefore, Internet service providers ("ISPs") and Internet users are, under the present UK law, technically infringing the copyright of the respective copyright owners each time information is transmitted and accessed (although, in reality, where copyright works are included on a website with the copyright owner's consent, there will probably be an implied licence for the website user to copy the works as necessary for accessing the website).

This problem of incidental copying by web browsers has been addressed recently by the new EC Copyright Directive. This Directive, which should be implemented by the EU Member States within 18 months of its publication date (22 June 2001), has provided some important clarification on this issue. The Copyright Directive makes it clear that transient or incidental acts of reproduction, which are an essential part of a technological process and whose sole purpose is to enable the intermediary to transmit works in a network between third parties (i.e. Internet users), will not infringe copyright. The provision also exempts caching of copyright works from being infringements.

The extent to which other forms of copyright infringement impact on the Internet is not yet clear. Given the scope of the Internet as a communication and information medium, it is certainly possible that it can be used to issue copies and show or play works to the public. Note though that in relation to showing or playing works, the CDPA states that the person responsible for merely conveying the information electronically will not be infringing, and therefore it seems ISPs would not be infringers in this respect. Furthermore, "cable program service" is defined rather broadly and potentially includes certain Internet-related activities.

Databases

The CDPA, section 3A defines a "database" as:

> "a collection of independent works, data or other materials which (a) are arranged in a systematic or methodical way, and (b) are individually accessible by electronic or other means."

Databases can be protected by copyright if they fulfil the requirements for copyright works under the CDPA in that by reason of the selection or arrangement of the contents of the database the database constitutes the author's own intellectual creation. If a database is not protected by copyright, it may still be protected by database right. The level of "originality" required for a database to be protected by database right is lower than is required for the database to be protected by copyright. This can be important where a database is merely a collection of readily available (*i.e.* not original) data.

A database will benefit from database right if there was a *substantial investment in obtaining, verifying or presenting* its contents (Copyright and Rights in Databases Regulations 1997, regulation 13). Database right lasts for 15 years from the end of the calendar year in which the database was completed (compared to the 70-year period under copyright protection). The first owner of database right is the "maker" of the database who is:

> "the person who takes the initiative in obtaining, verifying or presenting the contents of a database and assumes the risk of investing in the obtaining, verification or presentation".

As with copyright, where a database is made by an employee in the course of his employment, his employer is regarded as the maker of the database, subject to any agreement to the contrary.

The owner of the database right has the right to prevent the extraction and reutilisation of *all or a substantial part* of the database. For the purpose of database rights, the *repeated and systematic extraction of insubstantial parts* of the contents of a database may amount to the extraction or re-utilisation of a substantial part of those contents.

Whilst database rights are undoubtedly useful, particularly in relation to much information held on websites, there is still some uncertainty as to their scope. The English courts recently considered the scope of database rights in *British Horseracing Board & Ors* v *William Hill Organisation Ltd* [2001]. The British Horseracing Board sued the bookmakers William Hill for infringement of its database rights. William Hill were using various race details from the Board's database in their online betting service. On 31 July 2001 the Court of Appeal ruled that while the trial judge, Laddie J, had given a wide interpretation to database right and what was protected by database rights, the courts of other EU Member States had construed it more narrowly (the Copyright and Rights in Databases Regulations 1997 were the implementing legislation of an EC Database Directive). The European Court of Justice ("ECJ") had not yet given a ruling on the interpretation of database rights under the Directive and therefore the Court of Appeal was not prepared to give a definite ruling on interpretation either. Rather, it felt that the matter should be referred to the ECJ. Therefore, there remains some uncertainty as to the extent and applicability of database rights.

Moral rights

In addition to copyright, it is important to consider any applicable moral rights. Moral rights are the rights of the author of a copyright work to be recognised as the author and to prevent derogatory treatment of his work. Moral rights are separate rights from copyright and the author of a work retains his moral rights even when he has transferred (*i.e.* sold) the copyright to another person. However, the right to be recognised as author/director must be positively asserted and can be waived. In addition, moral rights do not apply to computer programs or computer-generated works.

3. Trade marks

What is a trade mark?

A trade mark is a badge or sign indicating the source of goods or services (*e.g.* a brand or logo). Trade marks can be very important and valuable assets and their protection should not be overlooked. Trade marks should not be confused with domain names or company names, which are simply administrative registrations having no innate IP significance.

Trade marks can be protected in the United Kingdom by registration at the Trade Marks Registry. Unregistered trade marks are also afforded a degree of protection if a significant reputation attaches to the trade mark. However, it is always advisable to register marks so far as is possible.

What can be registered?

Registered trade marks are territorial (*i.e.* are registered in individual territories) and are registered in respect of specified goods or services. The Trade Marks Act 1994 (the "TMA") governs the registration of trade marks in the United Kingdom. The TMA defines a trade mark as a sign that can be represented graphically and that can distinguish the goods or services of one business from another. Trade marks can (subject to certain restrictions in the TMA) consist of words, letters, numbers, images or even the shape of a product or its packaging. However, to be registrable, the trade mark must have a distinctive character. So, for example, provided they were distinctive, a company could register its name and/or logo and/or the name of any of its brands. In an online business, a trade mark can be a very powerful and valuable marketing tool if applied to a website and other related materials in that it enables users to easily identify the website as that of a given company.

Furthermore, the TMA widened the scope of what is registrable as a trade mark. For example, colour combinations and sounds can, in certain circumstances, be registrable. However, a mark that is purely descriptive of the goods or services is not registrable. This is particularly relevant where the mark being sought is simply a descriptive word with the letter "e" preceding it, or consists solely of the wording used in a descriptive domain name such as "business.com". Other restrictions on registration include marks whose usage has become commonplace in the industry (*i.e.* generic terms), or that are likely to mislead the public, or that include a protected emblem (*e.g.* a national flag), or are contrary to public policy or accepted principles of morality.

Trade mark infringement

When a person or business uses a trade mark without the consent of the trade mark owner, the trade mark owner may be able to bring an action for trade mark infringement or passing-off.

In the case of registered trade marks, the trade mark owner can bring an action against another person who uses an identical trade mark in the course of trade in respect of the same goods or services for which the trade mark is registered. If the trade mark being used is *similar* to the registered trade mark or being used in respect of *similar* goods or services the trade mark owner can bring an action for trade mark infringement if consumers are or are likely to be confused by the use of the competing trade mark.

In the case of very famous registered trade marks with a significant reputation associated with them, it may also be possible for the trade mark owner to bring an action for trade mark infringement against someone using an identical or similar trade mark in respect of goods or services which are not similar to those for which the trade mark is registered. However, in this case the trade mark owner must establish that the competing use takes unfair advantage of or is detrimental to the distinctive character or repute of the registered trade mark.

It is also possible for the owner of an unregistered trade mark or brand to bring an action in "passing-off" against someone who attempts to use the unregistered trade mark or brand. To bring an unsuccessful action in passing-off the trade mark owner must establish:

(1) that a sufficient reputation is associated with their trade mark or brand (in other words, that they own rights in the trade mark or brand);

(2) that the other person is misrepresenting that their goods or services are those of the trade mark or brand owner or associated or endorsed by them; and

(3) as a result of the misrepresentation the trade mark or brand owner has suffered or is likely to suffer damage (including damage to reputation).

It is often difficult to establish passing-off. In particular, it may be difficult and time-consuming (and therefore expensive) to gather evidence that shows that an unregistered trade mark or brand has a reputation attached to it. This is particularly true of newer brands or trade marks.

Why register?

It is always advisable to register a trade mark if registration is possible. Unregistered trade marks are not protected until they have been used. Also, as discussed above, passing-off is difficult and expensive to establish. In particular, it is often difficult and expensive to establish ownership of rights in an unregistered trade mark. When a trade mark is registered, the registration certificate provides evidence of ownership, thus avoiding the effort and expense of establishing ownership.

Registered trade marks are more likely to come to the attention of others who may be in the process of choosing their own trade marks because trade mark registries can be searched by those people wishing to register trade marks.

Registration

Before launching a new business or project it is important to ensure that the names or trade marks proposed to be used do not infringe the rights of others in similar or identical trade marks (see "Infringement" below) by conducting suitable searches including searches at relevant Trade Marks Registries.

Applications for trade mark registrations in the United Kingdom are made to the UK Trade Marks Registry. The application must be made for the class or classes of goods or services in which the trade mark will be used. The fee for a *single* class application is currently £200, with additional classes costing £50 each. If the trade mark application is accepted by the Trade Marks Registrar, it will be advertised in the *Trade Marks Journal*, allowing others the opportunity to oppose its registration. If there are no oppositions within three months of the publication in the *Trade Marks Journal*, the mark will be entered on the register. If there are no oppositions, the entire process takes about six months from the date of filing the application.

The initial period of registration is 10 years, after which time, the registration can be renewed (on payment of renewal fees) for additional 10-year periods. A registration can last indefinitely provided the renewal fees are paid. However, once a trade mark is registered it is possible for others to apply to remove the trade mark from the register. The TMA sets out various grounds on which a trade mark may be removed from the register. These grounds include non-use of the mark for a five-year period, that the mark has become misleading or that it has become a generic term for the goods or services for which it is registered.

It is also possible to apply for a Community Trade Mark ("CTM") whereby a single trade mark registration will give protection across the EU. Applications are made to the Office for Harmonisation in the Internal Market ("OHIM") in Alicante. A successful application will benefit from protection in all Member States in return for the payment of a single fee. However, the downside is that it is "all or nothing", so if the application fails in any one country, the whole application is lost. An alternative is to make separate national registrations but this is likely to be prohibitively expensive.

4. Patents

What is a patent?

Patents protect inventions. The owner of a patent is given a monopoly over the invention described in the patent. Patents are likely to be very relevant to a company or business that is involved in the development of technology and technological processes but currently, of less relevance to e-commerce businesses.

The UK and European Patent Offices will *not* grant patents in respect of a number of excluded categories of inventions. Of particular relevance to e-commerce businesses, patents will not be granted in respect of schemes or rules for performing mental acts, playing a game or *doing business*, or a *computer program* (although, as discussed above, computer programs are protectable by copyright), or the presentation of information. However, the European Patent Office is gradually changing its attitude in respect of computer programs that have or produce a novel technical effect, allowing patents to be granted in respect of the novel technical effect.

The situation is different in the United States, where it is possible to obtain patents for business methods. If an e-commerce business has a novel method for business that it wishes to protect in the United States, it could consider applying for a patent.

In all cases, if you have an invention which you believe may be patentable, advice should be sought from a patent agent.

In the United Kingdom the proprietor of a patent benefits from the exclusive use of the invention for up to 20 years from the "priority date" (generally, the date of filing the application).

A patent is property, and as such can be bought, sold and licensed, and gives its proprietor the right to take legal action against others who infringe the right by exploiting the invention without the proprietor's consent in the territories in which the patent is granted.

To be patentable, an invention must be new and not obvious to a notional person of ordinary skill experienced in the particular technology. It must also be capable of industrial application and not be of a class of inventions specifically excluded by law from being patentable (as discussed above).

The invention must be new

For the invention to be considered "new" it must never have been disclosed to the public before the "priority date". In principle the priority date will be the date on which the application for a patent is filed, but may be a date up to 12 months prior to this, if a patent application for essentially the same invention has been filed elsewhere in that period by the same applicant. The priority date marks the point at which the novelty and obviousness of the invention is assessed.

The invention must involve an inventive step

If something is to be considered inventive, it must not be technically or practically obvious to a notional person skilled in the area of technology in question.

The invention must be capable of industrial application

To be patentable, the invention must be capable of being made or used in some kind of industry, *i.e.* it must be a product or a process (and not just an abstract idea). Industry, for these purposes, has a very wide meaning and would include the Internet.

The invention must not be excluded by law

As discussed above, a number of things are excluded from qualifying as inventions in the United Kingdom and Europe for the purposes of a patent application. Some are excluded because they are better protected by other IP rights, such as computer programs (copyright). It is possible to patent software in the United States, and more recently in Europe too, but the circumstances in which this can be done are limited. It is also possible to patent certain business methods in the United States, but again, patentability in Europe is limited.

Obtaining international patent protection

UK patents only provide protection in the United Kingdom and the Isle of Man. If there is a possibility of expanding into foreign markets, either directly or via licensing arrangements, or if there is a concern that the invention may be copied by foreign competitors, then it will be necessary to consider other patent applications. In addition, there are alternatives to the national route for applying for a UK patent, which may be appropriate where protection is also sought in other countries.

It is possible to make a single international application, specifying those countries in which the applicant wishes to apply for a patent. The application is filed in one language and one search is conducted, potentially reducing costs. The next stage is to make filings in each of the desired countries, and from then on the applications proceed according to national requirements. The system is administered by the World Intellectual Property Organisation ("WIPO"), a UN agency in Geneva.

It is also possible to make one single European patent application for patents in one or more of the European Union countries and also some others. Where a patent is sought in more than one or two countries, this method is usually cheaper than applying in each individual country, as it avoids a certain amount of duplication of work. After the grant of the patent by the European Patent Office ("EPO"), the national laws of each country apply, for example, in relation to infringement. A UK patent granted by this route is known as a "European Patent (UK)", but is essentially the same as one obtained via the national route. The only significant difference is that within nine months of grant of a patent by the EPO, any interested party can oppose the patent, i.e. seek its revocation. A successful opposition will result in the revocation of the patent in all the European countries where the patent was granted.

Deciding which application system to use requires a careful consideration of the costs involved and the scope of protection required.

5. **Confidential information**

Confidential information or know-how is not property in the same way as intellectual property. However, many businesses use confidential information or know-how that gives them a competitive edge over their competitors.

A person or business who wishes to disclose their confidential information to another person but wishes to restrict that person's ability to disclose the information to others, could enter into a confidentiality agreement with that person. A confidentiality agreement can take many forms but, broadly, will describe the confidential information and restrict the receiving party's ability to disclose the information to others. Confidentiality agreements are commercially useful but it is very difficult to successfully bring an action for breach of contract against a party who breaches a confidentiality agreement.

Whilst it may be difficult to enforce terms of confidentiality agreements directly, it may instead be possible to bring an action for breach of confidence against a party making or threatening to make an unauthorised disclosure of confidential information. To bring a successful action for breach of confidence, the person alleging breach will have to show:

- the information must be capable of legal protection – in other words, it must have the necessary *"quality of confidence"* about it;
- the information must have been imparted by its owner in circumstances importing an obligation of confidence;
- there must be actual or threatened unauthorised use or disclosure of that information.

Confidentiality agreements may be difficult to enforce but provide useful evidence that the information was disclosed "in circumstances importing an obligation of confidence". It is also useful if all confidential information is clearly labelled as such and that any oral disclosures of confidential information are followed by written confirmation of what was disclosed. Again, this will assist in showing that the recipient was under an obligation of confidence.

As breach of confidence can be difficult to establish, it is worth considering what additional protection is available in relation to any particular confidential information. As discussed above, copyright can protect physical embodiment of any confidential information. However, copyright does not protect the confidential information itself. If the confidential information relates to a novel process or product, it may be possible to apply for a patent (see below).

6. **Exploiting intellectual property rights**

For many businesses, the value of their IP is realised by exploiting it in their business. However, it may be more practical or more profitable for a business to license its IP or, if they are of no further use, to assign (sell) them to a third party.

Licensing intellectual property rights

In granting a licence of IP, some of the main terms that should be considered are:
- whether the licence should be:
  - exclusive (only the licensee can use the licensed property),
  - sole (only the licensee and the licensor can use the licensed property); or
  - non-exclusive (the licensor can grant other licences if it wishes to do so);

- the scope of the licence (*i.e.* territory and content of the licence);
- the duration of the licence;
- royalties or fees payable;
- the extent of any warranties or indemnities; and
- the rights of the parties on termination of the licence (*e.g.* a period following termination during which use of the licensed property by the licensee can be "wound down").

Licensing variations

A licence could involve a "vertical agreement" or a "horizontal agreement". A common example of a vertical agreement would be where the owner of a patent grants a right to another entity to use the patented process. The owner of the patent can expect to command a higher fee if he grants an exclusive right to use the technology. Horizontal agreements include agreements made between two or more parties owning IPRs, under which the parties mutually agree to co-operate and share technology, or operate within certain agreed restrictions.

European competition law

When drafting licensing agreements, it is necessary to consider the impact of competition law on the agreement in relevant jurisdictions. Agreements such as IP licences, which restrict the activities of one or more parties may be contrary to European, UK or other countries' competition laws. In cases where there are serious breaches of competition law which result in significant distortion of the market, fines may be imposed. Expert advice in this area is essential.

7. **Summary**

- Copyright can exist in the text, graphics, sound recordings and video clips displayed on a website. It can also exist in the coding of the web pages.

- Copyright arises automatically and gives the owner the right to control the way in which the copyright work is exploited.

- The Copyright Directive states that transient or incidental acts of reproduction which are an essential part of a technological process and whose sole purpose is to enable the intermediary to transmit works in a network between third parties will not infringe copyright.

- Databases can be protected by copyright and/or database rights. The owner of a database right may prevent extraction and reutilisation of all or a substantial part of the database.

- Trade marks are used to distinguish the goods/services of one business from another. Whilst unregistered trade marks can be protected it is wise to register trade marks.

- Patents protect inventions. The general rule in Europe is that patents will not be granted in respect of business methods or computer programs. However, this attitude is changing slightly and computer programs that have or produce a novel technical effect may be capable of being patented.

Chapter 11

· Linking & Affiliate Deals ·

1. Introduction

When Tim Berners-Lee created the world wide web in 1989 its principal function was to enable the exchange of information between different academic institutions. One of the reasons why the world wide web became such a useful tool for the exchange of information was the ability to create hypertext links to other pages within the world wide web.

Since its inception the world wide web has changed beyond recognition but its defining feature remains the ability to link between web pages. Linking can obviously occur between web pages within the same website but can also be used to navigate to websites operated by third parties. The latter form of linking can have legal repercussions and in this chapter we will look at the legal issues that arise out of linking to or using content from a third party site. We will also discuss the legal implications of the use of other people's names as metatags and how banner ad keying may lead to potential liability for those engaged in such activities. In addition we will look at the issues, both legal and practical, which arise out of participating in a consensual linking or affiliate relationship.

2. What is linking?

It may be helpful to set out an example by way of illustration of how a hypertext link operates. If we imagine that an Internet user, Steve, visits the website www.example.com which has a hypertext link to www.illustration.com which appears in the format "illustration" on the Example.com website. In doing this proprietor of Example.com has placed a signpost to another web page within the world wide web. The hypertext link as we have just described it links to the Illustration.com homepage, what might be called a plain link. If the link to Illustration.com is to a page "deeper" within the Ilustration.com website (*i.e.* further in than the home page) the link is called a "deep link". The distinction between these two types of linking is important as the legal implications of establishing the two different types of link may vary and as we will see there can be problems associated with deep linking.

It is worth explaining how a hypertext link enables a user to switch from one web page to another and here we will continue to use our example. The hypertext link on Example.com contains a URL address which, when selected by Steve, acts as a request to the Illustration.com web servers to send a copy of the web page to Steve's computer (for the purpose of this chapter we will call the site or page requested the "target" site or page). This page is then broken down into a series of data packets which travel across the Internet before being reassembled at Steve's computer.

There are even more extensive forms of linking than deep linking. Framing is the placing of a frame around content downloaded from the target website. Example.com could therefore frame the Illustration.com website by designing a web page with a frame sitting around a "request bar" which requests the content from the Illustration.com website. It may even be possible to design the frame in such a way as to cover the distinguishing features of the target site and thereby deceive the user of the Example.com website into thinking that he is viewing content written and designed by Example.com.

3. Linking in US law

Before turning to how the issue of linking has been dealt with by European courts it is interesting to see how the issue has been dealt with by the US courts where there has been more case law on the subject. It is important to note that these decisions would not be binding on the English courts considering similar disputes but nevertheless they provide interesting background.

As regards a plain link to a website the US courts have held that whilst in its most basic form (*i.e.* a basic hyperlink) a hyperlink does not infringe the intellectual property rights of the target site, a link which somehow uses a registered trade mark of the target site may well infringe the intellectual property rights of the proprietors of the target site. A good illustration of this is provided in a case involving a link to the Playboy website from a pornographic website. Playboy successfully argued that the use of the Playboy trade mark and bunny logo as the basis of the hypertext link through to the Playboy website infringed the intellectual property rights of Playboy. They even managed to show that the use of the Playboy name and logo in association with the pornographic site would damage the reputation of Playboy.

One of the most important cases in this area in the United States is a case involving the use of deep linking.

Ticketmaster Corp v Tickets.com Inc

In this case the facts were that both the plaintiff and the defendant operated websites selling tickets to sporting and entertainment events. Tickets.com also displayed information regarding a number of events to which it did not have tickets for sale. For these events Tickets.com identified other websites where the tickets could be purchased and in some cases the Tickets.com website included a hypertext link to the relevant page of the Ticketmaster website. Ticketmaster objected to this deep linking to its website, presumably on the basis that the deep linking effectively by-passed the lucrative advertising within the main sections of the Ticketmaster website, and Ticketmaster sued Tickets.com under a number of heads of action.

One of the heads of action on which Ticketmaster based its claim was that the linking was a violation of the US Copyright Act. The US court held that there was no violation of the Copyright Act since no copying of the Ticketmaster website was involved. The customer was automatically transferred to the particular Ticketmaster web page and there was no deception in what was happening since it was clear to the users of the Tickets.com website that they were being transferred to the Ticketmaster website.

It was this last factor which seemed decisive in the judge's decision. Had it been unclear that the user was being transferred to another website there may have been a real risk that the hypertext link to the Ticketmaster website would have infringed Ticketmaster's copyright. This would certainly be the case where there was some positive deception involved in the deep link to the target site.

4.   Linking in German Law

The German courts have also been asked to hear a case concerning deep linking and in that case granted an injunction to stop linking activity. In *Stepstone* v *OfiR* Stepstone claimed that OfiR, the Danish media group, was using a link to Stepstone's online job advertisements to substantiate claims about the availability of jobs on its own websites. Again, in this case one of the motivating factors behind bringing the action was the fact that Stepstone objected to users being able to bypass the advertising elsewhere on the Stepstone site.

The German court held that it can intervene and require the removal of such links if the linking is extensive and prejudicial to the website which is the subject of the link. The court held that the links in the *Stepstone* case were extensive and prejudicial and granted an injunction requiring the removal of the links from the OfiR website.

5.   Linking in English law

As has been seen in Chapter 10, copyright may exist in the design and content of the website and, using our example, Illustration.com licenses all users of the world wide web to access and read the contents of its website. The implied licence must also extend to allowing a user to store a cache copy of the web page in the user's hard drive since this is an automatic consequence of viewing the web page. The question then is: does the implied licence to make limited use of the web page extend to linking to it or framing it? Does Example.com's link to Illustration.com's website infringe Illustration.com's copyright or other intellectual property rights?

As yet there are no simple answers to these questions since it has yet to be fully settled under English law whether the consent of the proprietor of a website is needed in order to link to that website although there has been some case law on the subject which may offer some guidance.

Shetland Times v Wills

This Scottish case involved unauthorised deep linking by Wills to sections of the *Shetland Times* website. The *Shetland Times* succeeded in obtaining an interim interdict in the Scottish court to prevent Wills from deep linking into the *Shetland Times* website. However, the case is of limited precedent value since the decision in the case was given at interlocutory level (*i.e.* at an interim stage rather than at full trial) and then the case was ultimately settled. In addition, the case was heard before the Scottish courts and whilst a Scottish decision can be considered by an English court, when, as is the case here, the legal principles are very similar, it is possible that an English court, with a more specialist intellectual property judge, would not find this Scottish precedent persuasive.

In the *Shetland Times* case the motivating factor behind the *Shetland Times'* action was the fact that the deep linking had the effect of enabling users to bypass the advertising on the *Shetland Times'* homepage. Such advertising tends to be the most valuable to any website and therefore it is not surprising that website proprietors are loath to allow deep linking to continue. Another reason why websites tend to object to deep linking is that it enables users to bypass terms and conditions of use of the website and possibly even registration procedures which may afford the website proprietor valuable contractual protection.

Haymarket Group Ltd v Burmah Castrol Plc

In this case Haymarket, the publishing company, made a claim against Burmah Castrol who were including content from Haymarket's website within a Castrol-branded frame on Castrol's website. Haymarket claimed copyright infringement, breach of its database rights and passing-off. The case, however, does not present much in the way of a precedent since Burmah Castrol dropped the relevant content and links after Haymarket commenced proceedings.

6.   Linking - practical advice

From the UK case law and from general principles of intellectual property law it is possible to draw together some basic guidance on how the different sorts of linking should be approached. Again we will look at how Example.com might approach the different sorts of linking.

In the case of the plain link from the Example.com website to the Illustration.com homepage, provided that there is nothing defamatory or damaging to the reputation of Illustration.com in the use of the hypertext link or the method in which it is presented, there is unlikely to be any problem. There can be no copyright infringement since there has been no copying of the Illustration.com content and since the user is being clearly directed to the Illustration.com website, which has been clearly identified as such, Illustration.com cannot claim that its rights to be identified as the author of copyright material have been infringed. In addition, it is extremely unlikely that the use of the link to the Illustration.com website could constitute passing-off although this rather depends on how the link to the Illustration.com website is used within the Example.com website.

There may be problems with the plain link if, as in the US *Playboy* case, a registered trade mark is used to form the plain link. In addition, it is possible that linking to the Illustration.com website breaches the terms of use of that website since it is increasingly common to see prohibitions in terms of use on any form of linking and framing without the permission of the proprietors of the website. It is arguable whether a website would take action to prevent linking based solely on a breach of contract claim since it may be difficult to show that a binding contract existed incorporating the terms of use and the costs of bringing the action may outweigh any benefit that may be gained. However, if the terms of use do contain a prohibition of linking, the possibility remains that the target site could commence a breach of contract claim and that such an action could be successful. Therefore the only cast iron method of linking to another website without fear of any resultant liability is to obtain the consent of the target site to the creation of the link.

A deep link from the Example.com website to a page within the Illustration.com website poses more problems. The *Shetland Times* case indicates that the Scottish courts would consider granting injunctive relief to prevent such linking as would the German courts, but only where the linking is extensive and prejudicial. Depending on the specific facts of the case there could be the possibility that Illustration.com would be able to take action successfully against Example.com to bring an end to the deep linking. Assuming that the deep linking is conducted in such a way as to mask the fact that the user is being transferred to another website, such an action could be founded on a violation of Illustration.com's copyright and there may also be grounds for a claim of passing-off. Consequently, again it is advisable to obtain the consent of the target site to any deep linking and it would be even better to conduct such linking as part of a structured and documented affiliate or linking contractual arrangement.

Finally, the use of framing is almost certain to infringe the copyright of the author or designer of the content which is being framed and it is likely that the framing also violates the author's or designer's moral rights to be identified as the author or designer of the content. Framing may also lead to a claim of passing-off where goods advertised within the framed content appear to be associated with the website framing the content. As with deep linking it would be extremely unwise to frame another website's content without the consent of the target site and preferably within the terms of an affiliate contractual arrangement.

7.   Metatags and banner ad keying

Metatags

A "metatag" is a piece of coding information within the HTML coding of a website that describes the website. This information is then used by search engines to categorise the website to enable the search engines users to find the site. The legal significance of metatags is that the inclusion of a competitor's name as a metatag within the coding of a site may amount to trade mark infringement as was the case in the following action.

Roadtech Computer System Ltd v Mandata (Management and Data Services) Ltd

In this case Roadtech had used the word "ROADRUNNER" as a trade mark in respect of certain computer software sold by Roadtech. The defendants, Mandata, had included "ROADTECH" and "ROADRUNNER" metatags within the coding of their website so that Internet searches against these names would list Mandata's website amongst the results. Mandata admitted infringement of Roadtech's trade marks and the court awarded damages.

Banner ad keying

"Keying" occurs where the banner advertisements shown on Internet search engine pages are selected according to the words typed into the search engine by the user. The operators of some search engines sell a given word to an advertiser so that the advertiser's banner will appear each time that word is used. Some of the words sold have been trade marks and this practice is therefore likely to lead to claims of trade mark infringement.

For instance, the Hamburg court in Germany prohibited Excite from causing any banners of a US-based cosmetics discounter, iBeauty.com, to be triggered by the words "Estée Lauder", "Clinique" or "Origins" all of which are trade marks belonging to Estée Lauder. The court held that this amounted to trade mark infringement. Excite has appealed.

Playboy Enterprises Inc v Netscape Communications Corp (1999)

In this US case Playboy brought an action against Netscape and Excite challenging their practice of "keying" advertisements to the words "Playboy" and "Playmate". Playboy argued that the practice of keying constituted trade mark infringement under Californian law. The US court disagreed and found that Playboy's claim failed for a number of reasons, including the fact that the defendants were not using Playboy's trade marks, but merely using words found in the English language over which Playboy did not have a monopoly.

8.   Linking and affiliate contracts

There are several commercial and legal considerations that arise out of a linking (sometimes called an "affiliate") arrangement. Assuming that the purpose of including a link to the Illustration.com website on the Example.com website is to drive Internet traffic through to Illustration.com website, the substance of an affiliate deal between Example.com will be that Example.com agrees to include a link (whether in the form of a text URL or a link in the form of a logo which itself contains the URL) on the Example.com website in return for some form of remuneration.

The important commercial considerations that arise in such a deal tend to centre around how the website hosting the link is rewarded. A common model is for commission to be payable on any goods and/or services purchased on the target site after the target site has been accessed via the link. Alternatively the site hosting the link can be rewarded on a clickthrough basis, charging a set tariff every time the target site is accessed via the link. Finally, the other common method of charging target sites for the establishment of a link is to charge a set monthly fee which applies irrespective of the number of clickthroughs to the target site or the number of sales that the target site makes. Whichever method of charging the target site uses, certain considerations will have to be dealt with in the contract.

Commission payment structure

Perhaps the most important issue to be dealt with is an affiliate agreement based on a commission payment structure in which goods or services will be subject to the commission payment. Will the commission attach to all goods sold on the target site or will the commission attach only to sales of certain goods? In addition, the contract must address whether the commission only applies to goods or services purchased when the user accesses the target site directly via the link or, once the user has accessed the target site via the link, all subsequent purchases made by that user on the target site. Obviously the latter approach will prove unpopular with the target site but the hosting site may well argue that the target site is being given access to the hosting site's customer base, a customer base which otherwise might not have visited the target site. In addition, this approach may reflect the fact that the visitors to the target site may continue to make purchases from the target site but only use the link from the hosting site the first time they visit the target site.

Another important issue to be dealt with in the commission-based affiliate agreement is the reporting of sales by the target site. Without accurate and timely reporting the hosting site will not be able to issue invoices for the commission on sales made. The contract must therefore specify when the report should be made and in what format. The hosting site will want to be sure that the reports submitted are accurate and therefore may wish the contract to specify exactly how the users entering the target site via the link and any purchases they may make should be tracked. This can be done, for example, by requiring that the URLs used by the target site in relation to the products on the target site include a reference to the hosting site (such a URL would look something like:
http://www.illustration.com/products.asp?id=345?Referrer=example).

The hosting site will also want to include a right to audit the books and records held by the target site so as to ensure that the reports submitted are accurate. Finally the hosting site needs to consider what action it will take in the event that the target site fails to submit reports at all. Whilst the hosting site will have its normal contractual remedies for breach of contract (namely, the right to terminate if the breach is unremedied following notice from the hosting site and damages to cover any loss flowing from the breach) it would be easier to include a minimum payment or a method of calculating commission which applies in the absence of any reports being submitted by the target site.

Clickthrough payment structure

This method of payment structure is somewhat simpler than the commission structure since the hosting site will be able to monitor, via its own web servers, the number of clickthroughs to the target site. Therefore there is no need for the hosting site to rely on reports submitted by the target site before submitting an invoice. It is worth noting that the target site will also be able to monitor the number of clickthroughs from the hosting site and the contract should therefore deal with how any disparity between the two sets of figures generated by the hosting site and target site should be resolved.

Regular fee payment structure

Fixed payments systems are often used by larger websites who are able to charge by merely including the link on their site by virtue of the large amount of traffic that they attract and are therefore able to pass on to the target site. This is the simplest arrangement to embody in the affiliate contract but the target site does need to be aware of exactly what it is buying for its fixed fee. With the other two structures the target site is at least paying for sales made or visitors transferred to its site. Without contractual protection the target site may pay its fixed fee without necessarily reaping the reward in terms of new users of its site.

Accordingly, the target site should ensure that the affiliate contract includes guaranteed user numbers with a provision enabling the clawback of some or all of the fees paid if the targets are not met. In addition, the positioning of the link will be important in determining how many users link through to the target site. If the target site is not able to negotiate a specific placement of its link or logo it should at least ensure that the link or logo appears "above the fold", that is, on the hosting website in view of users without the need to scroll down the page.

Legal issues

With each of these payment structures there are certain common legal issues which will have to be dealt with in the affiliate contract.

The hosting site will be concerned that its association with the target site does not damage its reputation in any way. Consequently, the hosting site should seek to include, within the affiliate agreement, a warranty from the target site that nothing within its site will be obscene, breach any law or regulation, or infringe any third party intellectual property rights. It is also important that this warranty should cover any wording or graphics given to the hosting site by the target site to display alongside, or as part of, the link. The particular concern to be addressed here is that if any logos or names given to the hosting site infringe any third party intellectual property rights the hosting site may incur liability for the display of those names or logos.

The parties to the affiliate agreement will also be concerned to ensure that the division of ownership of their own intellectual property is clearly stated. Consequently, the affiliate agreement should state that nothing in the agreement will operate to transfer any rights in the target site's content (or any content given to the hosting site for display) to the hosting site's owner. Similarly, the target site's owner should acquire no rights in the content displayed on the hosting site (or indeed any frame that may be applied to the target site as part of the affiliate arrangement).

It is easy to see the obvious benefits of an affiliate arrangement which should operate to the mutual benefit of both parties. However, the contract must deal with how the relationship can be brought to an end. The contract will no doubt contain all the usual termination provisions such as termination on material breach or insolvency of the other party. However, the agreement should also allow the immediate suspension of the link in circumstances which might damage a party's goodwill and reputation. For instance, if the target site were to start displaying obscene material, depending on the terms of the contract, a termination right (based on material breach of the warranty mentioned above) will be effective to bring the agreement to an end, at worst after the target site has been given an opportunity to rectify the breach and at best only after written notice has been served on the other party. In either scenario the damage to the hosting site's reputation will already have been done. A right of immediate suspension in such circumstances is therefore an important right to be included in the contract, and will be important to both parties since obscene content on the hosting site could be equally damaging to the target site.

9. **Summary**

- A plain text link to a website's homepage is unlikely to result in any legal liability unless there is something malicious or defamatory in the use of the link.

- Use of a trade mark, whether in the form of a name or a logo, as the link could result in a claim for trade mark infringement.

- Deep linking to another website or framing its content is much more likely to lead to legal liability. Such activity could constitute a violation of copyright and even passing-off. The website wishing to use deep linking or framing would be well advised to seek the consent of the target site.

- Use of another company's name as a metatag within the coding of a website may amount to trade mark infringement. Similarly the use of another company's name to trigger banner ads may lead to claims of trade mark infringement.

Chapter 12

· **Tax** ·

1. Introduction

Tax may often be about the last thing e-tailers wish to take an interest in. Nevertheless, considering tax issues at an early stage can help improve tax efficiency and avoid unexpected tax compliance issues coming to light at a later date. There are certain key tax issues this chapter will consider in establishing an e-tailing venture.

Foremost amongst these is structuring the e-tailing venture in a tax efficient manner. This includes avoiding "permanent establishments" abroad to avoid profits being subject to foreign tax – even an overseas server can be a "permanent establishment" if it carries out substantial elements of the e-tailing business such as concluding contracts or supplying "digitised products". This chapter will also identify and address certain VAT and customs duties issues that may arise on the new e-tailing business.

2. Structuring an e-tailing venture

A new UK Internet venture will be set up either as a business division of an existing trading company or as a new trading subsidiary. From a commercial and legal risk perspective, a new subsidiary provides a suitable vehicle for a future Initial Public Offering ("IPO") or sale if the Internet business is successful, as well as the benefit of limited liability if it is not.

From a tax perspective, the tax implications of setting up a new division or new company are similar – in each case the business will be subject to UK tax on its trading profits. If a new company structure is used and the business is loss-making the tax losses may generally be surrendered to offset taxable profits of the parent's "bricks and mortar" business during the same period. However, the flexibility to offset profits of the "bricks and mortar" business is generally greater if a divisional structure is used.

A separate subsidiary structure may also be advantageous from a tax perspective on an IPO – if the funds from the IPO go to the e-tailing subsidiary and not the "bricks and mortar" parent, then it may be possible to effect an IPO without triggering a taxable capital gain.

On either structure, a private sale (or sale of listed shares following an IPO) for a profit will normally trigger a taxable capital gain.

3.   International perspective – "permanent establishments"

Structuring can also become more important in an international perspective.

A UK-based e-tailer will generally not be subject to overseas tax on the profits of overseas sales unless the sales take place through a "permanent establishment" in the foreign country. This means, broadly, a geographically fixed location through which substantive aspects of the trade are carried on. Auxiliary activities overseas such as marketing or storage generally in most jurisdictions do not constitute "permanent establishments" and will not expose a UK e-tailer to local tax on its profits. However, it is always prudent to check the particular local rules before relying on this. A number of general points should be noted in the context of e-commerce and "permanent establishments."

A website or web page generally cannot, of itself, constitute a "permanent establishment" that would expose a UK e-tailer's profits to tax abroad.

Website hosting arrangements (which typically do not result in a server and its location being at the disposal of the e-tailer) also generally do not give rise to "permanent establishments" subject to foreign tax on profits.

An Internet service provider overseas will not normally constitute a "permanent establishment", assuming the ISP simply provides Internet services to the e-tailer and does not (and cannot) conclude contracts in the name of the e-tailer.

If an e-tailer owns or leases its own overseas server, this might potentially constitute a "permanent establishment" depending upon the activities performed by the server. If the server is only providing information about products, soliciting business or other auxiliary activities, it generally will not be a "permanent establishment". However if an overseas server performs functions that are a core or substantial element of the e-tailer's business enterprise (such as concluding contracts with customers or actually electronically supplying "digitised products" such as software or e-music to customers) the server could be a "permanent establishment" which causes a UK e-tailer's profits to become subject to foreign tax, even without any personnel being present in the foreign jurisdiction.

Overall, it is prudent to exercise caution in the choice of location of servers where the server will undertake any form of significant business activity for the e-tailer. Since the tax treatment of servers is a relatively new issue, it is advisable to check the applicable local tax treatment of servers in the relevant jurisdiction, as there may be considerable variation between jurisdictions.

Overseas sales can also raise VAT and customs duty issues – see Sections 5 and 6 below.

4.   Going offshore?

Internet businesses are, by their nature, geographically mobile. A real shop must be in a geographical location its customers can get to – not so a virtual shop whose customers need no more than a website address to gain access. Some companies seek to set up part or all of their Internet business offshore in order to reduce or eliminate the tax payable on their profits.

There are many obstacles that must be overcome in order to achieve that goal.

(1) The offshore subsidiary must be centrally managed and controlled from outside the United Kingdom. This will require a non-UK board of directors that exercises real, top-level strategic control over the company.

(2) The offshore subsidiary must not trade in the United Kingdom. Broadly speaking, its trading infrastructure and activities must be located outside the United Kingdom, and no significant elements of its trade should take place in the United Kingdom. In many cases it can be difficult in practice to locate business infrastructure in tax haven jurisdictions.

(3) The offshore subsidiary's activities will also need to be restricted to trading activities that are exempt from the "Controlled foreign companies" rules. Otherwise, the UK "bricks and mortar" parent will be taxed on the offshore e-tailing subsidiary's profits.

(4) Transactions between the offshore subsidiary and the UK parent (including loans, other finance and any support services) must be on arms' length terms.

(5)   Even if profits can be realised offshore at reduced tax rates, they
        will still be taxable in the United Kingdom when repatriated to
        the United Kingdom.

As a result, "going offshore" is rarely as attractive or viable as it may
first appear.

5.   **VAT**

Sales of electronically ordered goods or electronically supplied services
or "digitised products" (such as downloaded business software or
computer games and e-music) within the United Kingdom are subject to
UK value added tax ("VAT") at 17.5% in the same way as their
traditional retailing equivalents. However, the VAT position becomes
more complicated in the context of the international trading
environment provided by e-commerce, particularly between different
Member States of the European Union.

   Sales by a UK e-tailer to business customers in other EU Member
States (whether of electronically ordered physical goods or digitised
products or services) are generally not subject to UK VAT – but the
recipient will be required to charge itself VAT on its receipt of the
goods. Competing sales by a UK e-tailer's non-EU based competitors to
business customers in the EU would attract broadly similar VAT
treatment – save that EU VAT will generally apply when physical goods
are imported into the EU from outside it. Accordingly, within the B2B
sector the VAT rules generally do not interfere with the competitiveness
of EU e-tailers – and may even give them a slight advantage over non-
EU competitors in relation to electronically ordered but physically
delivered goods.

   In the B2C sector, sales by a UK e-tailer to an EU non-business
consumer will generally be subject to UK VAT (save that, in the case of
physical goods only, if the e-tailer's total sales into that EU state exceed
the applicable local threshold it will be required to register for and
charge customers the local VAT instead of UK VAT). Non-EU
competitor e-tailers in the B2C market are generally in a broadly
equivalent competitive position as regards electronically ordered
physical goods, since local VAT will arise on importing the goods into
the customer's EU state from outside the EU. However, UK and other
EU e-tailers have a competitive disadvantage against non-EU
competitors in the B2C market in respect of digitised products.

Currently, the overall sales levels of B2C digitised products such as downloaded computer games or music represent only a comparatively small proportion of the e-commerce market, but this is likely to increase as e-commerce develops.

Sales by UK (or other European) e-tailers outside the EU are generally not subject to VAT.

The EU has recognised the competitive disadvantage the EU VAT system gives EU B2C e-tailers of digitised products against their non-EU competitors, and has proposed that non-EU e-tailers should be required to register for VAT in a single EU Member State and charge that EU state's VAT on all supplies within the EU. However, the United Kingdom has objected to this on the grounds that such a proposal would impose unfair additional compliance burdens on non-EU suppliers which are not already registered for VAT in the EU, that it would be difficult for non-EU operators to comply with in practice, and near impossible for EU states to enforce in practice against suppliers wholly outside their jurisdictions.

Instead, the United Kingdom has proposed that, as a short term measure, all supplies of digitised products by non-EU e-tailers should be temporarily exempt from VAT. In the longer term the United Kingdom proposes that the EU should work with the OECD (whose review of VAT and e-commerce is still underway) to find an appropriate remedy for the existing gap in the EU VAT system. For the time being, though, it remains the position that VAT on digitised supplies in the B2C sector is chargeable on sales by EU e-tailers only.

6.   Customs duties

Customs duties are only an issue in e-commerce when physical goods are electronically ordered – digitised products and services are free of customs duties. Customs duties also do not apply to movements of goods within the EU.

However, EU customs duties generally do apply on any goods imported into the EU from outside the EU. Thus, a UK e-tailer sourcing its goods from within the EU enjoys a competitive advantage as regards customs duties over competitors importing goods from outside the EU. Importers of goods into the EU are advised to check the local customs duties rules of the EU state into which the goods are first imported.

7. **Summary**

- The tax structuring of an e-tailing venture should be considered at an early stage, particularly in respect of businesses that will operate internationally.

- Avoiding a "permanent establishment" in other jurisdictions will generally prevent a UK e-tailer's profits becoming subject to foreign tax. A server can constitute a permanent establishment if it performs substantial elements of the e-tailer's business (such as concluding contracts or supplying "digitised products").

- In rare cases it may be possible to establish e-tailing ventures in tax havens to take advantage of very low tax rates, but this is generally difficult to achieve in practice.

- The VAT and customs duties implications of a new e-tailing venture should be considered at an early stage.

Chapter 13

· **Employee Benefits** ·

1. **Introduction**

The recent fluctuations in the share prices of Internet and technology companies have been widely publicised. Despite this, companies may still consider that granting employees shares in their employing company is a valuable way to reward and motivate employees. This can particularly be the case with start-up companies where the perceived potential for future growth in share value can be considerable. Companies often want their employees to be able to share in any future successes – this can also have the useful effect of increasing employee loyalty to the company.

There are many possibilities open to a company that wishes to reward and incentivise its employees by reference to its equity. For example, employees can be given shares, rights to obtain shares at a future date or a cash bonus of an amount linked to the company's share price. Such awards will have tax consequences for both the employees and the company. However, it is possible for a company to establish Inland Revenue approved arrangements, thus minimising the tax payable by both the company and the employee.

2. **Inland Revenue approved share schemes**

There are advantages to using Inland Revenue approved schemes. A charge to income tax for employees does not generally arise on the exercise of options. Gains on shares are subject to capital gains tax only on ultimate sale; taper relief, annual exemption and other capital losses may be used to reduce or avoid any charge to tax. Costs incurred by a company in establishing an approved scheme are automatically deductible for corporation tax purposes. Benefits provided pursuant to approved schemes do not generally attract National Insurance contributions.

There are a number of different types of Inland Revenue approved schemes.

Company share option plans

Under a company share option plan, options are granted to acquire shares at their market value at the date of grant of the option. These plans are flexible and the exercise of options can, for instance, be linked to performance targets. Options can be to subscribe for new shares or to acquire shares from an existing holder (usually an employee trust). They do not require any employer contribution and employees need only make payment on exercise of options. The flexibility of such schemes makes them a popular means of incentivising employees.

There are a number of key features to this type of share option plan. The directors are free to select participants at their discretion – however, only employees or full-time directors can be eligible to participate. The total value of shares (calculated at the date of grant of the option) over which an employee can hold options at any one time must not exceed £30,000. In order for favourable tax treatment to apply an option must only be exercised between three and ten years after it is granted and must not be exercised within three years of a previous exercise of approved options (with income tax relief) under any other approved share option scheme (other than a savings-related scheme). Scheme documentation must be approved by the Inland Revenue in advance. The option price must not be less than the market value of the shares at the date of grant – unless the shares are listed on the London or New York Stock Exchange the market value of the shares has to be agreed in advance with the Inland Revenue. Finally, a participant will be liable to capital gains tax on any gain he makes on any eventual disposal of shares.

Savings-related share option schemes

Under a savings-related option scheme, employees are granted options to acquire shares and take out qualifying savings contracts to fund the exercise of the options. As with company share option plans no contribution is required from the company. Savings-related schemes are often attractive to companies as providing low cost incentives but may be less so to employees who are required to make a monthly contribution (non-deductible for tax purposes) without any immediate return or stake in the company.

A participating employee makes monthly contributions (maximum £250) for a minimum of three years into an SAYE savings contract with the bank or building society nominated by the company. The savings contract provides for repayment on maturity together with a tax free bonus. The employee is granted an option exercisable at the date of maturity of his SAYE contract (*i.e.* after either three, five or seven years) over that number of shares the total option exercise price for which equals the maturity value of the SAYE contract. Options can be granted at a discount of up to 20% of the market value of the shares at the date the option is granted.

All-employee share plan

This is a new type of employee share scheme introduced in the Finance Act 2000. The all-employee scheme is extremely flexible, allowing employers to award any combination of free shares, shares for which the employee pays ("partnership" shares) and further free shares based on the number of partnership shares bought by the employee ("matching" shares).

The main features of the scheme are:

- free shares can be awarded to an employee up to a maximum value of £3,000 per tax year; partnership shares can be purchased by the employee out of their gross salary, up to a limit of £125 per month (or 10% of their overall salary if less);
- up to two matching shares can be provided by the employer for each partnership share purchased by the employee;
- all employees who are invited to participate in the scheme must do so on the same terms, although the company can take account of level of pay, length of service or hours worked to vary the awards of free shares;
- the awards of free shares can also be subject to the employee reaching performance targets, provided that these are fair and objective;
- there must be a holding period of between three and five years for free and matching shares, during which time the employee must leave any such shares in the plan (unless they leave the company's employment) – this is to encourage long-term share ownership by employees;
- dividends received on shares whilst they remain in the plan can be re-invested in shares, up to a maximum value of £1,500 in a tax year; any shares bought with dividends must then themselves be held in the plan for three years;

- free and matching shares may be subject to forfeiture under certain conditions for a period of up to three years after the date of award; forfeiture cannot be linked to performance targets;
- provided that shares are left in the plan for at least five years, employees pay no income tax or National Insurance contributions on the shares; shares left in the plan for between three and five years will be subject to income tax and National Insurance contributions on the lesser of the initial value of the shares or their exit value – any gain in value whilst the shares remain in the plan is tax free; shares withdrawn from the plan within three years are chargeable to income tax and National Insurance contributions on the market value of the shares on the date on which they are withdrawn;
- no capital gains tax is payable by the employee until shares are removed from the plan and subsequently sold – tax is then due on any gain in value between the removal of the shares from the plan and the sale (although this may be reduced by taper relief);
- the employer obtains corporation tax relief on the costs of providing free and matching shares and shares for employees to purchase, to the extent that this exceeds any contributions by the employees.

Enterprise management incentives

Also introduced in the Finance Act 2000, this scheme is designed for small companies so that they can offer employees a substantial equity incentive to remain with the company. As such, it may be ideal for Internet start-ups, rather than already established businesses. The Finance Act 2001 has amended the EMI further.

Since the Finance Act 2001, the company may award EMI options to any number of employees, provided that they work for the company for at least 25 hours a week or 75% of their working time. Each employee may be granted options over shares worth up to £100,000. Since the Finance Act 2001, the company may award EMI options over shares with a value of up to £3 million.

In order to operate an EMI scheme the company must be an independent trading company with gross assets of no more than £15 million (there is a proposal that this limit may be raised to £30 million).

The scheme is more flexible in the conditions that can be attached to the options, including exercise period, option price and performance conditions.

The employee will not be taxed on the grant of the option. There will normally be no income tax or National Insurance contributions to pay when the options are exercised. Capital gains tax will only become payable by the employee when the shares are sold, but as taper relief will run from the date that the option is granted, there will be an effective charge to capital gains tax on 25% of the gain, provided that the shares are held for at least four years from the date on which the option is granted (reducing the effective rate of tax for higher rate taxpayers to 10%). From April 2002 taper relief will be accelerated, so that the maximum relief will be granted where shares are held for at least two years from the date on which the option was granted.

Unlike other Inland Revenue approved schemes, there are no approval or clearance procedures for the scheme – the company simply has to notify the Revenue when a grant under an EMI scheme is made. However, there is an informal advance clearance procedure for companies wishing to obtain comfort that they are qualified to grant EMI options.

Profit-sharing schemes

Unlike option schemes, a profit-sharing scheme requires contributions from the company but gives employees the opportunity to acquire shares at no cost to themselves. Profit-sharing schemes are being phased out under the Finance Act 2000 – no new schemes would have been approved unless an application was made to the Inland Revenue before 6 April 2001, and no appropriation of shares may be made under an existing scheme after 6 April 2002. It is intended that profit-sharing schemes will be replaced by the all-employee share plan described above.

Broadly, a profit-sharing scheme requires the company to form a trust, to which funds (not necessarily profits) are allocated each year. The trustees use these funds to purchase shares in the company, which are then appropriated amongst the participants in the scheme. All UK employees who have completed a qualifying period of service must be eligible to participate in the scheme. Each participant can receive shares with a maximum initial value of £3,000 per annum or, if greater, 10% of his salary (subject to an overriding maximum of £8,000). The shares must be held in the trust for a minimum period of two years; if they are withdrawn from the trust within three years then an income tax charge will arise. On a disposal of the shares by the employee a capital gains tax charge will arise.

Further information about Inland Revenue approved share schemes can be found on the Inland Revenue's website at: www.inlandrevenue.gov.uk/shareschemes.

3. Unapproved share schemes

Sometimes an Inland Revenue approved share scheme is not appropriate for a company because its terms are too restrictive. An unapproved scheme allows flexibility (subject to institutional investors' guidelines). There is no need to limit the value of share benefits provided; nor are there restrictions on the terms of the grant (including exercise price). Participation in an unapproved share scheme can be at the discretion of the company and no Inland Revenue approval is required for changes to such a scheme.

Tax treatment of unapproved schemes

There are a number of points to be aware of in considering how unapproved schemes are treated for tax purposes.

Employees will (in contrast to approved schemes) normally be charged to income tax where shares are acquired at an undervalue. Deferred purchase terms are also a taxable benefit.

Anti-avoidance rules may give rise to a further charge to income tax on any subsequent increase in value. The charge will not normally arise where the shares acquired are ordinary shares in a parent company not subject to any special rights or restrictions.

The grant of an option to purchase shares in the future will not usually give rise to any charge to income tax unless the option can be exercised more than ten years after the date of grant and the option price is less than the market value of the shares at the date of grant.

On the exercise of an option, an income tax charge will arise on the difference between the market value on the date of exercise of the shares acquired and the total amount paid by the employee for the option and the shares.

On a disposal of the shares on arm's length terms capital gains tax will be payable in the normal way. Credit will generally be given for any income tax paid on the exercise of an option.

PAYE and National Insurance

PAYE might have to be operated and National Insurance contributions are generally payable (by both the employer and the employee) in relation to unapproved share schemes and on the gift of shares or sale of shares at an undervalue to employees.

On the grant of an option, if income tax is payable then PAYE may in some cases need to be accounted for. National Insurance contributions were also due on the grant of options prior to 6 April 1999 if the market value of the shares at the date of grant exceeded the option price. In respect of options granted on or after 6 April 1999, income tax and National Insurance contributions will only be due on the grant of options on the difference between the market value of the shares at the date of grant and the option price if the option is exercisable more than ten years after the date of grant.

On the exercise of an option, PAYE will be due if an income tax charge arises. In respect of options granted on or after 6 April 1999, National Insurance contributions will also be due. However, neither PAYE needs to be operated nor will National Insurance contributions be due if the shares in question are not "readily convertible assets" (e.g. tradable on a recognised investment exchange or where other trading arrangements are or are likely to be in place to enable the employees concerned to sell on their shares).

If the shares in question are readily convertible assets, PAYE will have to be operated and National Insurance contributions will be due on the amount of any undervalue at which shares are sold or gifted to an employee outside an option scheme.

It is now possible for companies to pass on the cost of all or part of any employer's National Insurance contributions due on the exercise of a share option to the employee. This can be done by means of either a written agreement or by submitting a formal election to the Inland Revenue.

Unapproved share option schemes

Historically, unapproved share option schemes have proved to be the most popular with companies wishing to grant share options to employees. Unapproved schemes operate in the same way as approved company share option plans, but are not subject to Inland Revenue restrictions and therefore do not attract the tax advantages of approved plans.

Long-term incentive plans

Long-term incentive plans ("LTIPs") are a popular means of remunerating directors and senior executives. The three most common forms of LTIP are restricted share plans, performance based plans and deferred payment/bonus plans.

Restricted share plans are the simplest form of LTIP using a trust to purchase shares and allocate them to individual executives. They are termed "restricted" because the executive concerned only has a right to his shares after a certain period of time has elapsed and provided the executive is still employed by the company. Provision is often made to bring forward an entitlement in circumstances where the executive leaves the company as a "good leaver".

In performance-based plans, an employee trust will generally acquire shares which are from time to time earmarked for selected senior executives on the recommendation of the company's remuneration committee. The executive does not become entitled to the shares until normally three to five years have elapsed and the company has met its performance targets. If the company fails to meet its optimum target, a sliding scale is often used to determine the amount of benefit payable. Typical performance targets which are set include growth in earnings per share and total shareholders' return, frequently by reference to a group of competing companies.

Deferred payment/bonus plans again use trust arrangements to allow an executive to buy shares which are then matched by the company after a certain period of time. This can be combined with a performance-based plan to allow for the number of matching shares to be varied depending on performance.

In addition to the advantages provided by a traditional share option scheme, an LTIP allows for a number of benefits. A company's performance is more closely linked to executive remuneration. The executives are encouraged to hold a stable interest in their company - under traditional share option schemes it is common for executives to sell shares in order to fund exercise of the option. Tax relief can be obtained on contributions made to the employee trust. The real cost of putting the employee trust in funds can be more easily ascertained. Finally, the executives benefit not merely from the increase in value over the exercise price (as under an option scheme), but from the full value of the shares transferred.

4.   Employee share ownership trusts

ESOPs and QUESTs

An ESOP is an employee share ownership plan. They generally take the form of an employee trust (which may be an Inland Revenue approved employee share ownership trust or "QUEST") which purchases shares in the company, together with a share incentive scheme. The trust will provide shares for distribution to employees under that scheme. The trust will be funded by borrowings or by gifts from the company on a regular or ad hoc basis, or by borrowings from a third party. The trust may eventually become self-financing from the proceeds of sale of the shares and dividends received.

There are many benefits to ESOPs. For example, existing shares rather than new shares can be used to prevent dilution of existing equity. ESOPS create a market for employees' shares. The shares may be purchased in buy-outs or flotations for later distribution to employees. Such shares are held in "friendly" hands - the trustees, although independent, are unlikely to vote against recommendations of the board on a takeover. Finally, contributions will normally be tax deductible as trading expenses. Non-trading companies may claim a deduction as an expense of management.

In order to qualify as a QUEST the trust must satisfy various conditions, for example, it must be UK resident, have at least one professional trustee and half the non-professional trustees must themselves be employee representatives. The powers of the trustees are also restricted, for example, shares cannot be used to satisfy options under an unapproved scheme or a company share option plan. Both contributions made to, and the costs of setting up a QUEST, automatically qualify for a corporation tax deduction.

Further information on ESOPs can be found at the Employee Share Ownership Centre website: www.mhcc.co.uk/esop/esop/default.asp. The ESOP centre is a nonprofit organisation which aims to develop all forms of broad-based employee share ownership plans in the United Kingdom and Europe.

5.   Further information and advice

The Inland Revenue website (cited above) is extremely helpful and should provide the answers to many e-tailers' questions. Another website that an e-tailer may find useful is: www.proshare.org.uk.

6. **Summary**

- Inland Revenue approved share schemes provide a tax-efficient method of equity incentivisation. There are several types of approved share scheme to choose from. These schemes contain varying levels and types of restrictions on the awards that may be made under them.

- Unapproved share schemes are less tax efficient, but may prove to be more flexible as they can be individually tailored to meet the needs of the company.

- Where National Insurance contributions are payable on the exercise of an option, it is possible for the company to agree with the employee that the cost of some or all of the employer's National Insurance contributions will be met by the employee.

- Companies may wish to operate a share scheme in conjunction with a trust. This type of arrangement has many advantages, including tax-efficiency and the prevention of dilution of existing shareholdings by the award of shares to employees.

· Glossary of Internet Terms ·

The following is a glossary of some Internet and technology terms which may prove useful:

ADSL: an acronym for Asymmetric Digital Subscriber Line, ADSL is a method of transmitting digital data over traditional copper telephone lines at speeds higher than were previously possible and on a continuously available basis (*i.e.* an "always on" connection). Data can be downloaded at speeds of up to 1.544 Megabits per second and uploaded at speeds of 128 Kilobits per second (that's why it's termed asymmetric – data flows principally in one direction). This technology is well suited to broadband Internet access, where much more data is sent from a server to the consumer's computer than is sent by the consumer to the server.

Affiliate marketing: the use by an e-tailer of other websites (affiliates) to help market its products or services either through the affiliate providing a link through to the e-tailer's website or the affiliate displaying details of the e-tailer's products or services.

ASP (Application Service Provider): an organisation which offers access over the Internet to software applications which otherwise would have to be stored on the user's computer.

AUP (Acceptable Use Policy): a policy which must be signed up to by a user wishing to access a network, prior to and as a condition of using such network. An AUP provides rules of use of the network, any breach of which would allow the network provider to suspend or terminate provision of the network. The network provider will usually seek protection against any activities that are damaging to the reputation of the network provider or illegal.

B2B (Business to Business): the selling or transfer of products, services and/or information over the Internet by one business to another business.

B2C (Business to Customer): the selling or transfer of products, services and/or information from business to customer.

Bandwidth: if you think of the communications path as a pipe, then bandwidth represents the width of the pipe that determines how much data can flow through it all at once. It is a measure of the difference between the lowest and highest frequencies of an electromagnetic transmission (*i.e.* the width of the band of an electromagnetic transmission) and is used to mean both how fast data flows on a given bandwidth and the range of frequencies that an electronic signal occupies when transmitted on different transmission mediums.

Banner: a graphic image often used as a heading to a web page or as an advertisement displayed on the top of a web page.

Bitmap: defines a space representing text or graphics by rows or columns of single pixels.

Bit rate: a measure in digital telecommunications of the number of binary digits that pass a certain point on a network each second (or other length of time). "Kilobits", therefore, means one thousand bits per second. Bit rate is a synonym for "data transfer rate".

Broadband: high speed Internet services which allow users to view content which requires high bandwidth such as video clips. Broadband Internet access can be delivered via DSL and cable modems.

Browser: a software program that allows users to view and interact with various kinds of Internet resources available on the World Wide Web. A browser is commonly called a web browser.

Cable modem: a device connecting a PC to a fibre-optic cable, which due to the high bandwidth of the coaxial cable allows much faster access to the Internet than telephone modems – approximately 1.5mbps as compared to 28.8/56kps. A cable modem provides a similar data transfer rate to that provided to subscribers to a DSL service.

Cache: a way of storing something temporarily, *e.g.* web pages visited are stored in the cache directory of a browser allowing them to be called up directly rather than from the original server, ensuring quicker access. When you download a web page, the data is "cached," meaning it is temporarily stored on your computer. The next time you want that page, instead of requesting the file from the web server, your web browser just accesses it from the cache, so the page loads quickly.

Certificate Authority (CA): a trusted person or agency, who releases certificates in respect of an electronic signature verifying the identity of the sender of the electronic signature.

Chat room: part of a website which allows users to communicate in real time through text.

Checksum: the bit of coding attached to a transmission packet of data sent from one computer to another which enables the receiving computer to calculate whether it has received all of the data being transmited. The checksum is attached to the back of the transmission packet so that when it is received the checksum generated by the receiving computer should match that generated by the sending computer.

Cipher: a way of transforming text to disguise its meaning, such as by encryption.

Clickthrough: when a user clicks on an advertisement or hypertext link taking them through to another web page. The amount of clickthroughs an advertisement gets is used as a way of measuring its success and can be used as a measure of reward for the site hosting the advertisement or link.

Clicks and mortar: a business which uses both a physical location for its main activities as well as the World Wide Web. The term is often used to refer to a traditional old economy company that has begun to exploit the Internet in its marketing and sales, alongside its traditional methods of business.

Client/server: a network which contains a system whereby client software is used to request a service from a **server** with corresponding server software.

Colocation: location of telecommunications or network equipment on the premises of a service provider. For example, a website owner could place the site's own computer servers on the premises of an Internet service provider.

Conditional access: the encryption of a transmitted programme on digital TV and other forms of broadcast and interactive services, in order to limit access to authorised users.

Content: all materials and information provided on a website.

Cookie: a file sent to a web browser by a web server that is used to record a user's activities on a website. For instance, when a user buys items from a site and places them in a so-called virtual shopping cart, that information is stored in the cookie. When the browser requests additional files, the cookie information is sent back to the server. Cookies can remember other kinds of personal information, such as passwords and preferences, allowing users to be presented with customised information. Some people regard cookies as an invasion of privacy; others think they are a harmless way to make websites more personal. Most cookies have an expiration date and either reside in your computer's memory until you close your browser or are saved to your hard drive. Cookies cannot read information stored in your computer.

Cryptography: the science or actual process of security of information, using methods to make content indecipherable to anyone without the key. Cryptosystems are used for this purpose and in the modern context often involve complex mathematics and computer programs.

Cybersquatting: the purchase or use of a domain name with the intention of selling it to a someone else who may want it in the future.

Dark fibre: fibre/installed fibre optic cable infrastructure which is not actually carrying a signal or is not ready to use.

Decryption: the conversion of encrypted text back into its original form.

Deep link: a link to a page on a website which is not the home page of the website.

Denial of service: when a user or organisation is prevented access to a facility normally available to them through the actions of a third party. A denial of service attack may be maliciously instigated or accidental and can affect, for example, e-mail services or websites.

Dial up: the connection to a telephone line normally in a large system with many lines/users. The connection is maintained for a limited time (as opposed to a "dedicated" line). Dial-up lines are also referred to as switched lines (and dedicated lines as nonswitched lines). A dial-up connection can be initiated manually or automatically by a computer's modem or other device.

Digital cash: a method of payment over the Internet involving the purchase of "cash credits". They can be stored on the user's computer. They can then be used for purchasing goods and services over the online.

Digital signature: a way of authenticating the identity of the sender of a message or author of a document, and it allows the message recipient to see this. It may also be used to ensure that the content of a message or document remains unchanged from time of sending and as a time stamp.

DSL (Digital Subscriber Line): a technology offered by telephone companies to their users in which their ordinary copper telephone lines are used to provide a much faster service for the transmission of high bandwidth information. A DSL line can carry both data and voice signals and the data part of the line is continuously connected. One form of DSL is ADSL and the various forms of DSL are collectively known as xDSL.

Domain name: the location or address of an organisation on the Internet consisting of two main parts, *e.g.* .com, .org – reflecting the nature of the organisation, (for example, commercial, governmental or educational). Before this is an identification of the organisation, *e.g.* 'Britishairways.com'.

Downloading: transmission of a file from one computer to another.

Encryption: the conversion of data into a form that cannot be easily be read or understood by unauthorised people.

E-tailing: retailing on the Internet.

Firewall: a network security system designed to restrict external and internal traffic over the Internet.

Framing: a link in which the new page is framed so that it appears to be part of the initial site.

FTP: File Transfer Protocol – a means of transferring files (such as a computer program, image or document) across the Internet.

Hit: the sending of a single file, whether an HTML file, an image, audio or other type of file to a user's computer. A single web page request can bring with it a number of files and can therefore produce more than one hit.

Home page: the main or front page of a website.

HTML: an acronym for Hypertext Markup Language, HTML is the computer language used to create hypertext documents. HTML uses a finite list of tags that describe the general structure of various kinds of documents linked together on the World Wide Web.

Hypertext links: the links on a webpage which act as a request to the web servers of a web site owner requesting the display of another web page or different content.

ICANN: the Internet Corporation for Assigned Names and Numbers, which licenses domain name registrars, and operates a process for resolving domain name disagreements outside the regular court system.

In-lining: the display of graphic files on one site that are stored on another site.

Internet: a global network of interconnected computer networks using transmission control protocol or Internet protocol (TCP/IP) to transfer the data between one another. It is not only the World Wide Web that is transferred by the Internet. WAP services and certain interactive tv services are also carried over the Internet but have nothing to do with the World Wide Web.

IP: Internet Protocol, which is a technological means of transmitting packets of data from computer to computer.

IP address: the individual sequence of numbers allocated to each computer connected to the Internet.

ISP: an Internet service provider or access provider, ISP refers to the remote computer system to which you connect your personal computer and through which you connect to the Internet. ISPs that you access by modem and telephone line are often called dial-up services.

Java: a form of programing language.

LAN: Local Area Network – a computer network which operates within a confined area such as an office or a university.

Linking: the linking, by means of a hypertext link of one website to another, allowing users to transfer to the second website solely by clicking on the hypertext link.

Meta tag: a "coding statement" used in HTML to describe a part of a web page.

Modem: short for modulator/demodulator, a modem is a device that allows remote computers to communicate, to transmit and receive data using telephone lines.

MP3: compressed music files which can be transferred from one computer to another.

Netiquette: a form of online etiquette, an informal code of conduct that governs what is generally considered to be the acceptable way for users to interact with one another online.

Packet: a unit of data which travels across the Internet to its destination where it is assembled with the other packets making up the file.

Peer to peer: on the Internet, peer to peer is a type of network which allows a group of users with the same networking program to connect with each other and directly access files from one another's hard drives. The most famous example of this is Napster. Because this method avoids a central server, many businesses are considering peer to peer as a way of reducing costs of maintaining a central server.

Portal: a website which acts as a starting point for users. It can be either general or specialised (for particular themes, such as law or women's health). A "horizontal portal" is a more general one, which aims to provide a wide range of goods and services, whereas a "vertical portal" is of a more industry-specific nature.

Protocol: an agreed "language" which is used by networks to talk to one another.

Rich media: a media format containing elaborate perceptual or interactive elements such as video clips.

Router: a piece of hardware or software that connects two or more networks. A router functions as a sorter and interpreter as it looks at addresses and passes bits of information to their proper destinations. Software routers are sometimes referred to as gateways.

Server: a program or the computer on which a server program is run which provides services to other programs in the same computer or other computers on a network.

Simple link: linking where it is clear that a user is being taken from one website to the homepage of another.

SMTP: Simple Mail Transfer Protocol – the protocol used for sending e-mail across the Internet.

Splash page: a preliminary page preceding a home page to a website, usually promoting a particular site feature or providing advertising and often timed to move on to the home page automatically after a short time.

TCP: Transmission Control Protocol – a means of transmitting packets of data from computer to computer.

URL: an acronym for Uniform Resource Locator, a URL is the address for a resource or site (usually a directory or file) on the World Wide Web and the convention that web browsers use for locating files and other remote services.

World Wide Web: worldwide collection of text and multimedia files and other network services interconnected via a system of hypertext documents (the "http" which appears in your browser is short for hypertext transfer protocol). The World Wide Web sits on top of the Internet since the data that makes up the World Wide Web is transferred via the Internet.

· Useful Internet Sites ·

1. Competition law and policy

Competition Commission
http://www.competition-commission.gov.uk/. A full list of reports dating from 1950 and merger references dating from 1966 together with current inquiries, press releases and speeches.

Competition Directorate-General
http://europa.eu.int/comm/dgs/competition/index en.htm. Cases, legislation (EU and national), press releases, publications, speeches and articles

Competition Online
http://www.clubi.ie/competition/compframesite/index.htm. This site mainly consists of Irish material but includes links to world-wide anti-trust and regulatory sites. The site includes news, articles, and full-text Competition Authority decisions.

Department of Trade and Industry
http://www.dti.gov.uk/. Regulatory guidance and information on international trade and investment, competition policy and science and technology policy. The site includes publications, press releases and consultation documents.

Federal Trade Commission
http://www.ftc.gov/. News releases, guidance, speeches and Commission actions. This site is US specific.

Office of Fair Trading (OFT)
http://www.oft.gov.uk/. Publications and reports on competition law, consumer advice and consumer credit law. The site includes the OFT quarterly magazine.

Organisation for Economic Co-operation and Development
http://www.oecd.org/. Online documents, information on activities of committees including trade, taxation, environment, and competition.

2. Corporate

British-American Chamber of Commerce (BACC)
http://www.babinc.org/. Includes business development/intelligence and information about conducting business in the United States and United Kingdom.

Companies House

http://www.companies-house.gov.uk/. A searchable database of companies registered in England and Wales.

Corporate Information

http://www.corporateinformation.com/.Over 15,000 research reports on publicly traded companies, 20,000 company profiles. Search engines for United States, Canada, Germany, France, Italy, Japan, United Kingdom and ìother countriesî and access to a search engine for 300,000+ company profiles.

Economist Intelligence Unit (EIU)

http://www.eiu.com/. An information service for companies establishing and managing operations across national borders anywhere in the world. This provides objective analysis and forecasts of the political, economic and business environment in more than 180 countries.

Hoover's Online (USA)

http://www.hoovers.com/. An online search engine where information on US corporations can be accessed; particularly background corporation information including location, history, employees, market, competitors, financials, officers, news and analysis. Certain information is available only to Hoover.com members.

Insolvency Service

http://www.insolvency.gov.uk/. The site provides a searchable list of insolvency practitioners, a glossary of insolvency terms, statutory insolvency forms, and the names and addresses of Official Receivers.

Institute of Chartered Accountants in England and Wales

http://www.icaew.co.uk/. Useful notes on accountancy practice in the United Kingdom and a search engine of chartered accountants.

Institute of Chartered Secretaries and Administrators

http://www.icsa.org.uk/. An independent, self-regulating professional body for company secretaries and corporate administrators.

Institute of Directors

http://www.iod.co.uk/. Useful notes on business practice and issues in the United Kingdom.

Institute of Management

http://www.inst-mgt.org.uk/. Useful notes on management practice and issues in the United Kingdom.

Mondaq Business Briefing

http://www.mondaq.com/. A substantial collection of professional business advisors' knowledge and expertise, the site contains information on legislative and regulatory frameworks affecting business and investment around the world.

NASDAQ Europe

http://www.easdaq.be/default.asp. Formerly the EASDAQ site, this includes the listing rules, details of NASDAQ Europe trading system and a searchable membersí list. The site also provides an All Share Index broadcast which is calculated in real time.

Securities and Exchange Commission (SEC)
http://www.sec.gov/. Responsible for administering US federal securities laws the SECís site includes the EDGAR database; an SEC digest; public statements, proposals and final rules of the SEC; enforcement decisions (including opinions, orders and litigation releases) and links to related sites.

Takeover Panel
http://www.thetakeoverpanel.org.uk/. The site provides access to the City Code, SARs, Panel statements and annual reports and also includes a disclosure table and disclosure forms.

3. Directories and reference

Acronym Finder
http://www.acronymfinder.com/. Enter any acronym and this site will search the web for all its possible meanings.

American Bar Association
http://www.abanet.org/. A web site for US qualified lawyers this site includes news on the latest legal developments.

British Library
http://www.bl.uk/. The home page of the British Library.

BT Phone Directory
http://www.bt.com/directory-enquiries/dq home.jsp. An online telephone directory for homes and businesses within the United Kingdom.

Eurodicautom
http://eurodic.ip.lu/cgi-bin/edicbin/EuroDicWWW.pl. A multilingual terminology database managed by the European Commission's translation service this site covers 12 languages (the 11 official languages of the European Union, plus Latin).

International Centre for Commercial Law (ICC)
http://www.icclaw.com/. The official site of The Legal 500 Series this provides a guide to lawyers across the United Kingdom, Europe, the Asia Pacific region, the United States and the Middle East.

Martindale-Hubbell Lawyer Locator
http://www.martindale.com/xp/Martindale/home.xml. An online search facility profiling lawyers and law firms in over 160 countries via a variety of criteria, including name, geographic location, practice area, firm size, and languages spoken.

Notaries' Society
http://www.notaries.co.uk/. This site includes a geographical directory of notaries in England and Wales.

Solicitors in England and Wales
http://www.solicitors-online.com/. A directory run by the Law Society which includes all solicitors in private practice in England and Wales who hold current practising certificates. The site is updated daily.

UK-iNvest

http://www.uk-invest.com/. An investment and business resource page providing access to share, stock and portfolio information in the United Kingdom.

Wall Street Executive Library

http://www.executivelibrary.com/. Hundreds of links to a wide range of business and reference sites. This site has a North American bias.

4. European Union

Europa

http://www.europa.eu.int/index en.htm. The European Union's main server which provides access to the homepages of the EU institutions; EU news including press releases, statistics and a calendar of forthcoming events; EU legislative and common policy information including legal texts and publications; and basic information on the EU including Euro rates; citizensí rights.

Europa: EUR-Lex

http://europa.eu.int/eur-lex/en/. The European Commission's free European Union law service, with links to the Official Journal; treaties; legislation in force and in preparation; consolidated texts; Euro conversion rates; recent case law from the Court of Justice and the Court of First Instance, and documents of public interest. The site also provides a feedback forum.

Europa: Language Index

http://www.europa.eu.int/. The European Unionís web site language index which provides access to its main server in each of its 11 languages.

European Commission

http://www.europa.eu.int/comm/index en.htm. The home page of the European Commission with links to the Directorates-General and associated services.

European Court of Justice and Court of First Instance

http://www.europa.eu.int/cj/en/index.htm. Full text of judgments from the European Court of Justice and the Court of First Instance dating back to 1997. The site also provides an outline of jurisdiction procedures; the statutes of the courts; judicial statistics; a case diary and index of cases lodged; recent case law and press releases.

European Parliament

http://www.europarl.eu.int/home/default en.htm. Details of the activities and rules of procedure of the European Parliament.

European Union in the World

http://europa.eu.int/comm/world/. A site providing comprehensive and user-friendly access to a cross-section of information on the European Union's external relations.

Legislative Observatory (OEIL)

http://wwwdb.europarl.eu.int/dors/oeil/en/default.htm. This site tracks the progress of draft EU legislation and is divided into three main elements: "subjects of current interest"; "legislative dossiers"; and "activities of the institutions".

United Nations Economic Commission for Europe (UNECE)
http://www.unece.org/. A site containing news, press releases, publications and
the full text of some conventions.

5. Internet, information technology and e-commerce

**Central Computer and Telecommunications Agency (CCTA) (now the Office
of Government Commerce (OGC))**
http://www.ogc.gov.uk/ogc/ogchelp.nsf/pages/redirect.html. On 1 April 2001
the CCTA was taken over by the Office of Government Commerce which aims
to improve the delivery of public services through the best use of information
technology. The site provides information about the OCG including its aims,
products and services.

ebusiness Forum
http://www.ebusinessforum.com/. This site provides insight and analysis from
the Economist Intelligence Unit (EIU - part of the Economist Group) aimed at
helping senior executives build successful e-commerce strategies.

E-Centre UK
http://www.e-centre.org.uk/. The resource site for the Association for
Standards and Practices in Electronic Trade this is mainly targeted at businesses
but includes a useful glossary of e-commerce terms, and includes two
Electronic Data Interchange (EDI) standard agreements.

E-Commerce Law & Policy
http://www.e-comlaw.com/. This site features up-to-date articles on e-
commerce legal issues including domain names and data protection.

Electronic Commerce and the European Union
http://europa.eu.int/ISPO/ecommerce/. The site of the European Commission's
Electronic Commerce Unit, this provides information about e-commerce
including the latest news and access to relevant legislation.

Elexica
http://www.elexica.com/. The online legal resource powered by knowledge
from Simmons & Simmons.

Foundation for Information Policy Research (FIPR)
http://www.fipr.org/. An independent body that studies the interaction between
information technology and society, the FIPR's site provides breaking news;
archived documents; reports and conference details as well as policy
information centres and research tools. This is an excellent resource for e-
commerce issues.

Internet Chamber of Commerce (ICC)
http://www.icc.org/. This site contains a search engine and sets out the latest
Internet news and ideas including top stories. The site includes a catalogue of
ICC resources including a calendar of events, an ICC presentation archive,
Internet job postings, and a lending library.

Internet Corporation for Assigned Names and Numbers (ICANN)
http://www.icann.org/. ICANN was formed to take over responsibility for the internet protocol (IP) address space allocation, protocol parameter assignment, domain name system management, and root server system management functions currently performed by the IANA. This site provides news, IP resources and details ICANNís supporting organisations and advisory board committees.

Journal of Information Law and Technology (JILT)
http://elj.warwick.ac.uk/jilt/. An online journal run by Warwick University dealing with IT, e-commerce and Internet law issues.

Kuester Law
http://www.kuesterlaw.com/. A resource providing technology law and general patent and trade marks information for the United States.

NetNames
http://www.netnames.co.uk/dnrs/netnames.client.Login. An international domain name registration facility which provides information and advice on domain name problems; a search and alert function; technical support; and a search engine. New users are required to register.

Network Solutions, Inc. (NSI)
http://www.internic.net/. The site provides a domain name registry facility and links to information regarding the implementation of NSI's Shared Registration System; ICANN and the registrar accreditation process. In addition there is a link to Information regarding the US government's efforts to privatise the management of the domain name system and to increase competition in domain name registration services.

Nominet UK
http://www.nominet.org.uk/. The site details the domain registration process for .uk domain names. The site also contains a domain name search facility; dispute resolution service; membership information; procedures and documentation; news and press releases.

Office of the E-Envoy
http://www.e-envoy.gov.uk/. The UK government's e-commerce strategy website, containing an online discussion forum and a set of links to useful e-commerce websites.

PrivacyExchange
http://www.privacyexchange.org/. This site contains information on international laws relating to consumer privacy and data protection.

Society for Computers and Law (SCL)
http://www.scl.org/welcome.htm. A subscription web site detailing IT law and IT developments for lawyers. The site provides Information on a full range of SCL activities, meetings, publications and news.

WIPO Domain Name Dispute Resolution Service
http://arbiter.wipo.int/domains/index.html. A site detailing cybersquatting and other domain name disputes both before and resolved by the WIPO.

Wired News

http://www.wired.com/. A site providing the latest news and developments in the digital world including analysis of the technologies, companies, and people driving the information age.

6. Telecommunications and broadcasting

British Telecom Carrier Services Interconnect

http://www.btwebworld.com/interconnect/. A site containing British Telecom's ("BT's") pricing and contractual information; codes of practice; interconnection news; and carrier pre-selection information for use by operators seeking to interconnect with BT.

Federal Communications Commission (FCC)

http://www.fcc.gov/. A site containing information about the FCC and its resources, commissioners, major initiatives, bureaux and offices. The site also contains press releases and regulatory news updates.

Home Office: Interception of Communications

http://www.homeoffice.gov.uk/ripa/ripact.htm. Information and guidance on the Regulation of Investigatory Powers Act 2000 and subordinate legislation (together with a full legislative text).

Independent Committee for the Supervision of Standards of Telephone **Information Services (ICSTIS)**

http://www.icstis.org.uk/. The site provides the ICSTIS Code of Practice and guidelines relating to the regulation of premium rate telephone services in the United Kingdom.

Independent Regulators Group Information Sharing (IRG)

http://irgis.icp.pt/site/. This site includes information provided by 19 tele-communications regulators from across Europe (including European Union and EFTA Member States) on a range of regulatory matters. The siteís contents are available in 13 languages.

Independent Television Commission (ITC)

http://www.itc.org.uk/. This site sets out the ITCís role in licensing and regulating commercial TV (including internet and digital broadcasting issues) and contains ITC announcements; policy decisions; public consultation documents and monthly programmes and advertising complaints reports.

Information, Communications, Culture and Audio Visual Directorate-General (DGX)

http://www.europa.eu.int/comm/dg10/index.html. This site includes the European Union's audiovisual police and information on communications and media regulation and initiatives and cultural activities.

Office of Communications (OFCOM)

http://www.ofcom.gov.uk/. The site for the proposed UK communications industry regulator (currently at Green Paper stage). OFCOM is intended to combine the existing functions of the Broadcasting Standards Commission, Independent Television Commission, Oftel, Radio Authority, and Radiocommunications Agency.

Office of Telecommunications (OFTEL)

http://www.oftel.org.uk/. This site provides a comprehensive list of press releases and publications from OFTEL (together with a search facility). A list of telecoms licensees is also available together with the full text of applicable industry guidelines.

Radiocommunications Agency

http://www.radio.gov.uk/. This site includes consultation documents, information sheets, guidance notes and other publications and users are able to download licence application forms.

Telecoms Advice

http://www.telecomsadvice.org.uk/. This site is funded by the telecoms industry and OFTEL and offers practical and impartial advice to UK small businesses with a limited knowledge of the potential of modern telecoms.

TMA Ventures

http://www.tmav-online.com/preferred/preferred_1.htm. This site provides explanations of telecoms jargon.

Whatis.com

http://whatis.techtarget.com/. This site provides telecommunications and IT news and information, and includes explanations about the relevant technology, its effects and the issues it raises.

7. Trade associations

Advertising Standards Authority (ASA)

http://www.asa.org.uk/. This site includes the text for the British Codes of Advertising and Sales Promotion.

Alternative Investment Management Association

http://www.aima.org/. This site includes news items and other resources relating to hedge funds, managed futures and currency management (including regulatory information). Some items on this site require payment of a subscription.

Association of British Insurers

http://www.abi.org.uk/. This site includes consumer advice and information relating to insurance, press releases, research papers and briefing material together with links to related sites. Some items require registration and/or payment of a subscription.

Association of Chartered Certified Accountants

http://www.acca.co.uk/. This site contains general information relating to accountancy practice in the United Kingdom together with a database of accountants.

Association of Unit Trusts and Investment Funds

http://www.investmentfunds.org.uk/. This site includes a directory of UK investment funds, fact sheets, fund prices and yield information.

British Bankers' Association (BBA)

http://www.bba.org.uk/. This site is split into three sections for use by consumers, businesses and for media and research use. The site includes Libor rates, publications and information on EMU issues.

Chartered Institute of Management Accountants

http://www.cima.org.uk/. This site provides news and publications relating to management accounting and contains a database of UK and international practitioners.

Chartered Insurance Institute

http://www.cii.co.uk/index.php. This site provides a database of insurance professionals within the United Kingdom together with related links.

Council of Mortgage Lenders (CML)

http://www.cml.org.uk/servlet/dycon/zt-cml/cml/live/en/cml/home. A number of resources are available from this site including publications, statistics, code of practice, submissions and responses to consultation papers.

Financial Law Panel (FLP)

http://www.flpanel.demon.co.uk/. This site contains publications and opinions relating to legal uncertainties within the UK wholesale financial market. Some of these documents are only available to site sponsors.

Financial Markets Lawyers Group (FMLG)

http://www.ny.frb.org/fmlg/index.html. Users are able to access a range of documents and opinions regarding foreign exchange markets, including market standard documents (*e.g.* the Foreign Exchange and Options Master Agreement (FEOMA)).

Institute of Financial Services

http://www.ifslearning.com/y2000/index.htm. This site provides details of corporate and educational services available relating to financial services (including in the field of e-commerce and technology). A library and research facility is available to members.

International Chamber of Commerce (ICC)

http://www.iccwbo.org/home/menu_international_arbitration.asp. Users can access information relating to the ICCís international arbitration procedure, including the text of its 1998 International Rules of Arbitration and appropriate guidelines.

International Financial Services, London

http://www.bi.org.uk/. This site provides information on trade policy, reports and statistics on individual countries and their markets and information on various products. Users are also able to access conference information and press releases. Certain areas of the site are only available to members.

Securities Institute

http://www.siservices.co.uk/. Users can access information on membership and a glossary of financial terms.

8. Government and regulatory

British Standards Institution
http://www.bsi-global.com/index.html. Users can access information on product testing, product marking, inspections and information security.

Cabinet Office
http://www.cabinet-office.gov.uk/. Users can access information on the operation of the cabinet, the public sector, the civil service and details of ministers and government organisations.

Charity Commission
http://www.charity-commission.gov.uk/. Users can access news, events, publications and guidance relevant to the UK charities sector. In addition, the Register of Charities is available online with search facilities.

DTI Export Control Organisation
http://www.dti.gov.uk/export.control/. Users can access a list of current UK Open General Export Licences, Notices to Exporters since 1997 and documents relating to applications for UK export licences.

Euro Information
http://www.euro.gov.uk/home.asp?f=1. HM Treasury's publications and guidelines for UK businesses following the introduction of the Euro in 2002 and its impact on businesses.

Foreign and Commonwealth Office
http://www.fco.gov.uk/. Users can access briefing papers, news, speeches and publications on UK foreign policy issues, travel overseas and visa information. Information is also available on human rights policy and international treaties.

Foreign Government Resources on the Web
http://www.lib.umich.edu/govdocs/foreign.html. An index of foreign government resources available on the Internet. This site is maintained by the University of Michigan.

Her Majesty's Stationery Office (HMSO)
http://www.hmso.gov.uk/. Users can access the full text of UK Acts since 1988, Statutory Instruments since 1987 and Local Acts since 1991. Scottish and Welsh legislation is also available.

HM Customs & Excise
http://www.hmce.gov.uk/. Users can access UK government materials on VAT, customs and excise duties. The site includes press releases, legislation, consultation documents and reports.

HM Treasury
http://www.hm-treasury.gov.uk/. The site sets out Budget and Treasury speeches, reports and related news releases and publications including consultation papers. Users can also access economic information, including an overview of the UK economy and economic forecasts.

Home Office
http://www.homeoffice.gov.uk/. Users can access publications, guidelines,

policy documents and legislative texts relating to constitutional issues, criminal justice and immigration.

Information Commissioner's Office

http://www.dataprotection.gov.uk/. Formerly the Office of the Data Protection Commissioner this site provides guidelines and advice on compliance with the Data Protection Act 1998 together with access to the Data Protection Register and the text of tribunal decisions.

Inland Revenue

http://www.inlandrevenue.gov.uk/. The site provides information and guidance on direct taxes, National Insurance contributions and pensions targeted towards individuals, businesses, employers, practitioners, non-residents and charities. Users can access press releases, leaflets, consultation documents, reports, tax tables and draft legislation.

Law Commission

http://www.lawcom.gov.uk/. Users can access consultation reports, documents and details of law reviews currently being conduced in the United Kingdom.

Lord Chancellor's Department (LCD)

http://www.lcd.gov.uk/. The site contains information about the UK court system, judiciary, QCs, legal aid, civil and criminal issues and human rights.

National Assembly for Wales

http://www.wales.gov.uk/. This site includes news, press releases, publications, legislation and details of the Assemblyís membership.

Office of the Rail Regulator (ORR)

http://www.rail-reg.gov.uk/. Users can access publications, press notices, speeches and policy documents relating to the regulation of the UK railway industry together with links to related organisations.

Office of Gas and Electricity Markets (OFGEM)

http://www.ofgem.gov.uk/. Users can access information on the UK gas and electricity industries including news releases, publications, policy documents and industry and customer information.

Office of Water Services (OFWAT)

http://www.ofwat.gov.uk/. Users can access information on the UK water industry including news releases, publications, policy and competition documents and speeches.

Privacy Laws & Business

http://www.privacylaws.co.uk/. Users can access advice on a number of world-wide data protection and privacy laws and links to national data protection/privacy authorities.

Regulatory Law

http://www.regulatorylaw.co.uk/. This is an online journal designed for regulatory lawyers in a variety of fields from financial services to trade regulation. Users can access commentary on recent legislation and case law together with the relevant text.

Scottish Executive
http://www.scotland.gov.uk/. Users can access press releases, publications and policy documents relating to Scotland together with links to other useful sites.

Scottish Parliament
http://www.scottish.parliament.uk/. This site provides details of the structure and membership of the Scottish Parliament together with information on Bills before it and news releases.

Stationery Office
http://www.the-stationery-office.co.uk/. This site provides official UK Parliamentary and government documents (either online or by mail order). Some documents require payment of a fee. Users can also access a ìsite springboardî to aid in navigating around other UK government sites.

Strategic Rail Authority (SRA)
http://www.sra.gov.uk/. Users can access annual reports, information on UK national rail trends, consultation documents, press releases and information on the UK passenger and freight rail industries.

UK Official Documents
http://www.official-documents.co.uk/. Run by the Stationery Office this site allows users to search for legislative and policy documents issued by the UK Parliament, government and Hansard.

UK online
http://www.ukonline.gov.uk. A UK government site allowing users to access links to central and local government sites, departmental and topic indexes. The site includes a ìWhat's Newî feature and can provide email updates.

The White House
http://www.whitehouse.gov/. This site provides information on all branches and agencies of the US federal government.

9. Intellectual property

American Intellectual Property Law Association (AIPLA)
http://www.aipla.org/. Users can access information on AIPLA meetings, committee reports, newsletters. Testimony, statements and commentary from AIPLA members are also available. This site is US specific.

Chartered Institute of Patent Agents (CIPA)
http://www.cipa.org.uk/. A site providing basic intellectual property information, users can access a directory of patent agents together with briefing papers and links to other relevant sites.

Copyright Licensing Agency (CLA)
http://www.cla.co.uk/. This site provides users with a rapid clearance service for copyright works together with a list of excluded works and information on licensing procedures. Users can also access information on other reproduction rights organisations and copyright information sources.

Copyright Website

http://www.benedict.com/. A site providing information on US copyright law users can access examples of cases of infringement in the visual, audio and digital arts including real life examples.

Delphion Intellectual Property Network (IPN)

http://www.delphion.com/. This site provides access to a wide variety of patent data collections and research. Users must register to search, browse and view online patents (this facility is free). Access to the Derwent World Patent Index is subject to a charge.

European Patent Office (EPO)

http://www.european-patent-office.org/. Users can access guidelines on applying for a European patent, the EPOís Official Journal, annual reports or the decisions of the administrative council. The site also provides the text of tender documents and provides links to patent information centres across Europe.

Intellectual Property

http://www.intellectual-property.gov.uk/. This site is sponsored and maintained by the UK Patent Office and provides basic information on intellectual property issues and news together with resources and links to related sites.

MARQUES: Association of European Trade Mark Owners

http://www.martex.co.uk/marques/index.htm. This site aims to assist European-based brand owners in the selection, management and protection of their trade marks and includes a case commentary section.

Mayall's IP Links

http://www.mayallj.freeserve.co.uk/. A comprehensive site this has links to various international patent, trade mark and design right databases and supplies the text for the patent laws of 25 countries. The sites contents are available in six languages.

Office for Harmonization in the Internal Market (OHIM)

http://oami.eu.int/en/default.htm. This site includes OHIM decisions, Community trade mark forms and guidance and links to other trade mark offices across Europe.

Patent Office (UK)

http://www.patent.gov.uk/. This site contains information, advice and resources concerning copyright, designs, patents, trade marks, etc. Users can access patent decisions since 1998 but please note that some decisions may have been overturned on appeal, either in whole or part.

Patents Court Diary

http://www.courtservice.gov.uk/lists/pat_list.htm. This site displays pending patent actions before the English courts and allows users to access the results of recent trials and applications. An archive of trials and applications since 4/12/97 is also available.

US Patent and Trademark Office (USPTO)

http://www.uspto.gov/. A comprehensive site this provides US patent, trade mark and copyright information and resources including a Trade Mark Electronic Search System, Patent Grants and Patent Applications databases.

World Intellectual Property Organisation (WIPO)
http://www.wipo.org/. Users can access the text of international intellectual property treaties and guidelines together with a "magazine" of the latest developments. In addition the site contains a database of member statesí national intellectual property legislation.

10. International trade

North American Free Trade Agreement (NAFTA)
http://www.dfait-maeci.gc.ca/nafta-alena/agree-e.asp. This site sets out what NAFTA is together with the text of the main agreement and its side agreements and institutions doing business in the NAFTA region.

UN Commission on International Trade Law (UNCITRAL)
http://www.uncitral.org/. This site provides information about the UN Commission together with the full text of UN conventions and model laws plus texts, information and documents from its working groups. The site is available in six languages.

World Trade Organisation (WTO)
http://www.wto.org/. This is the only international organisation dealing with the global rules of trade between nations and its site contains information archives on a variety of trade topics and offers users access to online trade resources.

11. Legal resources - UK

Butterworths Lexis Direct (subscription)
http://www.butterworths.co.uk/. This site offers a range of full-text sources including *Halsbury's Laws, All England Law Reports* since 1936, and consolidated statutes and statutory instruments in force together with articles on the latest legal developments and services aimed at specific practice areas including crime, employment and personal injury. Some services are only available on a subscription basis.

Casetrack
http://www.casetrack.com/. A subscription service, this site provides full text judgments from the UK Court of Appeal, High Court, and Employment Appeals Tribunal.

Scottish Courts
http://www.scotcourts.gov.uk/. This site sets out details of the Scottish legal system, including the Courts of Session, High Court, Sheriffís Courts and District Courts. The site includes the procedural rules of each court and the full text of court opinions since September 1998.

Daily Law Notes

http://www.lawreports.co.uk/. A service provided by the Royal Courts of Justice this summarises important decisions issued by the court during the previous 24 hours.

Hansard

http://www.publications.parliament.uk/pa/ This site provides the full text of the Hansard reports on the debates of both the House of Commons and House of Lords plus future Parliamentary business.

Infolaw

http://www.infolaw.co.uk/. A portal aimed at practising lawyers this site includes "Lawfinder", a searchable source for primary law on the web.

Justis (subscription)

http://www.justis.com/navigate/main.html. This site provides access to a range of legal materials including the *Law Reports*, *Weekly Law Reports*, *Common Market Law Reports*, *CELEX* and *Official Journal C Series*.

Law Society of England and Wales

http://www.lawsociety.org.uk/. A site provided by the UK solicitorís professional body offering a directory of specialist practitioners licensed to practice in England and Wales.

Lawtel

http://www.lawtel.co.uk/. A leading provider of online legal information this site allows subscribers to access articles, text and other materials on UK and EU law together with information on the specific areas of personal injury, local government, human rights and civil practice and procedure.

Legal Resources in the UK and Ireland

http://www.venables.co.uk/. A wide-ranging portal maintained by Delia Venables which includes information and guidance for legal practitioners, companies and students using the Internet.

Lexis-Nexis

http://web.lexis-nexis.com/professional. A site providing legal and business information which includes a large number of full text sources such as cases and journals on a subscription only basis.

PLC Publications

http://www.practicallaw.com/. This site provides summaries of the latest and archive articles from PLC magazine, *European Counsel* magazine and *PLC Practice Manuals* on a subscription basis.

Sweet & Maxwell Ltd

http://www.smlawpub.co.uk/. Users can access various products provided by Sweet & Maxwell including alerting services, Current Legal Information and European Union News. Some services require subscription.

Westlaw UK (subscription)

http://www.westlaw.co.uk/. A major online legal database provided by Sweet & Maxwell containing full text cases, consolidated legislation, journal articles, current awareness.

12. Legal resources – non-UK

CELEX - EN
http://europa.eu.int/celex/htm/celex_en.htm. A link to the European Celex database providing information on European Union documents.

Conseil Constitutionnel (France)
http://www.conseil-constitutionnel.fr/. A site providing decisions of the Council in four languages.

Cornell Law School
http://www.law.cornell.edu/. A comprehensive site providing the text of the US constitution and codes, court opinions, guides to different areas of law; US Supreme and Federal Court decisions and New York Court of Appeal decisions. Users can also use a search facility by source or jurisdiction.

Council of Europe Treaty Office
http://conventions.coe.int/treaty/EN/cadreprincipal.htm. This site provides the full text of treaties entered into by members of the Council.

Internet Law Library
http://www.lawguru.com/. A substantial US legal research source which includes an online library facility.

Internet Legal Resource Guide
http://www.ilrg.com/. An international guide, including lists of law firms and legal associations and legal research sites.

Law Library of Ireland
http://www.lawlibrary.ie/. Information on the Irish courts, bar, the work of barristers and qualifying as a lawyer in Ireland.

Lexpert
http://www.lexpert.ca/. A directory of legal practitioners and experts in Canada.

New York State Department of State
http://www.dos.state.ny.us/. A site setting out the responsibilities of the Department of State together with local government services, business and licensing services, committees and commissions, offices and press releases.

New Zealand Court of Appeal Judgments
http://www.brookers.co.nz/. Users can access the text of New Zealand legislation and judgments dating from November 1995 together with related links.

South African Courts
http://www.law.wits.ac.za/. A site providing access to South African legal materials including links to various legal resources.

Supreme Court of Canada
http://www.scc-csc.gc.ca/. Users can access recent judgments of the court together with the text of Supreme Court Reports since 1985. This site is available in English or French.

United States Department of Justice

http://www.ins.usdoj.gov/graphics/index.htm. A site providing the text of laws, regulations and guidelines on immigration and naturalisation; law enforcement and border management together with a schedule of immigration fees and forms and FAQs.

United States House of Representatives

http://www.house.gov/. Users can access information on the operations of the House, details of legislative process together with access to US federal statutes; the annual congressional schedule and current house floor proceedings and details of the US constitution and amendments.

United States Senate

http://www.senate.gov/. This site provides basic information about how the Senate works, its history; details of various standing committees including the Special Committee on the Year 2000 Technology Problem for transportation, healthcare, telecoms, utilities, financial services etc together with news, hearings, speeches and statements, and FAQ's.

United States Supreme Court

http://www.supremecourtus.gov/. Users can access the opinions of the court and text versions of the court rules.

13. Tax

Accounting Web

http://www.accountingweb.co.uk/. A site providing tax facts, news, analysis and links.

Chartered Institute of Taxation

http://www.tax.org.uk/. A site providing advice and publications on professional practice and tax technical matters, both in the United Kingdom and internationally.

European Commission: DG Taxation and Customs

http://europa.eu.int/comm/dgs/taxation_customs/index_en.htm. A site providing a staff directory, working papers, proposals, reports and other official Commission documents on tax policy.

ICAEW Tax Faculty

http://www.taxfac.co.uk/. An online resource for tax professionals offering access to technical tax information, facts and figures and topical tax news items. There are also additional features for members of the Tax Faculty.

Institute for Fiscal Studies

http://www1.ifs.org.uk/. An independent research organisation, providing economic analysis of public policy, including tax policies.

Internal Revenue Service (IRS)

http://www.irs.ustreas.gov/. This site includes news and information for tax professionals and is US specific.

Taxman International

http://www.taxman.nl/. A gateway to tax and customs administrations on the Internet.

Appendix 1

· E-Commerce Directive ·

Directive 2000/31/EC of the European Parliament and of the Council of 8 June 2000 on certain legal aspects of information society services, in particular electronic commerce, in the Internal Market (Directive on electronic commerce)*

THE EUROPEAN PARLIAMENT AND THE COUNCIL OF THE EUROPEAN UNION,

Having regard to the Treaty establishing the European Community, and in particular Articles 47(2), 55 and 95 thereof,

Having regard to the proposal from the Commission[1],

Having regard to the opinion of the Economic and Social Committee[2],

Acting in accordance with the procedure laid down in Article 251 of the Treaty[3],

Whereas:

(1) The European Union is seeking to forge ever closer links between the States and peoples of Europe, to ensure economic and social progress; in accordance with Article 14(2) of the Treaty, the internal market comprises an area without internal frontiers in which the free movements of goods, services and the freedom of establishment are ensured; the development of information society services within the area without internal frontiers is vital to eliminating the barriers which divide the European peoples.

(2) The development of electronic commerce within the information society offers significant employment opportunities in the Community, particularly in small and medium-sized enterprises, and will stimulate economic growth and investment in innovation by European companies, and can also enhance the competitiveness of European industry, provided that everyone has access to the Internet.

(3) Community law and the characteristics of the Community legal order are a

---

* OJ 2000 L178/1.
1 OJ C 30. 5.2.1999, p. 4.
2 OJ C 169, 16.6.1999, p. 36.
3 Opinion of the European Parliament of 6 May 1999 (OJ C 279, 1.10.1999, p. 389), Council common position of 28 February 2000 (OJ C 128, 8.5.2000, p. 32) and Decision of the European Parliament of 4 May 2000 (not yet published in the Official Journal).

vital asset to enable European citizens and operators to take full advantage, without consideration of borders, of the opportunities afforded by electronic commerce; this Directive therefore has the purpose of ensuring a high level of Community legal integration in order to establish a real area without internal borders for information society services.

(4) It is important to ensure that electronic commerce could fully benefit from the internal market and therefore that, as with Council Directive 89/552/EEC of 3 October 1989 on the coordination of certain provisions laid down by law, regulation or administrative action in Member States concerning the pursuit of television broadcasting activities⁴, a high level of Community integration is achieved.

(5) The development of information society services within the Community is hampered by a number of legal obstacles to the proper functioning of the internal market which make less attractive the exercise of the freedom of establishment and the freedom to provide services; these obstacles arise from divergences in legislation and from the legal uncertainty as to which national rules apply to such services; in the absence of coordination and adjustment of legislation in the relevant areas, obstacles might be justified in the light of the case-law of the Court of Justice of the European Communities; legal uncertainty exists with regard to the extent to which Member States may control services originating from another Member State.

(6) In the light of Community objectives, of Articles 43 and 49 of the Treaty and of secondary Community law, these obstacles should be eliminated by coordinating certain national laws and by clarifying certain legal concepts at Community level to the extent necessary for the proper functioning of the internal market; by dealing only with certain specific matters which give rise to problems for the internal market, this Directive is fully consistent with the need to respect the principle of subsidiarity as set out in Article 5 of the Treaty.

(7) In order to ensure legal certainty and consumer confidence, this Directive must lay down a clear and general framework to cover certain legal aspects of electronic commerce in the internal market.

(8) The objective of this Directive is to create a legal framework to ensure the free movement of information society services between Member States and not to harmonise the field of criminal law as such.

(9) The free movement of information society services can in many cases be a specific reflection in Community law of a more general principle, namely freedom of expression as enshrined in Article 10(1) of the Convention for the Protection of Human Rights and Fundamental Freedoms, which has been ratified by all the Member States; for this reason, directives covering the supply of information society services must ensure that this activity

---

4 OJ L 298, 17.10.1989, p. 23. Directive as amended by Directive 97/36/EC of the European Parliament and of the Council (OJ L 202, 30.7.1997, p. 60).

may be engaged in freely in the light of that Article, subject only to the restrictions laid down in paragraph 2 of that Article and in Article 46(1) of the Treaty; this Directive is not intended to affect national fundamental rules and principles relating to freedom of expression.

(10) In accordance with the principle of proportionality, the measures provided for in this Directive are strictly limited to the minimum needed to achieve the objective of the proper functioning of the internal market; where action at Community level is necessary, and in order to guarantee an area which is truly without internal frontiers as far as electronic commerce is concerned, the Directive must ensure a high level of protection of objectives of general interest, in particular the protection of minors and human dignity, consumer protection and the protection of public health; according to Article 152 of the Treaty, the protection of public health is an essential component of other Community policies.

(11) This Directive is without prejudice to the level of protection for, in particular, public health and consumer interests, as established by Community acts; amongst others, Council Directive 93/13/EEC of 5 April 1993 on unfair terms in consumer contracts[5] and Directive 97/7/EC of the European Parliament and of the Council of 20 May 1997 on the protection of consumers in respect of distance contracts[6] from a vital element for protecting consumers in contractual matters; those Directives also apply in their entirety to information society services; that same Community acquis, which is fully applicable to information society services, also embraces in particular Council Directive 84/450/EEC of 10 September 1984 concerning misleading and comparative advertising[7], Council Directive 87/102/EEC of 22 December 1986 for the approximation of the laws, regulations and administrative provisions of the Member States concerning consumer credit[8], Council Directive 93/22/EEC of 10 May 1993 on investment services in the securities field[9], Council Directive 90/314/EEC of 13 June 1990 on package travel, package holidays and package tours[10], Directive 98/6/EC of the European Parliament and of the Council of 16 February 1998 on consumer production in the indication of prices of products offered to consumers[11],

---

4   OJ L 298, 17.10.1989, p. 23. Directive as amended by Directive 97/36/EC of the European Parliament and of the Council (OJ L 202, 30.7.1997, p. 60).
5   OJ L 95, 21.4.1993, p. 29.
6   OJ L 144, 4.6.1999, p. 19.
7   OJ L 250, 19.9.1984, p. 17. Directive as amended by Directive 97/55/EC of the European Parliament and of the Council (OJ L 290, 23.10.1997, p. 18).
8   OJ L 42, 12.2.1987, p. 48. Directive as last amended by Directive 98/7/EC of the European Parliament and of the Council (OJ L 101, 1.4.1998, p. 17).
9   OJ L 141, 11.6.1993, p. 27. Directive as last amended by Directive 97/9/EC of the European Parliament and of the Council (OJ L 84, 26.3.1997, p. 22).
10 OJ L 158, 23.6.1990, p. 59.

Council Directive 92/59/EEC of 29 June 1992 on general product safety[12], Directive 94/47/EC of the European Parliament and of the Council of 26 October 1994 on the protection of purchasers in respect of certain aspects on contracts relating to the purchase of the right to use immovable properties on a timeshare basis[13], Directive 98/27/EC of the European Parliament and of the Council of 19 May 1998 on injunctions for the protection of consumers' interests[14], Council Directive 85/374/EEC of 25 July 1985 on the approximation of the laws, regulations and administrative provisions concerning liability for defective products[15], Directive 1999/44/EC of the European Parliament and of the Council of 25 May 1999 on certain aspects of the sale of consumer goods and associated guarantees[16], the future Directive of the European Parliament and of the Council concerning the distance marketing of consumer financial services and Council Directive 92/28/EEC of 31 March 1992 on the advertising of medicinal products[17]; this Directive should be without prejudice to Directive 98/43/EC of the European Parliament and of the Council of 6 July 1998 on the approximation of the laws, regulations and administrative provisions of the Member States relating to the advertising and sponsorship of tobacco products[18] adopted within the framework of the internal market, or to directives on the protection of public health; this Directive complements information requirements established by the abovementioned Directives and in particular Directive 97/7/EC.

(12) It is necessary to exclude certain activities from the scope of this Directive, on the grounds that the freedom to provide services in these fields cannot, at this stage, be guaranteed under the Treaty or existing secondary legislation, excluding these activities does not preclude any instruments which might prove necessary for the proper functioning of the internal market; taxation, particularly value added tax imposed on a large number of the services covered by this Directive, must be excluded form the scope of this Directive.

(13) This Directive does not aim to establish rules on fiscal obligations nor does it pre-empt the drawing up of Community instruments concerning fiscal aspects of electronic commerce.

(14) The protection of individuals with regard to the processing of personal

---

11 OJ L 80, 18.3.1998, p. 27.
12 OJ L 228, 11.8.1992, p. 24.
13 OJ L 280, 29.10.1994, p. 83.
14 OJ L 166, 11.6.1998, p. 51. Directive as amended by Directive 1999/44/EC (OJ L 171 7.7.1999, p. 12).
15 OJ L 210, 7.8.1985, p. 29. Directive as amended by Directive 1999/34/EC (OJ L 141, 4.6.1999, p. 20).
16 OJ L 171, 7.7.1999, p. 12.
17 OJ L 113, 30.4.1992, p. 13.
18 OJ L 213, 30.7.1998, p. 9.

data is solely governed by Directive 95/46/EC of the European Parliament and of the Council of 24 October 1995 on the protection of individuals with regard to the processing of personal data and on the free movement of such data[19] and Directive 97/66/EC of the European Parliament and of the Council of 15 December 1997 concerning the processing of personal data and the protection of privacy in the telecommunications sector[20] which are fully applicable to information society services; these Directives already establish a Community legal framework in the field of personal data and therefore it is not necessary to cover this issue in this Directive in order to ensure the smooth functioning of the internal market, in particular the free movement of personal data between Member States; the implementation and application of this Directive should be made in full compliance with the principles relating to the protection of personal data, in particular as regards unsolicited commercial communication and the liability of intermediaries; this Directive cannot prevent the anonymous use of open networks such as the Internet.

(15) The confidentiality of communications is guaranteed by Article 5 Directive 97/66/EC; in accordance with that Directive, Member States must prohibit any kind of interception or surveillance of such communications by others than the senders and receivers, except when legally authorised.

(16) The exclusion of gambling activities from the scope of application of this Directive covers only games of chance, lotteries and betting transactions, which involve wagering a stake with monetary value; this does not cover promotional competitions or games where the purpose is to encourage the sale of goods or services and where payments, if they arise, serve only to acquire the promoted goods or services.

(17) The definition of information society services already exists in Community law in Directive 98/34/EC of the European Parliament and of the Council of 22 June 1998 laying down a procedure for the provision of information in the field of technical standards and regulations and of rules on information society services[21] and in Directive 98/84/EC of the European Parliament and of the Council of 20 November 1998 on the legal protection of services based on, or consisting of, conditional access[22]; this definition covers any service normally provided for remuneration, at a distance, by means of electronic equipment for the processing (including digital compression) and storage of data, and at the individual request of a recipient of a service; those services referred to in

---

19 OJ L 281, 23.11.1995, p. 31.
20 OJ L 24, 30.1.1998, p. 1.
21 OJ L 204, 21.7.1998, p. 37. Directive as amended by Directive 98/48/EC
    (OJ L 217, 5.8.1998, p. 18).
22 OJ L 320, 28.11.1998, p. 54.

the indicative list in Annex V to Directive 98/34/EC which do not imply data processing and storage are not covered by this definition.

(18) Information society services span a wide range of economic activities which take place on-line; these activities can, in particular, consist of selling goods on-line; activities such as the delivery of goods as such or the provision of services off-line are not covered; information society services are not solely restricted to services giving rise to on-line contracting but also, in so far as they represent an economic activity, extend to services which are not remunerated by those who receive them, such as those offering on-line information or commercial communications, or those providing tools allowing for search, access and retrieval of data; information society services also include services consisting of the transmission of information via a communication network, in providing access to a communication network or in hosting information provided by a recipient of the service; television broadcasting within the meaning of Directive EEC/89/552 and radio broadcasting are not information society services because they are not provided at individual request; by contrast, services which are transmitted point to point, such as video-on-demand or the provision of commercial communications by electronic mail are information society services; the use of electronic mail or equivalent individual communications for instance by natural persons acting outside their trade, business or profession including their use for the conclusion of contracts between such persons is not an information society service; the contractual relationship between an employee and his employer is not an information society service; activities which by their very nature cannot be carried out at a distance and by electronic means, such as the statutory auditing of company accounts or medical advice requiring the physical examination of a patient are not information society services.

(19) The place at which a service provider is established should be determined in conformity with the case-law of the Court of Justice according to which the concept of establishment involves the actual pursuit of an economic activity through a fixed establishment for an indefinite period; this requirement is also fulfilled where a company is constituted for a given period; the place of establishment of a company providing services via an Internet website is not the place at which the technology supporting its website is located or the place at which its website is accessible but the place where it pursues its economic activity; in cases where a provider has several places of establishment it is important to determine from which place of establishment the service concerned is provided; in cases where it is difficult to determine from which of several places of establishment a given service is provided, this is the place where the provider has the centre of his activities relating to this particular service.

(20) The definition of 'recipient of a service' covers all types of usage of

information society services, both by persons who provide information on open networks such as the Internet and by persons who seek information on the Internet for private or professional reasons.

(21) The scope of the coordinated field is without prejudice to future Community harmonisation relating to information society services and to future legislation adopted at national level in accordance with Community law; the coordinated field covers only requirements relating to on-line activities such as on-line information, on-line advertising, on-line shopping, on-line contracting and does not concern Member States' legal requirements relating to goods such as safety standards, labelling obligations, or liability for goods, or Member States' requirements relating to the delivery or the transport of goods, including the distribution of medicinal products; the coordinated field does not cover the exercise of rights of pre-emption by public authorities concerning certain goods such as works of art.

(22) Information society services should be supervised at the source of the activity, in order to ensure an effective protection of public interest objectives; to that end, it is necessary to ensure that the competent authority provides such protection not only for the citizens of its own country but for all Community citizens; in order to improve mutual trust between Member States, it is essential to state clearly this responsibility on the part of the Member State where the services originate; moreover, in order to effectively guarantee freedom to provide services and legal certainty for suppliers and recipients of services, such information society services should in principle be subject to the law of the Member State in which the service provider is established.

(23) This Directive neither aims to establish additional rules on private international law relating to conflicts of law nor does it deal with the jurisdiction of Courts; provisions of the applicable law designated by rules of private international law must not restrict the freedom to provide information society services as established in this Directive.

(24) In the context of this Directive, notwithstanding the rule on the control at source of information society services, it is legitimate under the conditions established in this Directive for Member States to take measures to restrict the free movement of information society services.

(25) National courts, including civil courts, dealing with private law disputes can take measures to derogate from the freedom to provide information society services in conformity with conditions established in this Directive.

(26) Member States, in conformity with conditions established in this Directive, may apply their national rules on criminal law and criminal proceedings with a view to taking all investigative and other measures necessary for the detection and prosecution of criminal offences, without

there being a need to notify such measures to the Commission.

(27) This Directive, together with the future Directive of the European Parliament and of the Council concerning the distance marketing of consumer financial services, contributes to the creating of a legal framework for the on-line provision of financial services; this Directive does not pre-empt future initiatives in the area of financial services in particular with regard to the harmonisation of rules of conduct in this field; the possibility for Member States, established in this Directive, under certain circumstances of restricting the freedom to provide information society services in order to protect consumers also covers measures in the area of financial services in particular measures aiming at protecting investors.

(28) The Member States' obligation not to subject access to the activity of an information society service provider to prior authorisation does not concern postal services covered by Directive 97/67/EC of the European Parliament and of the Council of 15 December 1997 on common rules for the development of the internal market of Community postal services and the improvement of quality of service[23] consisting of the physical delivery of a printed electronic mail message and does not affect voluntary accreditation systems, in particular for providers of electronic signature certification service.

(29) Commercial communications are essential for the financing of information society services and for developing a wide variety of new, charge-free services; in the interests of consumer protection and fair trading, commercial communications, including discounts, promotional offers and promotional competitions or games, must meet a number of transparency requirements; these requirements are without prejudice to Directive 97/7/EC; this Directive should not affect existing Directives on commercial communications, in particular Directive 98/43/EC.

(30) The sending of unsolicited commercial communications by electronic mail may be undesirable for consumers and information society service providers and may disrupt the smooth functioning of interactive networks; the question of consent by recipient of certain forms of unsolicited commercial communications is not addressed by this Directive, but has already been addressed, in particular, by Directive 97/7/EC and by Directive 97/66/EC; in Member States which authorise unsolicited commercial communications by electronic mail, the setting up of appropriate industry filtering initiatives should be encouraged and facilitated; in addition it is necessary that in any event unsolicited commercial communities are clearly identifiable as such in order to improve transparency and to facilitate the functioning of such industry

---

23 OJ L 15, 21.1.1998, p. 14.

initiatives; unsolicited commercial communications by electronic mail should not result in additional communication costs for the recipient.

(31) Member States which allow the sending of unsolicited commercial communications by electronic mail without prior consent of the recipient by service providers established in their territory have to ensure that the service providers consult regularly and respect the optout registers in which natural persons not wishing to receive such commercial communications can register themselves.

(32) In order to remove barriers to the development of cross-border services within the Community which members of the regulated professions might offer on the Internet, it is necessary that compliance be guaranteed at Community level with professional rules aiming, in particular, to protect consumers or public health; codes of conduct at Community level would be the best means of determining the rules on professional ethics applicable to commercial communication; the drawing-up or, where appropriate, the adaptation of such rules should be encouraged without prejudice to the autonomy of professional bodies and associations.

(33) This Directive complements Community law and national law relating to regulated professions maintaining a coherent set of applicable rules in this field.

(34) Each Member State is to amend its legislation containing requirements, and in particular requirements as to form, which are likely to curb the use of contracts by electronic means; the examination of the legislation requiring such adjustment should be systematic and should cover all the necessary stages and acts of the contractual process, including the filing of the contract; the result of this amendment should be to make contracts concluded electronically workable; the legal effect of electronic signatures is dealt with by Directive 1999/93/EC of the European Parliament and of the Council of 13 December 1999 on a Community framework for electronic signatures[24]; the acknowledgement of receipt by a service provider may take the form of the on-line provision of the service paid for.

(35) This Directive does not affect Member States' possibility of maintaining or establishing general or specific legal requirements for contracts which can be fulfilled by electronic means, in particular requirements concerning secure electronic signatures.

(36) Member States may maintain restrictions for the use of electronic contracts with regard to contracts requiring by law the involvement of courts, public authorities, or professions exercising public authority; this possibility also covers contracts which require the involvement of courts, public authorities, or professions exercising public authority in order to

---

24 OJ L 13, 19.1.2000, p. 12.

have an effect with regard to third parties as well as contracts requiring by law certification or attestation by a notary.

(37) Member States' obligation to remove obstacles to the use of electronic contracts concerns only obstacles resulting from legal requirements and not practical obstacles resulting from the impossibility of using electronic means in certain cases.

(38) Member States' obligation to remove obstacles to the use of electronic contracts is to be implemented in conformity with legal requirements for contracts enshrined in Community law.

(39) The exceptions to the provisions concerning the contracts concluded exclusively by electronic mail or by equivalent individual communications provided for by this Directive, in relation to information to be provided and the placing of orders, should not enable, as a result, the by-passing of those provisions by providers of information society services.

(40) Both existing and emerging disparities in Member States' legislation and case-law concerning liability of service providers acting as intermediaries prevent the smooth functioning of the internal market, in particular by impairing the development of cross-border services and producing distortions of competition; service providers have a duty to act, under certain circumstances, with a view to preventing or stopping illegal activities; this Directive should constitute the appropriate basis for the development of rapid and reliable procedures for removing and disabling access to illegal information; such mechanisms could be developed on the basis of voluntary agreements between all parties concerned and should be encouraged by Member States; it is in the interest of all parties involved in the provision of information society services to adopt and implement such procedures; the provisions of this Directive relating to liability should not preclude the development and effective operation, by the different interested parties, of technical systems of protection and identification and of technical surveillance instruments made possible by digital technology within the limits laid down by Directives 95/46/EC and 97/66/EC.

(41) This Directive strikes a balance between the different interests at stake and establishes principles upon which industry agreements and standards can be based.

(42) The exemptions from liability established in this Directive cover only cases where the activity of the information society service provider is limited to the technical process of operating and giving access to a communication network over which information made available by third parties is transmitted or temporarily stored, for the sole purpose of making the transmission more efficient; this activity is of a mere technical, automatic and passive nature, which implies that the

information society service provider has neither knowledge of nor control over the information which is transmitted or stored.

(43) A service provider can benefit from the exemptions for 'mere conduit' and for 'caching' when he is in no way involved with the information transmitted; this requires among other things that he does not modify the information that he transmits; this requirement does not cover manipulations of a technical nature which take place in the course of the transmission as they do not alter the integrity of the information contained in the transmission.

(44) A service provider who deliberately collaborates with one of the recipients of his service in order to undertake illegal acts goes beyond the activities of 'mere conduit' or 'caching' and as a result cannot benefit from the liability exemptions established for these activities.

(45) The limitations of the liability of intermediary service providers established in this Directive do not affect the possibility of injunctions of different kinds; such injunctions can in particular consist of orders by courts or administrative authorities requiring the termination or prevention of any infringement, including the removal of illegal information or the disabling of access to it.

(46) In order to benefit from a limitation of liability, the provider of an information society service, consisting of the storage of information, upon obtaining actual knowledge or awareness of illegal activities has to act expeditiously to remove or to disable access to the information concerned; the removal or disabling of access has to be undertaken in the observance of the principle of freedom of expression and of procedures established for this purpose at national level; this Directive does not affect Member States' possibility of establishing specific requirements which must be fulfilled expeditiously prior to the removal or disabling of information.

(47) Member States are prevented from imposing a monitoring obligation on service providers only with respect to obligations of a general nature; this does not concern monitoring obligations in a specific case and, in particular, does not affect orders by national authorities in accordance with national legislation.

(48) This Directive does not affect the possibility for Member States of requiring service providers, who host information provided by recipients of their service, to apply duties of care, which can reasonably be expected from them and which are specified by national law, in order to detect and prevent certain types of illegal activities.

(49) Member States and the Commission are to encourage the drawing-up of codes of conduct; this is not to impair the voluntary nature of such codes and the possibility for interested parties of deciding freely whether to adhere to such codes.

(50) It is important that the proposed directive on the harmonisation of certain aspects of copyright and related rights in the information society and this Directive come into force within a similar time scale with a view to establishing a clear framework of rules relevant to the issue of liability of intermediaries for copyright and relating rights infringements at Community level.

(51) Each Member State should be required, where necessary, to amend any legislation which is liable to hamper the use of schemes for the out-of-court settlement of disputes through electronic channels; the result of this amendment must be to make the functioning of such schemes genuinely and effectively possible in law and in practice, even across borders.

(52) The effective exercise of the freedoms of the internal market makes it necessary to guarantee victims effective access to means of settling disputes; damage which may arise in connection with information society services is characterised both by its rapidity and by its geographical extent; in view of this specific character and the need to ensure that national authorities do not endanger the mutual confidence which they should have in one another, this Directive requests Member States to ensure that appropriate court actions are available; Member States should examine the need to provide access to judicial procedures by appropriate electronic means.

(53) Directive 98/27/EC, which is applicable to information society services, provides a mechanism relating to actions for an injunction aimed at the protection of the collective interests of consumers; this mechanism will contribute to the free movement of information society services by ensuring a high level of consumer protection.

(54) The sanctions provided for under this Directive are without prejudice to any other sanction or remedy provided under national law; Member States are not obliged to provide criminal sanctions for infringement of national provisions adopted pursuant to this Directive.

(55) This Directive does not affect the law applicable to contractual obligations relating to consumer contracts; accordingly, this Directive cannot have the result of depriving the consumer of the protection afforded to him by the mandatory rules relating to contractual obligations of the law of the Member State in which he has his habitual residence.

(56) As regards the derogation contained in this Directive regarding contractual obligations concerning contracts concluded by consumers, those obligations should be interpreted as including information on the essential elements of the content of the contract, including consumer rights, which have a determining influence on the decision to contract.

(57) The Court of Justice has consistently held that a Member State retains the right to take measures against a service provider that is established in

another Member State but directs all or most of his activity to the territory of the first Member State if the choice of establishment was made with a view to evading the legislation that would have applied to the provider had he been established on the territory of the first Member State.

(58) This Directive should not apply to services supplied by service providers established in a third country; in view of the global dimension of electronic commerce, it is, however, appropriate to ensure that the Community rules are consistent with international rules; this Directive is without prejudice to the results of discussions within international organisations (amongst others WTO, OECD, Uncitral) on legal issues.

(59) Despite the global nature of electronic communications, coordination of national regulatory measures at European Union level is necessary in order to avoid fragmentation of the internal market, and for the establishment of an appropriate European regulatory framework; such coordination should also contribute to the establishment of a common and strong negotiating position in international forums.

(60) In order to allow the unhampered development of electronic commerce, the legal framework must be clear and simple, predictable and consistent with the rules applicable at international level so that it does not adversely affect the competitiveness of European industry or impede innovation in that sector.

(61) If the market is actually to operate by electronic means in the context of globalisation, the European Union and the major non-European areas need to consult each other with a view to making laws and procedures compatible.

(62) Cooperation with third countries should be strengthened in the area of electronic commerce, in particular with applicant countries, the developing countries and the European Union's other trading partners.

(63) The adoption of this Directive will not prevent the Member States from taking into account the various social, societal and cultural implications which are inherent in the advent of the information society; in particular it should not hinder measures which Member States might adopt in conformity with Community law to achieve social, cultural and democratic goals taking into account their linguistic diversity, national and regional specificities as well as their cultural heritage, and to ensure and maintain public access to the widest possible range of information society services; in any case, the development of the information society is to ensure that Community citizens can have access to the cultural European heritage provided in the digital environment.

(64) Electronic communication offers the Member States an excellent means of providing public services in the cultural, educational and linguistic fields.

(65) The Council, in its resolution of 19 January 1999 on the consumer dimension of the information society[25], stressed that the protection of consumers deserved special attention in this field; the Commission will examine the degree to which existing consumer protection rules provide insufficient protection in the context of the information society and will identify, where necessary, the deficiencies of this legislation and those issues which could require additional measures; if need be, the Commission should make specific additional proposals to resolve such deficiencies that will thereby have been identified,

HAVE ADOPTED THIS DIRECTIVE:

CHAPTER I—GENERAL PROVISIONS
Article 1
Objective and scope

1. This Directive seeks to contribute to the proper functioning of the internal market by ensuring the free movement of information society services between the Member States.

2. This Directive approximates, to the extent necessary for the achievement of the objective set out in paragraph 1, certain national provisions on information society services relating to the internal market, the establishment of service providers, commercial communications, electronic contracts, the liability of intermediaries, codes of conduct, out-of-court dispute settlements, court actions and cooperation between Member States.

3. This Directive complements Community law applicable to information society services without prejudice to the level of protection for, in particular, public health and consumer interests, as established by Community acts and national legislation implementing them in so far as this does not restrict the freedom to provide information society services.

4. This Directive does not establish additional rules on private international law nor does it deal with the jurisdiction of Courts.

5. This Directive shall not apply to:
    (a) the field of taxation;
    (b) questions relating to information society services covered by Directives 95/46/EC and 97/66/EC;
    (c) questions relating to agreements or practices governed by cartel law;
    (d) the following activities of information society services:
    – the activities of notaries or equivalent professions to the extent that they involve a direct and specific connection with the exercise of public authority,

---

25 OJ C 23, 28.1.1999, p. 1.

- the representation of a client and defence of his interests before the courts,
- gambling activities which involve wagering a stake with monetary value in games of chance, including lotteries and betting transactions.

6. This Directive does not affect measures taken at Community or national level, in the respect of Community law, in order to promote cultural and linguistic diversity and to ensure the defence of pluralism.

Article 2
Definitions

For the purpose of this Directive, the following terms shall bear the following meanings:

(a) 'information society services': services within the meaning of Article 1(2) of Directive 98/34/EC as amended by Directive 98/48/EC;

(b) 'service provider': any natural or legal person providing an information society service;

(c) 'established service provider': a service provider who effectively pursues an economic activity using a fixed establishment for an indefinite period. The presence and use of the technical means and technologies required to provide the service do not, in themselves, constitute an establishment of the provider;

(d) 'recipient of the service': any natural or legal person who, for professional ends or otherwise, uses an information society service, in particular for the purposes of seeking information or making it accessible;

(e) 'consumer': any natural person who is acting for purposes which are outside his or her trade, business or profession;

(f) 'commercial communication': any form of communication designed to promote, directly or indirectly, the goods, services or image of a company, organisation or person pursuing a commercial, industrial or craft activity or exercising a regulated profession. The following do not in themselves constitute commercial communications:

- information allowing direct access to the activity of the company, organisation or person, in particular a domain name or an electronic-mail address,

- communications relating to the goods, services or image of the company, organisation or person compiled in an independent manner, particularly when this is without financial consideration;

(g) 'regulated profession': any profession within the meaning of either Article 1(d) of Council Directive 89/48/EEC of 21 December 1988 on a general system for the recognition of higher-education diplomas awarded on

---

26 OJ L 19, 24.1.1989, p. 16.

completion of professional education and training of at least three-years' duration[26] or of Article 1(f) of Council Directive 92/51/EEC of 18 June 1992 on a second general system for the recognition of professional education and training to supplement Directive 89/48/EEC[27];

(h)'coordinated field': requirements laid down in Member States' legal systems applicable to information society service providers or information society services, regardless of whether they are of a general nature or specifically designed for them.

(i) The coordinated field concerns requirements with which the service provider has to comply in respect of:

– the taking up of the activity of an information society service, such as requirements concerning qualifications, authorisation or notification,

– the pursuit of the activity of an information society service, such as requirements concerning the behaviour of the service provider, requirements regarding the quality or content of the service including those applicable to advertising and contracts, or requirements concerning the liability of the service provider;

(ii)The coordinated field does not cover requirements such as:

    – requirements applicable to goods as such,

    – requirements applicable to the delivery of goods,

    – requirements applicable to services not provided by electronic means.

Article 3
Internal market

1. Each Member State shall ensure that the information society services provided by a service provider established on its territory comply with the national provisions applicable in the Member State in question which fall within the coordinated field.

2. Member States may not, for reasons falling within the coordinated field, restrict the freedom to provide information society services from another Member State.

3. Paragraphs 1 and 2 shall not apply to the fields referred to in the Annex.

4. Member States may take measures to derogate from paragraph 2 in respect of a given information society service if the following conditions are fulfilled:

(a)the measures shall be:

(i) necessary for one of the following reasons:

---

26 OJ L 19, 24.1.1989, p. 16.
27 OJ L 209, 24.7.1992, p. 25. Directive as last amended by Commission Directive 97/38/EC (OJ L 184, 12.7.1997, p. 31).

– public policy, in particular the prevention, investigation, detection and prosecution of criminal offences, including the protection of minors and the fight against any incitement to hatred on grounds of race, sex, religion or nationality, and violations of human dignity concerning individual persons,

– the protection of public health,

– public security, including the safeguarding of national security and defence,

– the protection of consumers, including investors;

(ii) taken against a given information society service which prejudices the objectives referred to in point (i) or which presents a serious and grave risk of prejudice to those objectives;

(iii) proportionate to those objectives;

(b) before taking the measures in question and without prejudice to court proceedings, including preliminary proceedings and acts carried out in the framework of a criminal investigation, the Member State has:

– asked the Member State referred to in paragraph 1 to take measures and the latter did not take such measures, or they were inadequate,

– notified the Commission and the Member State referred to in paragraph 1 of its intention to take such measures.

5. Member States may, in the case of urgency, derogate from the conditions stipulated in paragraph 4(b). Where this is the case, the measures shall be notified in the shortest possible time to the Commission and to the Member State referred to in paragraph 1, indicating the reasons for which the Member State considers that there is urgency.

6. Without prejudice to the Member State's possibility of proceeding with the measures in question, the Commission shall examine the compatibility of the notified measures with Community law in the shortest possible time; where it comes to the conclusion that the measure is incompatible with Community law, the Commission shall ask the Member State in question to refrain from taking any proposed measures or urgently to put an end to the measures in question.

CHAPTER II—PRINCIPLES

Section 1: Establishment and information requirements

Article 4
Principle excluding prior authorisation

1. Member States shall ensure that the taking up and pursuit of the activity of an information society service provider may not be made subject to prior authorisation or any other requirement having equivalent effect.

2. Paragraph 1 shall be without prejudice to authorisation schemes which are not specifically and exclusively targeted at information society services, or

which are covered by Directive 97/13/EC of the European Parliament and of the Council of 10 April 1997 on a common framework for general authorisations and individual licences in the field of telecommunications services.[28]

Article 5
General information to be provided

1. In addition to other information requirements established by Community law, Member States shall ensure that the service provider shall render easily, directly and permanently accessible to the recipients of the service and competent authorities, at least the following information:

   (a) the name of the service provider;

   (b) the geographic address at which the service provider is established;

   (c) the details of the service provider, including his electronic mail address, which allow him to be contacted rapidly and communicated with in a direct and effective manner;

   (d) where the service provider is registered in a trade or similar public register, the trade register in which the service provider is entered and his registration number, or equivalent means of identification in that register;

   (e) where the activity is subject to an authorisation scheme, the particulars of the relevant supervisory authority;

   (f) as concerns the regulated professions:

   – any professional body or similar institution with which the service provider is registered,

   – the professional title and the Member State where it has been granted,

   – a reference to the applicable professional rules in the Member State of establishment and the means to access them;

   (g) where the service provider undertakes an activity that is subject to VAT, the identification number referred to in Article 22(1) of the sixth Council Directive 77/388/EEC of 17 May 1977 on the harmonisation of the laws of the Member States relating to turnover taxes — Common system of value added tax: uniform basis of assessment[29].

2. In addition to other information requirements established by Community law, Member States shall at least ensure that, where information society services refer to prices, these are to be indicated clearly and unambiguously and, in particular, must indicate whether they are inclusive of tax and delivery costs.

---

28 OJ L 117, 7.5.1997, p. 15.
29 OJ L 145, 13.6.1977, p. 1. Directive as last amended by Directive 1999/85/EC (OJ L 277, 28.10.1999, p. 34).

Section 2: Commercial communications
Article 6
Information to be provided

In addition to other information requirements established by Community law, Member States shall ensure that commercial communications which are part of, or constitute, an information society service comply at least with the following conditions:

(a) the commercial communication shall be clearly identifiable as such;

(b) the natural or legal person on whose behalf the commercial communication is made shall be clearly identifiable;

(c) promotional offers, such as discounts, premiums and gifts, where permitted in the Member State where the service provider is established, shall be clearly identifiable as such, and the conditions which are to be met to qualify for them shall be easily accessible and be presented clearly and unambiguously;

(d) promotional competitions or games, where permitted in the Member State where the service provider is established, shall be clearly identifiable as such, and the conditions for participation shall be easily accessible and be presented clearly and unambiguously.

Article 7
Unsolicited commercial communication

1. In addition to other requirements established by Community law, Member States which permit unsolicited commercial communication by electronic mail shall ensure that such commercial communication by a service provider established in their territory shall be identifiable clearly and unambiguously as such as soon as it is received by the recipient.

2. Without prejudice to Directive 97/7/EC and Directive 97/66/EC, Member States shall take measures to ensure that service providers undertaking unsolicited commercial communications by electronic mail consult regularly and respect the opt-out registers in which natural persons not wishing to receive such commercial communications can register themselves.

Article 8
Regulated professions

1. Member States shall ensure that the use of commercial communications which are part of, or constitute, an information society service provided by a member of a regulated profession is permitted subject to compliance with the professional rules regarding, in particular, the independence, dignity and honour of the profession, professional secrecy and fairness towards clients and other members of the profession.

2. Without prejudice to the autonomy of professional bodies and associations, Member States and the Commission shall encourage professional associations and bodies to establish codes of conduct at Community level in order to determine the types of information that can be given for the purposes of commercial communication in conformity with the rules referred to in paragraph 1

3. When drawing up proposals for Community initiatives which may become necessary to ensure the proper functioning of the Internal Market with regard to the information referred to in paragraph 2, the Commission shall take due account of codes of conduct applicable at Community level and shall act in close cooperation with the relevant professional associations and bodies.

4. This Directive shall apply in addition to Community Directives concerning access to, and the exercise of, activities of the regulated professions.

Section 3: Contracts concluded by electronic means
Article 9
Treatment of contracts

1. Member States shall ensure that their legal system allows contracts to be concluded by electronic means. Member States shall in particular ensure that the legal requirements applicable to the contractual process neither create obstacles for the use of electronic contracts nor result in such contracts being deprived of legal effectiveness and validity on account of their having been made by electronic means.

2. Member States may lay down that paragraph 1 shall not apply to all or certain contracts falling into one of the following categories:

(a) contracts that create or transfer rights in real estate, except for rental rights;

(b) contracts requiring by law the involvement of courts, public authorities or professions exercising public authority;

(c) contracts of suretyship granted and on collateral securities furnished by persons acting for purposes outside their trade, business or profession;

(d) contracts governed by family law or by the law of succession.

3. Member States shall indicate to the Commission the categories referred to in paragraph 2 to which they do not apply paragraph 1. Member States shall submit to the Commission every five years a report on the application of paragraph 2 explaining the reasons why they consider it necessary to maintain the category referred to in paragraph 2(b) to which they do not apply paragraph 1.

Article 10
Information to be provided

1. In addition to other information requirements established by Community law, Member States shall ensure, except when otherwise agreed by parties who are not consumers, that at least the following information is given by the service provider clearly, comprehensibly and unambiguously and prior to the order being placed by the recipient of the service:

(a) the different technical steps to follow to conclude the contract;

(b) whether or not the concluded contract will be filed by the service provider and whether it will be accessible;

(c) the technical means for identifying and correcting input errors prior to the placing of the order;

(d) the languages offered for the conclusion of the contract.

2. Member States shall ensure that, except when otherwise agreed by parties who are not consumers, the service provider indicates any relevant codes of conduct to which he subscribes and information on how those codes can be consulted electronically.

3. Contract terms and general conditions provided to the recipient must be made available in a way that allows him to store and reproduce them.

4. Paragraphs 1 and 2 shall not apply to contracts concluded exclusively by exchange of electronic mail or by equivalent individual communications.

Article 11
Placing of the order

1. Member States shall ensure, except when otherwise agreed by parties who are not consumers, that in cases where the recipient of the service places his order through technological means, the following principles apply:

– the service provider has to acknowledge the receipt of the recipient's order without undue delay and by electronic means,

– the order and the acknowledgement of receipt are deemed to be received when the parties to whom they are addressed are able to access them.

2. Member States shall ensure that, except when otherwise agreed by parties who are not consumers, the service provider makes available to the recipient of the service appropriate, effective and accessible technical means allowing him to identify and correct input errors, prior to the placing of the order.

3. Paragraph 1, first indent, and paragraph 2 shall not apply to contracts concluded exclusively by exchange of electronic mail or by equivalent individual communications.

Section 4: Liability of intermediary service providers
Article 12
'Mere conduit'

1. Where an information society service is provided that consists of the transmission in a communication network of information provided by a recipient of the service, or the provision of access to a communication network, Member States shall ensure that the service provider is not liable for the information transmitted, on condition that the provider:

    (a) does not initiate the transmission;

    (b) does not select the receiver of the transmission; and

    (c) does not select or modify the information contained in the transmission.

2. The acts of transmission and of provision of access referred to in paragraph 1 include the automatic, intermediate and transient storage of the information transmitted in so far as this takes place for the sole purpose of carrying out the transmission in the communication network, and provided that the information is not stored for any period longer than is reasonably necessary for the transmission.

3. This Article shall not affect the possibility for a court or administrative authority, in accordance with Member States' legal systems, of requiring the service provider to terminate or prevent an infringement.

Article 13
'Caching'

1. Where an information society service is provided that consists of the transmission in a communication network of information provided by a recipient of the service, Member States shall ensure that the service provider is not liable for the automatic, intermediate and temporary storage of that information, performed for the sole purpose of making more efficient the information's onward transmission to other recipients of the service upon their request, on condition that:

    (a) the provider does not modify the information;

    (b) the provider complies with conditions on access to the information;

    (c) the provider complies with rules regarding the updating of the information, specified in a manner widely recognised and used by industry;

    (d) the provider does not interfere with the lawful use of technology, widely recognised and used by industry, to obtain data on the use of the information; and

    (e) the provider acts expeditiously to remove or to disable access to the information it has stored upon obtaining actual knowledge of the fact that the information at the initial source of the transmission has been removed from the network, or access to it has been disabled, or that a court or an administrative authority has ordered such removal or disablement.

2. This Article shall not affect the possibility for a court or administrative authority, in accordance with Member States' legal systems, of requiring the service provider to terminate or prevent an infringement.

Article 14
Hosting

1. Where an information society service is provided that consists of the storage of information provided by a recipient of the service, Member States shall ensure that the service provider is not liable for the information stored at the request of a recipient of the service, on condition that:

(a) the provider does not have actual knowledge of illegal activity or information and, as regards claims for damages, is not aware of facts or circumstances from which the illegal activity or information is apparent; or

(b) the provider, upon obtaining such knowledge or awareness, acts expeditiously to remove or to disable access to the information.

2. Paragraph 1 shall not apply when the recipient of the service is acting under the authority or the control of the provider.

3. This Article shall not affect the possibility for a court or administrative authority, in accordance with Member States' legal systems, of requiring the service provider to terminate or prevent an infringement, nor does it affect the possibility for Member States of establishing procedures governing the removal or disabling of access to information.

Article 15
No general obligation to monitor

1. Member States shall not impose a general obligation on providers, when providing the services covered by Articles 12, 13 and 14, to monitor the information which they transmit or store, nor a general obligation activity to seek facts or circumstances indicating illegal activity.

2. Member States may establish obligations for information society service providers promptly to inform the competent public authorities of alleged illegal activities undertaken or information provided by recipients of their service or obligations to communicate to the competent authorities, at their request, information enabling the identification of recipients of their service with whom they have storage agreements.

CHAPTER III—IMPLEMENTATION
Article 16
Codes of conduct

1. Member States and the Commission shall encourage:

(a) the drawing up of codes of conduct at Community level, by trade, professional and consumer associations or organisations, designed to contribute to the proper implementation of Articles 5 to 15;

(b) the voluntary transmission of draft codes of conduct at national or Community level to the Commission;

(c) the accessibility of these codes of conduct in the Community languages by electronic means;

(d) the communication to the Member States and the Commission, by trade, professional and consumer associations or organisations, of their assessment of the application of their codes of conduct and their impact upon practices, habits or customs relating to electronic commerce;

(e) the drawing up of codes of conduct regarding the protection of minors and human dignity.

2. Member States and the Commission shall encourage the involvement of associations or organisations representing consumers in the drafting and implementation of codes of conduct affecting their interests and drawn up in accordance with paragraph 1(a). Where appropriate, to take account of their specific needs, associations representing the visually impaired and disabled should be consulted.

Article 17
Out-of-court dispute settlement

1. Member States shall ensure that, in the event of disagreement between an information society service provider and the recipient of the service, their legislation does not hamper the use of out-of-court schemes, available under national law, for dispute settlement, including appropriate electronic means.

2. Member States shall encourage bodies responsible for the out-of-court settlement of, in particular, consumer disputes to operate in a way which provides adequate procedural guarantees for the parties concerned.

3. Member States shall encourage bodies responsible for out-of-court dispute settlement to inform the Commission of the significant decisions they take regarding information society services and to transmit any other information on the practices, usages or customs relating to electronic commerce.

Article 18
Court actions

1. Member States shall ensure that court actions available under national law concerning information society services' activities allow for the rapid adoption of measures, including interim measures, designed to terminate any alleged infringement and to prevent any further impairment of the interests involved.

2. The Annex to Directive 98/27/EC shall be supplemented as follows:

'11. Directive 2000/31/EC of the European Parliament and of the Council of 8 June 2000 on certain legal aspects on information society services, in particular electronic commerce, in the internal market (Directive on electronic commerce) (OJ L 178, 17.7.2000, p. 1).'

Article 19
Cooperation

1. Member States shall have adequate means of supervision and investigation necessary to implement this Directive effectively and shall ensure that service providers supply them with the requisite information.

2. Member States shall cooperate with other Member States; they shall, to that end, appoint one or several contact points, whose details they shall communicate to the other Member States and to the Commission.

3. Member States shall, as quickly as possible, and in conformity with national law, provide the assistance and information requested by other Member States or by the Commission, including by appropriate electronic means.

4. Member States shall establish contact points which shall be accessible at least by electronic means and from which recipients and service providers may:

   (a) obtain general information on contractual rights and obligations as well as on the complaint and redress mechanisms available in the event of disputes, including practical aspects involved in the use of such mechanisms;

   (b) obtain the details of authorities, associations or organisations from which they may obtain further information or practical assistance.

5. Member States shall encourage the communication to the Commission of any significant administrative or judicial decisions taken in their territory regarding disputes relating to information society services and practices, usages and customs relating to electronic commerce. The Commission shall communicate these decisions to the other Member States.

Article 20
Sanctions

Member States shall determine the sanctions applicable to infringements of national provisions adopted pursuant to this Directive and shall take all measures necessary to ensure that they are enforced. The sanctions they provide for shall be effective, proportionate and dissuasive.

CHAPTER IV—FINAL PROVISIONS
Article 21
Re-examination

1. Before 17 July 2003, and thereafter every two years, the Commission shall submit to the European Parliament, the Council and the Economic and

Social Committee a report on the application of this Directive, accompanied, where necessary, by proposals for adapting it to legal, technical and economic developments in the field of information society services, in particular with respect to crime prevention, the protection of minors, consumer protection and to the proper functioning of the internal market.

2. In examining the need for an adaptation of this Directive, the report shall in particular analyse the need for proposals concerning the liability of providers of hyperlinks and location tool services, 'notice and take down' procedures and the attribution of liability following the taking down of content. The report shall also analyse the need for additional conditions for the exemption from liability, provided for in Articles 12 and 13, in the light of technical developments, and the possibility of applying the internal market principles to unsolicited commercial communications by electronic mail.

Article 22
Transposition

1. Member States shall bring into force the laws, regulations and administrative provisions necessary to comply with this Directive before 17 January 2002. They shall forthwith inform the Commission thereof.

2. When Member States adopt the measures referred to in paragraph 1, these shall contain a reference to this Directive or shall be accompanied by such reference at the time of their official publication. The methods of making such reference shall be laid down by Member States.

Article 23
Entry into force

This Directive shall enter into force on the day of its publication in the Official Journal of the European Communities.

Article 24
Addressees

This Directive is addressed to the Member States.

Done at Luxemburg, 8 June 2000.

Annex
Derogations from Article 3

As provided for in Article 3(3), Article 3(1) and (2) do not apply to:
- copyright, neighbouring rights, rights referred to in Directive 87/54/EEC[30]

---

30 OJ L 24, 27.1.1987, p. 36.

and Directive 96/9/EC[31] as well as industrial property rights,

– the emission of electronic money by institutions in respect of which Member States have applied one of the derogations provided for in Article 8(1) of Directive 2000/46/EC[32],

– Article 44(2) of Directive 85/611/EEC[33],

– Article 30 and Title IV of Directive 92/49/EEC[34], Title IV of Directive 92/96/EEC[35], Articles 7 and 8 of Directive 88/357/EEC[36] and Article 4 of Directive 90/619/EEC[37],

– the freedom of the parties to choose the law applicable to their contract,

– contractual obligations concerning consumer contacts,

– formal validity of contracts creating or transferring rights in real estate where such contracts are subject to mandatory formal requirements of the law of the Member State where the real estate is situated,

– the permissibility of unsolicited commercial communications by electronic mail.

---

31 OJ L 77, 27.3.1996, p. 20.
32 Not yet published in the Official Journal.
33 OJ L 375, 31.12.1985, p. 3. Directive as last amended by Directive 95/26/EC (OJ L 168, 18.7.1995, p. 7).
34 OJ L 228, 11.8.1992, p. 1. Directive as last amended by Directive 95/26/EC.
35 OJ L 360, 9.12.1992, p. 2. Directive as last amended by Directive 92/49/EC.
36 OJ L 172, 4.7.1988, p. 1. Directive as last amended by Directive 92/49/EC.
37 OJ L 330, 29.11.1990, p. 50. Directive as last amended by Directive 92/96/EC.

Appendix 2

· Electronic Cash Directive ·

Directive 2000/46/EC of the European Parliament and of the Council of 18 September 2000 on the taking up, pursuit of and prudential supervision of the business of electronic money institutions*

THE EUROPEAN PARLIAMENT AND THE COUNCIL OF THE EUROPEAN UNION,

Having regard to the Treaty establishing the European Community, and in particular the first and third sentences of Article 47(2) thereof,

Having regard to the proposal from the Commission[1],

Having regard to the opinion of the Economic and Social Committee[2],

Having regard to the opinion of the European Central Bank[3],

Acting in accordance with the procedure laid down in Article 251 of the Treaty[4],

Whereas:

(1) Credit institutions within the meaning of Article 1, point 1, first subparagraph (b) of Directive 2000/12/EC[5] are limited in the scope of their activities.

(2) It is necessary to take account of the specific characteristics of these institutions and to provide the appropriate measures necessary to coordinate and harmonise Member States' laws, regulations and administrative provisions relating to the taking up, pursuit and prudential supervision of the business of electronic money institutions.

(3) For the purposes of this Directive, electronic money can be considered an electronic surrogate for coins and banknotes, which is stored on an

---

* OJ 2000 L275/39

1 OJ C 317, 15.10.1998, p. 7.

2 OJ C 101, 12.4.1999, p. 64.

3 OJ C 189, 6.7.1999, p. 7.

4 Opinion of the European Parliament of 15 April 1999 (OJ C 219, 30.7.1999, p. 415), confirmed on 27 October 1999, Council Common Position of 29 November 1999 (OJ C 26, 28.1.2000, p. 1) and Decision of the European Parliament of 11 April 2000 (not yet published in the Official journal). Decision of the Council of 16 June 2000.

5 Directive 2000/12/EC of the European Parliament and of the Council of 20 March 2000 relating to the taking up and pursuit of the business of credit institutions (OJ L 126, 26.5.2000, p. 1). Directive as last amended by Directive 2000/28/EC (see page 37 of this Official Journal).

electronic device such as a chip card or computer memory and which is generally intended for the purpose of effecting electronic payments of limited amounts.

(4) The approach adopted is appropriate to achieve only the essential harmonisation necessary and sufficient to secure the mutual recognition of authorisation and prudential supervision of electronic money institutions, making possible the granting of a single licence recognised throughout the Community and designed to ensure bearer confidence and the application of the principle of home Member State prudential supervision.

(5) Within the wider context of the rapidly evolving electronic commerce it is desirable to provide a regulatory framework that assists electronic money in delivering its full potential benefits and that avoids hampering technological innovation in particular. Therefore, this Directive introduces a technology-neutral legal framework that harmonises the prudential supervision of electronic money institutions to the extent necessary for ensuring their sound and prudent operation and their financial integrity in particular.

(6) Credit institutions, by virtue of point 5 of Annex I to Directive 2000/12/EC, are already allowed to issue and administer means of payment including electronic money and to carry on such activities Community-wide subject to mutual recognition and to the comprehensive prudential supervisory system applying to them in accordance with the European banking Directives.

(7) The introduction of a separate prudential supervisory regime for electronic money institutions, which, although calibrated on the prudential supervisory regime applying to other credit institutions and Directive 2000/12/EC except Title V, Chapters 2 and 3 thereof in particular, differs from that regime, is justified and desirable because the issuance of electronic money does not constitute in itself, in view of its specific character as an electronic surrogate for coins and banknotes, a deposit-taking activity pursuant to Article 3 of Directive 2000/12/EC, if the received funds are immediately exchanged for electronic money.

(8) The receipt of funds from the public in exchange for electronic money, which results in a credit balance left on account with the issuing institution, constitutes the receipt of deposits or other repayable funds for the purpose of Directive 2000/12/EC.

(9) It is necessary for electronic money to be redeemable to ensure bearer confidence. Redeemability does not imply, in itself, that the funds received in exchange for electronic money shall be regarded as deposits or other repayable funds for the purpose of Directive 2000/12/EC.

(10) Redeemability should always be understood to be at par value.

(11) In order to respond to the specific risks associated with the issuance of electronic money this prudential supervisory regime must be more targeted

and, accordingly, less cumbersome than the prudential supervisory regime applying to credit institutions, notably as regards reduced initial capital requirements and the non-application of Directive 93/6/EEC[6] and Title V, Chapter 2, Sections II and III of Directive 2000/12/EC.

(12) However, it is necessary to preserve a level playing field between electronic money institutions and other credit institutions issuing electronic money and, thus, to ensure fair competition among a wider range of institutions to the benefit of bearers. This is achieved since the abovementioned less cumbersome features of the prudential supervisory regime applying to electronic money institutions are balanced by provisions that are more stringent than those applying to other credit institutions, notably as regards restrictions on the business activities which electronic money institutions may carry on and, particularly, prudent limitations of their investments aimed at ensuring that their financial liabilities related to outstanding electronic money are backed at all times by sufficiently liquid low risk assets.

(13) Pending the harmonisation of prudential supervision of outsourced activities for credit institutions it is appropriate that electronic money institutions have sound and prudent management and control procedures. With a view to the possibility of operational and other ancilliary functions related to the issuance of electronic money being performed by undertakings which are not subject to prudential supervision it is essential that electronic money institutions have in place internal structures which should respond to the financial and non-financial risks to which they are exposed.

(14) The issuance of electronic money may affect the stability of the financial system and the smooth operation of payments systems. Close cooperation in assessing the integrity of electronic money schemes is called for.

(15) It is appropriate to afford competent authorities the possibility of waiving some or all of the requirements imposed by this Directive for electronic money institutions which operate only within the territories of the respective Member States.

(16) Adoption of this Directive constitutes the most appropriate means of achieving the desired objectives. This Directive is limited to the minimum necessary to achieve these objectives and does not go beyond what is necessary for this purpose.

(17) Provision should be made for the review of this Directive in the light of experience of developments in the market and the protection of bearers of electronic money.

---

6 Council Directive 93/6/EEC of 15 March 1993 on the capital adequacy of investment firms and credit institutions (OJ L 141, 11.6.1993, p. 1). Directive as last amended by Directive 98/33/EC (OJ L 204, 21.7.1998, p. 29).

(18) The Banking Advisory Committee has been consulted on the adoption of this Directive,

HAVE ADOPTED THIS DIRECTIVE:

Article 1
Scope, definitions and restriction of activities

1. This Directive shall apply to electronic money institutions.

2. It shall not apply to the institutions referred to in Article 2(3) of Directive 2000/12/EC.

3. For the purposes of this Directive:

   (a) 'electronic money institution' shall mean an undertaking or any other legal person, other than a credit institution as defined in Article 1, point 1, first subparagraph (a) of Directive 2000/12/EC which issues means of payment in the form of electronic money;

   (b) 'electronic money' shall mean monetary value as represented by a claim on the issuer which is:

   (i) stored on an electronic device;

   (ii) issued on receipt of funds of an amount not less in value than the monetary value issued;

   (iii) accepted as means of payment by undertakings other than the issuer.

4. Member States shall prohibit persons or undertakings that are not credit institutions, as defined in Article 1, point 1, first subparagraph of Directive 2000/12/EC, from carrying on the business of issuing electronic money.

5. The business activities of electronic money institutions other than the issuing of electronic money shall be restricted to:

   (a) the provision of closely related financial and non-financial services such as the administering of electronic money by the performance of operational and other ancillary functions related to its issuance, and the issuing and administering of other means of payment but excluding the granting of any form of credit; and

   (b) the storing of data on the electronic device on behalf of other undertakings or public institutions.

Electronic money institutions shall not have any holdings in other undertakings except where these undertakings perform operational or other ancillary functions related to electronic money issued or distributed by the institution concerned.

Article 2
Application of Banking Directives

1. Save where otherwise expressly provided for, only references to credit

institutions in Directive 91/308/EEC[7] and Directive 2000/12/EC except Title V, Chapter 2 thereof shall apply tò electronic money institutions.

2. Articles 5, 11, 13, 19, 20(7), 51 and 59 of Directive 2000/12/EC shall not apply. The mutual recognition arrangements provided for in Directive 2000/12/EC shall not apply to electronic money institutions' business activities other than the issuance of electronic money.

3. The receipt of funds within the meaning of Article 1(3)(b)(ii) does not constitute a deposit or other repayable funds according to Article 3 of Directive 2000/12/EC, if the funds received are immediately exchanged for electronic money.

Article 3
Redeemability

1. A bearer of electronic money may, during the period of validity, ask the issuer to redeem it at par value in coins and bank notes or by a transfer to an account free of charges other than those strictly necessary to carry out that operation.

2. The contract between the issuer and the bearer shall clearly state the conditions of redemption.

3. The contract may stipulate a minimum threshold for redemption. The threshold may not exceed EUR 10.

Article 4
Initial capital and ongoing own funds requirements

1. Electronic money institutions shall have an initial capital, as defined in Article 34(2), subparagraphs (1) and (2) of Directive 2000/12/EC, of not less than EUR 1 million. Notwithstanding paragraphs 2 and 3, their own funds, as defined in Directive 2000/12/EC, shall not fall below that amount.

2. Electronic money institutions shall have at all times own funds which are equal to or above 2% of the higher of the current amount or the average of the preceding six months' total amount of their financial liabilities related to outstanding electronic money.

3. Where an electronic money institution has not completed a six months' period of business, including the day it starts up, it shall have own funds which are equal to or above 2% of the higher of the current amount or the six months' target total amount of its financial liabilities related to outstanding electronic money. The six months' target total amount of the institution's financial liabilities related to outstanding electronic money shall

---

7 Council Directive 91/308/EEC of 10 June 1991 on prevention of the use of the financial system for the purpose of money laundering (OJ L 166, 28.6.1991, p. 77).

be evidenced by its business plan subject to any adjustment to that plan having been required by the competent authorities.

Article 5

Limitations of investments

1. Electronic money institutions shall have investments of an amount of no less than their financial liabilities related to outstanding electronic money in the following assets only:

   (a) asset items which according to Article 43(1)(a) (1), (2), (3) and (4) and Article 44(1) of Directive 2000/12/EC attract a zero credit risk weighting and which are sufficiently liquid;

   (b) sight deposits held with Zone A credit institutions as defined in Directive 2000/12/EC; and

   (c) debt instruments which are:

   (i) sufficiently liquid;

   (ii) not covered by paragraph 1(a);

   (iii) recognised by competent authorities as qualifying items within the meaning of Article 2(12) of Directive 93/6/EEC; and

   (iv) issued by undertakings other than undertakings which have a qualifying holding, as defined in Article 1 of Directive 2000/12/EC, in the electronic money institution concerned or which must be included in those undertakings' consolidated accounts.

2. Investments referred to in paragraph 1(b) and (c) may not exceed 20 times the own funds of the electronic money institution concerned and shall be subject to limitations which are at least as stringent as those applying to credit institutions in accordance with Title V, Chapter 2, Section III of Directive 2000/12/EC.

3. For the purpose of hedging market risks arising from the issuance of electronic money and from the investments referred to in paragraph 1, electronic money institutions may use sufficiently liquid interest-rate and foreign-exchange-related off balance-sheet items in the form of exchange-traded (i.e. not OTC) derivative instruments where they are subject to daily margin requirements or foreign exchange contracts with an original maturity of 14 calendar days or less. The use of derivative instruments according to the first sentence is permissible only if the full elimination of market risks is intended and, to the extent possible, achieved.

4. Member States shall impose appropriate limitations on the market risks electronic money institutions may incur from the investments referred to in paragraph 1.

5. For the purpose of applying paragraph 1, assets shall be valued at the lower of cost or market value.

6. If the value of the assets referred to in paragraph 1 falls below the amount of financial liabilities related to outstanding electronic money, the competent authorities shall ensure that the electronic money institution in question takes appropriate measures to remedy that situation promptly. To this end, and for a temporary period only, the competent authorities may allow the institution's financial liabilities related to outstanding electronic money to be backed by assets other than those referred to in paragraph 1 up to an amount not exceeding the lower of 5% of these liabilities or the institution's total amount of own funds.

Article 6
Verification of specific requirements by the competent authorities

The competent authorities shall ensure that the calculations justifying compliance with Article 4 and 5 are made, not less than twice each year, either by electronic money institutions themselves, which shall communicate them, and any component data required, to the competent authorities, or by competent authorities, using data supplied by the electronic money institutions.

Article 7
Sound and prudent operation

Electronic money institutions shall have sound and prudent management, administrative and accounting procedures and adequate internal control mechanisms. These should respond to the financial and non-financial risks to which the institution is exposed including technical and procedural risks as well as risks connected to its cooperation with any undertaking performing operational or other ancillary functions related to its business activities.

Article 8
Waiver

1. Member States may allow their competent authorities to waive the application of some or all of the provisions of this Directive and the application of Directive 2000/12/EC to electronic money institutions in cases where either:

(a) the total business activities of the type referred to in Article 1(3)(a) of this Directive of the institution generate a total amount of financial liabilities related to outstanding electronic money that normally does not exceed EUR 5 million and never exceeds EUR 6 million; or

(b) the electronic money issued by the institution is accepted as a means of payment only by any subsidiaries of the institution which perform operational or other ancillary functions related to electronic money issued or distributed by the institution, any parent undertaking of the institution or any other subsidiaries of that parent undertaking; or

(c) electronic money issued by the institution is accepted as payment only by a limited number of undertakings, which can be clearly distinguished by:

(i) their location in the same premises or other limited local area; or

(ii) their close financial or business relationship with the issuing institution, such as a common marketing or distribution scheme.

The underlying contractual arrangements must provide that the electronic storage device at the disposal of bearers for the purpose of making payments is subject to a maximum storage amount of not more than EUR 150.

2. An electronic money institution for which a waiver has been granted under paragraph 1 shall not benefit from the mutual recognition arrangements provided for in Directive 2000/12/EC.

3. Member States shall require that all electronic money institutions to which the application of this Directive and Directive 2000/12/EC has been waived report periodically on their activities including the total amount of financial liabilities related to electronic money.

Article 9
Grandfathering

Electronic money institutions subject to this Directive which have commenced their activity in accordance with the provisions in force in the Member State in which they have their head office before the date of entry into force of the provisions adopted in implementation of this Directive or the date referred to in Article 10(1), whichever date is earlier, shall be presumed to be authorised. The Member States shall oblige such electronic money institutions to submit all relevant information to the competent authorities in order to allow them to assess within six months from the date of entry into force of the provisions adopted in implementation of this Directive, whether the institutions comply with the requirements pursuant to this Directive, which measures need to be taken in order to ensure compliance, or whether a withdrawal of authorisation is appropriate. If compliance is not ensured within six months from the date referred to in Article 10(1), the electronic money institution shall not benefit from mutual recognition after that time.

Article 10
Implementation

1. Member States shall bring into force the laws, regulations and administrative provisions necessary to comply with this Directive not later than 27 April 2002. They shall immediately inform the Commission thereof.

When Member States adopt these measures, they shall contain a reference to this Directive or shall be accompanied by such reference on the occasion of their official publication. The methods of making such a reference shall be laid down by the Member States.

2. Member States shall communicate to the Commission the text of the main

provisions of national law, which they adopt in the field covered by this Directive.

Article 11
Review

Not later than 27 April 2005 the Commission shall present a report to the European Parliament and the Council on the application of this Directive, in particular on:
- the measures to protect the bearers of electronic money, including the possible need to introduce a guarantee scheme,
- capital requirements,
- waivers, and
- the possible need to prohibit interest being paid on funds received in exchange for electronic money,

accompanied where appropriate by a proposal for its revision.

Article 12
Entry into force

This Directive shall enter into force on the day of its publication in the Official Journal of the European Communities.

Article 13

This Directive is addressed to the Member States.

Done at Brussels, 18 September 2000.

· Copyright Directive ·

**Directive 2001/29/EC of the European Parliament and of the
Council of 22 May 2001 on the harmonisation of certain
aspects of copyright and related rights
in the information society***

THE EUROPEAN PARLIAMENT AND THE COUNCIL OF THE
EUROPEAN UNION,

Having regard to the Treaty establishing the European Community, and in
particular Articles 47(2), 55 and 95 thereof,

Having regard to the proposal from the Commission[1],

Having regard to the opinion of the Economic and Social Committee[2],

Acting in accordance with the procedure laid down in Article 251 of the
Treaty[3],

Whereas:

(1) The Treaty provides for the establishment of an internal market and the
    institution of a system ensuring that competition in the internal market is not
    distorted. Harmonisation of the laws of the Member States on copyright and
    related rights contributes to the achievement of these objectives.

(2) The European Council, meeting at Corfu on 24 and 25 June 1994, stressed
    the need to create a general and flexible legal framework at Community
    level in order to foster the development of the information society in
    Europe. This requires, inter alia, the existence of an internal market for
    new products and services. Important Community legislation to ensure
    such a regulatory framework is already in place or its adoption is well
    under way. Copyright and related rights play an important role in this
    context as they protect and stimulate the development and marketing of
    new products and services and the creation and exploitation of their
    creative content.

---

* OJ 2001 L167/10.

1 OJ C 108, 7.4.1998, p. 6 and OJ C 180, 25.6.1999, p. 6.

2 OJ C 407, 28.12.1998, p. 30.

3 Opinion of the European Parliament of 10 February 1999 (OJ C 150. 28.5.1999, p. 171).
  Council Common Position of 28 September 2000 (OJ C 344, 1.12.2000, p. 1) and Decision of
  the European Parliament of 14 February 2001 (not yet published in the Official Journal).
  Council Decision of 9 April 2001.

(3) The proposed harmonisation will help to implement the four freedoms of the internal market and relates to compliance with the fundamental principles of law and especially of property, including intellectual property, and freedom of expression and the public interest.

(4) A harmonised legal framework on copyright and related rights, through increased legal certainty and while providing for a high level of protection of intellectual property, will foster substantial investment in creativity and innovation, including network infrastructure, and lead in turn to growth and increased competitiveness of European industry, both in the area of content provision and information technology and more generally across a wide range of industrial and cultural sectors. This will safeguard employment and encourage new job creation.

(5) Technological development has multiplied and diversified the vectors for creation, production and exploitation. While no new concepts for the protection of intellectual property are needed, the current law on copyright and related rights should be adapted and supplemented to respond adequately to economic realities such as new forms of exploitation.

(6) Without harmonisation at Community level, legislative activities at national level which have already been initiated in a number of Member States in order to respond to the technological challenges might result in significant differences in protection and thereby in restrictions on the free movement of services and products incorporating, or based on, intellectual property, leading to a refragmentation of the internal market and legislative inconsistency. The impact of such legislative differences and uncertainties will become more significant with the further development of the information society, which has already greatly increased transborder exploitation of intellectual property. This development will and should further increase. Significant legal differences and uncertainties in protection may hinder economies of scale for new products and services containing copyright and related rights.

(7) The Community legal framework for the protection of copyright and related rights must, therefore, also be adapted and supplemented as far as is necessary for the smooth functioning of the internal market. To that end, those national provisions on copyright and related rights which vary considerably from one Member State to another or which cause legal uncertainties hindering the smooth functioning of the internal market and the proper development of the information society in Europe should be adjusted, and inconsistent national responses to the technological developments should be avoided, whilst differences not adversely affecting the functioning of the internal market need not be removed or prevented.

(8) The various social, societal and cultural implications of the information society require that account be taken of the specific features of the content of products and services.

(9)   Any harmonisation of copyright and related rights must take as a basis a high level of protection, since such rights are crucial to intellectual creation. Their protection helps to ensure the maintenance and development of creativity in the interests of authors, performers, producers, consumers, culture, industry and the public at large. Intellectual property has therefore been recognised as an integral part of property.

(10) If authors or performers are to continue their creative and artistic work, they have to receive an appropriate reward for the use of their work, as must producers in order to be able to finance this work. The investment required to produce products such as phonograms, films or multimedia products, and services such as 'on-demand' services, is considerable. Adequate legal protection of intellectual property rights is necessary in order to guarantee the availability of such a reward and provide the opportunity for satisfactory returns on this investment.

(11) A rigorous, effective system for the protection of copyright and related rights is one of the main ways of ensuring that European cultural creativity and production receive the necessary resources and of safeguarding the independence and dignity of artistic creators and performers.

(12) Adequate protection of copyright works and subject-matter of related rights is also of great importance from a cultural standpoint. Article 151 of the Treaty requires the Community to take cultural aspects into account in its action.

(13) A common search for, and consistent application at European level of, technical measures to protect works and other subject-matter and to provide the necessary information on rights are essential insofar as the ultimate aim of these measures is to give effect to the principles and guarantees laid down in law.

(14) This Directive should seek to promote learning and culture by protecting works and other subject-matter while permitting exceptions or limitations in the public interest for the purpose of education and teaching.

(15) The Diplomatic Conference held under the auspices of the World Intellectual Property Organisation (WIPO) in December 1996 led to the adoption of two new Treaties, the 'WIPO Copyright Treaty' and the 'WIPO Performances and Phonograms Treaty', dealing respectively with the protection of authors and the protection of performers and phonogram producers. Those Treaties update the international protection for copyright and related rights significantly, not least with regard to the so-called 'digital agenda', and improve the means to fight piracy world-wide. The Community and a majority of Member States have already signed the Treaties and the process of making arrangements

for the ratification of the Treaties by the Community and the Member States is under way. This Directive also serves to implement a number of the new international obligations.

(16) Liability for activities in the network environment concerns not only copyright and related rights but also other areas, such as defamation, misleading advertising, or infringement of trademarks, and is addressed horizontally in Directive 2000/31/EC of the European Parliament and of the Council of 8 June 2000 on certain legal aspects of information society services, in particular electronic commerce, in the internal market ('Directive on electronic commerce')[4], which clarifies and harmonises various legal issues relating to information society services including electronic commerce. This Directive should be implemented within a time scale similar to that for the implementation of the Directive on electronic commerce, since that Directive provides a harmonised framework of principles and provisions relevant inter alia to important parts of this Directive. This Directive is without prejudice to provisions relating to liability in that Directive.

(17) It is necessary, especially in the light of the requirements arising out of the digital environment, to ensure that collecting societies achieve a higher level of rationalisation and transparency with regard to compliance with competition rules.

(18) This Directive is without prejudice to the arrangements in the Member States concerning the management of rights such as extended collective licences.

(19) The moral rights of rightholders should be exercised according to the legislation of the Member States and the provisions of the Berne Convention for the Protection of Literary and Artistic Works, of the WIPO Copyright Treaty and of the WIPO Performances and Phonograms Treaty. Such moral rights remain outside the scope of this Directive.

(20) This Directive is based on principles and rules already laid down in the Directives currently in force in this area, in particular Directives 91/250/EEC[5], 92/100/EEC[6], 93/83/EEC[7], 93/98/EEC[8] and 96/9/EC[9], and it

---

4 OJ L 178. 17.7.2000, p. 1.
5 Council Directive 91/250/EEC of 14 May 1991 on the legal protection of computer programs (OJ L 122, 17.5.1991, p. 42). Directive as amended by Directive 93/98/EEC.
6 Council Directive 92/100/EEC of 19 November 1992 on rental right and lending right and on certain rights related to copyright in the field of intellectual property (OJ L 346, 27.11.1992, p. 61). Directive as amended by Directive 93/98/EEC.
7 Council Directive 93/83/EEC of 27 September 1993 on the coordination of certain rules concerning copyright and rights related to copyright applicable to satellite broadcasting and cable retransmission (OJ L 248, 6.10.1993, p. 15).
8 Council Directive 93/98/EEC of 29 October 1993 harmonising the term of protection of copyright and certain related rights (OJ L 290, 24.11.1993, p. 9).
9 Directive 96/9/EC of the European Parliament and of the Council of 11 March 1996 on the legal protection of databases (OJ L 77, 27.3.1996, p. 20).

develops those principles and rules and places them in the context of the information society. The provision of this Directive should be without prejudice to the provisions of those Directives, unless otherwise provided in this Directive.

(21) This Directive should define the scope of the acts covered by the reproduction right with regard to the different beneficiaries. This should be done in conformity with the acquis communautaire. A broad definition of these acts is needed to ensure legal certainty within the internal market.

(22) The objective of proper support for the dissemination of culture must not be achieved by sacrificing strict protection of rights or by tolerating illegal forms of distribution of counterfeited or pirated works.

(23) This Directive should harmonise further the author's right of communication to the public. This right should be understood in a broad sense covering all communication to the public not present at the place where the communication originates. This right should cover any such transmission or retransmission of a work to the public by wire or wireless means, including broadcasting. This right should not cover any other acts.

(24) The right to make available to the public subject-matter referred to in Article 3(2) should be understood as covering all acts of making available such subject-matter to members of the public not present at the place where the act of making available originates, and as not covering any other acts.

(25) The legal uncertainty regarding the nature and the level of protection of acts of on-demand transmission of copyright works and subject-matter protected by related rights over networks should be overcome by providing for harmonised protection at Community level. It should be made clear that all rightholders recognised by this Directive should have an exclusive right to make available to the public copyright works or any other subject-matter by way of interactive on-demand transmissions. Such interactive on-demand transmissions are characterised by the fact that members of the public may access them from a place and at a time individually chosen by them.

(26) With regard to the making available in on-demand services by broadcasters of their radio or television productions incorporating music from commercial phonograms as an integral part thereof, collective licensing arrangements are to be encouraged in order to facilitate the clearance of the rights concerned.

(27) The mere provision of physical facilities for enabling or making a communication does not in itself amount to communication within the meaning of this Directive.

(28) Copyright protection under this Directive includes the exclusive right to

control distribution of the work incorporated in a tangible article. The first sale in the Community of the original of a work or copies thereof by the rightholder or with his consent exhausts the right to control resale of that object in the Community. This right should not be exhausted in respect of the original or of copies thereof sold by the rightholder or with his consent outside the Community. Rental and lending rights for authors have been established in Directive 92/100/EEC. The distribution right provided for in this Directive is without prejudice to the provisions relating to the rental and lending rights contained in Chapter I of that Directive.

(29) The question of exhaustion does not arise in the case of services and on-line services in particular. This also applies with regard to a material copy of a work or other subject-matter made by a user of such a service with the consent of the rightholder. Therefore, the same applies to rental and lending of the original and copies of works or other subject-matter which are services by nature. Unlike CD-ROM or CD-I, where the intellectual property is incorporated in a material medium, namely an item of goods, every on-line service is in fact an act which should be subject to authorisation where the copyright or related right so provides.

(30) The rights referred to in this Directive may be transferred, assigned or subject to the granting of contractual licences, without prejudice to the relevant national legislation on copyright and related rights.

(31) A fair balance of rights and interests between the different categories of rightholders, as well as between the different categories of rightholders and users of protected subject-matter must be safeguarded. The existing exceptions and limitations to the rights as set out by the Member States have to be reassessed in the light of the new electronic environment. Existing differences in the exceptions and limitations to certain restricted acts have direct negative effects on the functioning of the internal market of copyright and related rights. Such differences could well become more pronounced in view of the further development of transborder exploitation of works and cross-border activities. In order to ensure the proper functioning of the internal market, such exceptions and limitations should be defined more harmoniously. The degree of their harmonisation should be based on their impact on the smooth functioning of the internal market.

(32) This Directive provides for an exhaustive enumeration of exceptions and limitations to the reproduction right and the right of communication to the public. Some exceptions or limitations only apply to the reproduction right, where appropriate. This list takes due account of the different legal traditions in Member States, while, at the same time, aiming to ensure a functioning internal market. Member States should arrive at a coherent application of these exceptions and limitations, which will be assessed when reviewing implementing legislation in the future.

(33) The exclusive right of reproduction should be subject to an exception to allow certain acts of temporary reproduction, which are transient or incidental reproductions, forming an integral and essential part of a technological process and carried out for the sole purpose of enabling either efficient transmission in a network between third parties by an intermediary, or a lawful use of a work or other subject-matter to be made. The acts of reproduction concerned should have no separate economic value on their own. To the extent that they meet these conditions, this exception should include acts which enable browsing as well as acts of caching to take place, including those which enable transmission systems to function efficiently, provided that the intermediary does not modify the information and does not interfere with the lawful use of technology, widely recognised and used by industry, to obtain data on the use of the information. A use should be considered lawful where it is authorised by the rightholder or not restricted by law.

(34) Member States should be given the option of providing for certain exceptions or limitations for cases such as educational and scientific purposes, for the benefit of public institutions such as libraries and archives, for purposes of news reporting, for quotations, for use by people with disabilities, for public security uses and for uses in administrative and judicial proceedings.

(35) In certain cases of exceptions or limitations, rightholders should receive fair compensation to compensate them adequately for the use made of their protected works or other subject-matter. When determining the form, detailed arrangements and possible level of such fair compensation, account should be taken of the particular circumstances of each case. When evaluating these circumstances, a valuable criterion would be the possible harm to the rightholders resulting from the act in question. In cases where rightholders have already received payment in some other form, for instance as part of a licence fee, no specific or separate payment may be due. The level of fair compensation should take full account of the degree of use of technological protection measures referred to in this Directive. In certain situations where the prejudice to the rightholder would be minimal, no obligation for payment may arise.

(36) The Member States may provide for fair compensation for rightholders also when applying the optional provisions on exceptions or limitations which do not require such compensation.

(37) Existing national schemes on reprography, where they exist, do not create major barriers to the internal market. Member States should be allowed to provide for an exception or limitation in respect of reprography.

(38) Member States should be allowed to provide for an exception or limitation to the reproduction right for certain types of reproduction of audio, visual and audiovisual material for private use, accompanied by

fair compensation. This may include the introduction or continuation of remuneration schemes to compensate for the prejudice to rightholders. Although differences between those remuneration schemes affect the functioning of the internal market, those differences, with respect to analogue private reproduction, should not have a significant impact on the development of the information society. Digital private copying is likely to be more widespread and have a greater economic impact. Due account should therefore be taken of the differences between digital and analogue private copying and a distinction should be made in certain respects between them.

(39) When applying the exception or limitation on private copying, Member States should take due account of technological and economic developments, in particular with respect to digital private copying and remuneration schemes, when effective technological protection measures are available. Such exceptions or limitations should not inhibit the use of technological measures or their enforcement against circumvention.

(40) Member States may provide for an exception or limitation for the benefit of certain non-profit making establishments, such as publicly accessible libraries and equivalent institutions, as well as archives. However, this should be limited to certain special cases covered by the reproduction right. Such an exception or limitation should not cover uses made in the context of on-line delivery of protected works or other subject-matter. This Directive should be without prejudice to the Member States' option to derogate from the exclusive public lending right in accordance with Article 5 of Directive 92/100/EEC. Therefore, specific contracts or licences should be promoted which, without creating imbalances, favour such establishments and the disseminative purposes they serve.

(41) When applying the exception or limitation in respect of ephemeral recordings made by broadcasting organisations it is understood that a broadcaster's own facilities include those of a person acting on behalf of and under the responsibility of the broadcasting organisation.

(42) When applying the exception or limitation for non-commercial educational and scientific research purposes, including distance learning, the non-commercial nature of the activity in question should be determined by that activity as such. The organisational structure and the means of funding of the establishment concerned are not the decisive factors in this respect.

(43) It is in any case important for the Member States to adopt all necessary measures to facilitate access to works by persons suffering from a disability which constitutes an obstacle to the use of the works themselves, and to pay particular attention to accessible formats.

(44) When applying the exceptions and limitations provided for in this Directive, they should be exercised in accordance with international

obligations. Such exceptions and limitations may not be applied in a way which prejudices the legitimate interests of the rightholder or which conflicts with the normal exploitation of his work or other subject-matter. The provision of such exceptions or limitations by Member States should, in particular, duly reflect the increased economic impact that such exceptions or limitations may have in the context of the new electronic environment. Therefore, the scope of certain exceptions or limitations may have to be even more limited when it comes to certain new uses of copyright works and other subject-matter.

(45) The exceptions and limitations referred to in Article 5(2), (3) and (4) should not, however, prevent the definition of contractual relations designed to ensure fair compensation for the rightholders insofar as permitted by national law.

(46) Recourse to mediation could help users and rightholders to settle disputes. The Commission, in cooperation with the Member States within the Contact Committee, should undertake a study to consider new legal ways of settling disputes concerning copyright and related rights.

(47) Technological development will allow rightholders to make use of technological measures designed to prevent or restrict acts not authorised by the rightholders of any copyright, rights related to copyright or the sui generis right in databases. The danger, however, exists that illegal activities might be carried out in order to enable or facilitate the circumvention of the technical protection provided by these measures. In order to avoid fragmented legal approaches that could potentially hinder the functioning of the internal market, there is a need to provide for harmonised legal protection against circumvention of effective technological measures and against provision of devices and products or services to this effect.

(48) Such legal protection should be provided in respect of technological measures that effectively restrict acts not authorised by the rightholders of any copyright, rights related to copyright or the sui generis right in databases without, however, preventing the normal operation of electronic equipment and its technological development. Such legal protection implies no obligation to design devices, products, components or services to correspond to technological measures, so long as such device, product, component or service does not otherwise fall under the prohibition of Article 6. Such legal protection should respect proportionality and should not prohibit those devices or activities which have a commercially significant purpose or use other than to circumvent the technical protection. In particular, this protection should not hinder research into cryptography.

(49) The legal protection of technological measures is without prejudice to the application of any national provisions which may prohibit the private

possession of devices, products or components for the circumvention of technological measures.

(50) Such a harmonised legal protection does not affect the specific provisions on protection provided for by Directive 91/250/EEC. In particular, it should not apply to the protection of technological measures used in connection with computer programs, which is exclusively addressed in that Directive. It should neither inhibit nor prevent the development or use of any means of circumventing a technological measure that is necessary to enable acts to be undertaken in accordance with the terms of Article 5(3) or Article 6 of Directive 91/250/EEC. Articles 5 and 6 of that Directive exclusively determine exceptions to the exclusive rights applicable to computer programs.

(51) The legal protection of technological measures applies without prejudice to public policy, as reflected in Article 5, or public security. Member States should promote voluntary measures taken by rightholders, including the conclusion and implementation of agreements between rightholders and other parties concerned, to accommodate achieving the objectives of certain exceptions or limitations provided for in national law in accordance with this Directive. In the absence of such voluntary measures or agreements within a reasonable period of time, Member States should take appropriate measures to ensure that rightholders provide beneficiaries of such exceptions or limitations with appropriate means of benefiting from them, by modifying an implemented technological measure or by other means. However, in order to prevent abuse of such measures taken by rightholders, including within the framework of agreements, or taken by a Member State, any technological measures applied in implementation of such measures should enjoy legal protection.

(52) When implementing an exception or limitation for private copying in accordance with Article 5(2)(b), Member States should likewise promote the use of voluntary measures to accommodate achieving the objectives of such exception or limitation. If, within a reasonable period of time, no such voluntary measures to make reproduction for private use possible have been taken, Member States may take measures to enable beneficiaries of the exception or limitation concerned to benefit from it. Voluntary measures taken by rightholders, including agreements between rightholders and other parties concerned, as well as measures taken by Member States, do not prevent rightholders from using technological measures which are consistent with the exceptions or limitations on private copying in national law in accordance with Article 5(2)(b), taking account of the condition of fair compensation under that provision and the possible differentiation between various conditions of use in accordance with Article 5(5), such as controlling the number of reproductions. In order to prevent abuse of such measures, any

technological measures applied in their implementation should enjoy legal protection.

(53) The protection of technological measures should ensure a secure environment for the provision of interactive on-demand services, in such a way that members of the public may access works or other subject-matter from a place and at a time individually chosen by them. Where such services are governed by contractual arrangements, the first and second subparagraphs of Article 6(4) should not apply. Non-interactive forms of online use should remain subject to those provisions.

(54) Important progress has been made in the international standardisation of technical systems of identification of works and protected subject-matter in digital format. In an increasingly networked environment, differences between technological measures could lead to an incompatibility of systems within the Community. Compatibility and interoperability of the different systems should be encouraged. It would be highly desirable to encourage the development of global systems.

(55) Technological development will facilitate the distribution of works, notably on networks, and this will entail the need for rightholders to identify better the work or other subject-matter, the author or any other rightholder, and to provide information about the terms and conditions of use of the work or other subject-matter in order to render easier the management of rights attached to them. Rightholders should be encouraged to use markings indicating, in addition to the information referred to above, inter alia their authorisation when putting works or other subject-matter on networks.

(56) There is, however, the danger that illegal activities might be carried out in order to remove or alter the electronic copyright-management information attached to it, or otherwise to distribute, import for distribution, broadcast, communicate to the public or make available to the public works or other protected subject-matter from which such information has been removed without authority. In order to avoid fragmented legal approaches that could potentially hinder the functioning of the internal market, there is a need to provide for harmonised legal protection against any of these activities.

(57) Any such rights-management information systems referred to above may, depending on their design, at the same time process personal data about the consumption patterns of protected subject-matter by individuals and allow for tracing of on-line behaviour. These technical means, in their technical functions, should incorporate privacy safeguards in accordance with Directive 9546/EC of the European Parliament and of the Council of 24 October 1995 on the protection of individuals with regard to the processing of personal data and the free movement of such data[10].

---

10 OJ L 281, 23.11.1995, p. 31.'

(58) Member States should provide for effective sanctions and remedies for infringements of rights and obligations as set out in this Directive. They should take all the measures necessary to ensure that those sanctions and remedies are applied. The sanctions thus provided for should be effective, proportionate and dissuasive and should include the possibility of seeking damages and/or injunctive relief and, where appropriate, of applying for seizure of infringing material.

(59) In the digital environment, in particular, the services of intermediaries may increasingly be used by third parties for infringing activities. In many cases such intermediaries are best placed to bring such infringing activities to an end. Therefore, without prejudice to any other sanctions and remedies available, rightholders should have the possibility of applying for an injunction against an intermediary who carries a third party's infringement of a protected work or other subject-matter in a network. This possibility should be available even where the acts carried out by the intermediary are exempted under Article 5. The conditions and modalities relating to such injunctions should be left to the national law of the Member States.

(60) The protection provided under this Directive should be without prejudice to national or Community legal provisions in other areas, such as industrial property, data protection, conditional access, access to public documents, and the rule of media exploitation chronology, which may affect the protection of copyright or related rights.

(61) In order to comply with the WIPO Performances and Phonograms Treaty, Directives 92/100/EEC and 93/98/EEC should be amended,

HAVE ADOPTED THIS DIRECTIVE:

CHAPTER 1—OBJECTIVE AND SCOPE
Article 1
Scope

1. This Directive concerns the legal protection of copyright and related rights in the framework of the internal market, with particular emphasis on the information society.

2. Except in the cases referred to in Article 11, this Directive shall leave intact and shall in no way affect existing Community provisions relating to:

(a) the legal protection of computer programs;

(b) rental right, lending right and certain rights related to copyright in the field of intellectual property;

(c) copyright and related rights applicable to broadcasting of programmes by satellite and cable retransmission;

(d) the term of protection of copyright and certain related rights;

(e) the legal protection of databases.

CHAPTER II—RIGHTS AND EXCEPTIONS

Article 2

Reproduction right

Member States shall provide for the exclusive right to authorise or prohibit direct or indirect, temporary or permanent reproduction by any means and in any form, in whole or in part:

(a) for authors, of their works;

(b) for performers, of fixations of their performances;

(c) for phonogram producers, of their phonograms;

(d) for the producers of the first fixations of films, in respect of the original and copies of their films;

(e) for broadcasting organisations, of fixations of their broadcasts, whether those broadcasts are transmitted by wire or over the air, including by cable or satellite.

Article 3

Right of communication to the public of works and right of making available to the public other subject-matter

1. Member States shall provide authors with the exclusive right to authorise or prohibit any communication to the public of their works, by wire or wireless means, including the making available to the public of their works in such a way that members of the public may access them from a place and at a time individually chosen by them.

2. Member States shall provide for the exclusive right to authorise or prohibit the making available to the public, by wire or wireless means, in such a way that members of the public may access them from a place and at a time individually chosen by them:

    (a) for performers, of fixations of their performances;

    (b) for phonogram producers, of their phonograms;

    (c) for the producers of the first fixations of films, of the original and copies of their films;

    (d)for broadcasting organisations, of fixations of their broadcasts, whether these broadcasts are transmitted by wire or over the air, including by cable or satellite.

3. The rights referred to in paragraphs 1 and 2 shall not be exhausted by any act of communication to the public or making available to the public as set out in this Article.

Article 4
Distribution right

1. Member States shall provide for authors, in respect of the original of their works or of copies thereof, the exclusive right to authorise or prohibit any form of distribution to the public by sale or otherwise.

2. The distribution right shall not be exhausted within the Community in respect of the original or copies of the work, except where the first sale or other transfer of ownership in the Community of that object is made by the rightholder or with his consent.

Article 5
Exceptions and limitations

1. Temporary acts of reproduction referred to in Article 2, which are transient or incidental [and] an integral and essential part of a technological process and whose sole purpose is to enable:

(a) a transmission in a network between third parties by an intermediary, or

(b) a lawful use

   of a work or other subject-matter to be made, and which have no independent economic significance, shall be exempted from the reproduction right provided for in Article 2.

2. Member States may provide for exceptions or limitations to the reproduction right provided for in Article 2 in the following cases:

(a) in respect of reproductions on paper or any similar medium, effected by the use of any kind of photographic technique or by some other process having similar effects, with the exception of sheet music, provided that the rightholders receive fair compensation;

(b) in respect of reproductions on any medium made by a natural person for private use and for ends that are neither directly nor indirectly commercial, on condition that the rightholders receive fair compensation which takes account of the application or non-application of technological measures referred to in Article 6 to the work or subject-matter concerned;

(c) in respect of specific acts of reproduction made by publicly accessible libraries, educational establishments or museums, or by archives, which are not for direct or indirect economic or commercial advantage;

(d) in respect of ephemeral recordings of works made by broadcasting organisations by means of their own facilities and for their own broadcasts; the preservation of these recordings in official archives may, on the grounds of their exceptional documentary character, be permitted;

(e) in respect of reproductions of broadcasts made by social institutions pursuing non-commercial purposes, such as hospitals or prisons, on condition that the rightholders receive fair compensation.

3. Member States may provide for exceptions or limitations to the rights provided for in Articles 2 and 3 in the following cases:

(a) use for the sole purpose of illustration for teaching or scientific research, as long as the source, including the author's name, is indicated, unless this turns out to be impossible and to the extent justified by the non-commercial purpose to be achieved;

(b) uses, for the benefit of people with a disability, which are directly related to the disability and of a non-commercial nature, to the extent required by the specific disability;

(c) reproduction by the press, communication to the public or making available of published articles on current economic, political or religious topics or of broadcast works or other subject-matter of the same character, in cases where such use is not expressly reserved, and as long as the source, including the author's name, is indicated, or use of works or other subject-matter in connection with the reporting of current events, to the extent justified by the informatory purpose and as long as the source, including the author's name, is indicated, unless this turns out to be impossible;

(d) quotations for purposes such as criticism or review, provided that they relate to a work or other subject-matter which has already been lawfully made available to the public, that, unless this turns out to be impossible, the source, including the author's name, is indicated, and that their use is in accordance with fair practice, and to the extent required by the specific purpose;

(e) use for the purposes of public security or to ensure the proper performance or reporting of administrative, parliamentary or judicial proceedings;

(f) use of political speeches as well as extracts of public lectures or similar works or subject-matter to the extent justified by the informatory purpose and provided that the source, including the author's name, is indicated, except where this turns out to be impossible;

(g) use during religious celebrations or official celebrations organised by a public authority;

(h) use of works, such as works of architecture or sculpture, made to be located permanently in public places;

(i) incidental inclusion of a work or other subject-matter in other material;

(j) use for the purpose of advertising the public exhibition or sale of artistic works, to the extent necessary to promote the event, excluding any other commercial use;

(k) use for the purpose of caricature, parody or pastiche;

(l) use in connection with the demonstration or repair of equipment;

(m) use of an artistic work in the form of a building or a drawing or plan of a building for the purposes of reconstructing the building;

(n) use by communication or making available, for the purpose of research or private study, to individual members of the public by dedicated terminals on the premises of establishments referred to in paragraph 2(c) of works and other subject-matter not subject to purchase or licensing terms which are contained in their collections;

(o) use in certain other cases of minor importance where exceptions or limitations already exist under national law, provided that they only concern analogue uses and do not affect the free circulation of goods and services within the Community, without prejudice to the other exceptions and limitations contained in this Article.

4. Where the Member States may provide for an exception or limitation to the right of reproduction pursuant to paragraphs 2 and 3, they may provide similarly for an exception or limitations to the right of distribution as referred to in Article 4 to the extent justified by the purpose of the authorised act of reproduction.

5. The exceptions and limitations provided for in paragraphs 1, 2, 3 and 4 shall only be applied in certain special cases which do not conflict with a normal exploitation of the work or other subject-matter and do not unreasonably prejudice the legitimate interests of the rightholder.

CHAPTER III—PROTECTION OF TECHNOLOGICAL MEASURES AND RIGHTS-MANAGEMENT INFORMATION

Article 6
Obligations as to technological measures

1. Member States shall provide adequate legal protection against the circumvention of any effective technological measures, which the person concerned carries out in the knowledge, or with reasonable grounds to know, that he or she is pursuing that objective.

2. Member States shall provide adequate legal protection against the manufacture, import, distribution, sale, rental, advertisement for sale or rental, or possession for commercial purposes of devices, products or components or the provision of services which:

(a) are promoted, advertised or marketed for the purpose of circumvention of, or

(b) have only a limited commercially significant purpose or use other than to circumvent, or

(c) are primarily designed, produced, adapted or performed for the purpose of enabling or facilitating the circumvention of,

any effective technological measures.

3. For the purposes of this Directive, the expression 'technological measures' means any technology, device or component that, in the normal course of its operation, is designed to prevent or restrict acts, in respect of works or other subject-matter, which are not authorised by the rightholder of any copyright or any right related to copyright as provided for by law or the sui

generis right provided for in Chapter III of Directive 96/9/EC. Technological measures shall be deemed 'effective' where the use of a protected work or other subject-matter is controlled by the rightholders through application of an access control or protection process, such as encryption, scrambling or other transformation of the work or other subject-matter or a copy control mechanism, which achieves the protection objective.

4. Notwithstanding the legal protection provided for in paragraph 1, in the absence of voluntary measures taken by rightholders, including agreements between rightholders and other parties concerned, Member States shall take appropriate measures to ensure that rightholders make available to the beneficiary of an exception or limitation provided for in national law in accordance with Article 5(2)(a), (2)(c), (2)(d), (2)(e), (3)(a), (3)(b) or (3)(e) the means of benefiting from that exception or limitation, to the extent necessary to benefit from that exception or limitation and where that beneficiary has legal access to the protected work or subject-matter concerned.

A Member State may also take such measures in respect of a beneficiary of an exception or limitation provided for in accordance with Article 5(2)(b), unless reproduction for private use has already been made possible by rightholders to the extent necessary to benefit from the exception or limitation concerned and in accordance with the provisions of Article 5(2)(b) and (5), without preventing rightholders from adopting adequate measures regarding the number of reproductions in accordance with these provisions.

The technological measures applied voluntarily by rightholders, including those applied in implementation of voluntary agreements, and technological measures applied in implementation of the measures taken by Member States, shall enjoy the legal protection provided for in paragraph 1.

The provisions of the first and second subparagraphs shall not apply to works or other subject-matter made available to the public on agreed contractual terms in such a way that members of the public may access them from a place and at a time individually chosen by them.

When this Article is applied in the context of Directives 92/100/EEC and 96/9/EC, this paragraph shall apply mutatis mutandis.

Article 7
Obligations concerning rights-management information

1. Member States shall provide for adequate legal protection against any person knowingly performing without authority any of the following acts:

(a) the removal or alteration of any electronic rights-management information;

(b) the distribution, importation for distribution, broadcasting, communication or making available to the public of works or other subject-matter protected under this Directive or under Chapter III of

Directive 96/9/EC from which electronic rights-management information has been removed or altered without authority,

if such person knows, or has reasonable grounds to know, that by so doing he is inducing, enabling, facilitating or concealing an infringement of any copyright or any rights related to copyright as provided by law, or of the sui generis right provided for in Chapter III of Directive 96/9/EC.

2. For the purposes of this Directive, the expression 'rights-management information' means any information provided by rightholders which identifies the work or other subject-matter referred to in this Directive or covered by the sui generis right provided for in Chapter III of Directive 96/9/EC, the author or any other rightholder, or information about the terms and conditions of use of the work or other subject-matter, and any numbers or codes that represent such information.

The first subparagraph shall apply when any of these items of information is associated with a copy of, or appears in connection with the communication to the public of, a work or other subjectmatter referred to in this Directive or covered by the sui generis right provided for in Chapter III of Directive 96/9/EC.

CHAPTER IV—COMMON PROVISIONS
Article 8
Sanctions and remedies

1. Member States shall provide appropriate sanctions and remedies in respect of infringements of the rights and obligations set out in this Directive and shall take all the measures necessary to ensure that those sanctions and remedies are applied. The sanctions thus provided for shall be effective, proportionate and dissuasive.

2. Each Member State shall take the measures necessary to ensure that rightholders whose interests are affected by an infringing activity carried out on its territory can bring an action for damages and/or apply for an injunction and, where appropriate, for the seizure of infringing material as well as of devices, products or components referred to in Article 6(2).

3. Member States shall ensure that rightholders are in a position to apply for an injunction against intermediaries whose services are used by a third party to infringe a copyright or related right.

Article 9
Continued application of other legal provisions

This Directive shall be without prejudice to provisions concerning in particular patent rights, trade marks, design rights, utility models, topographies of semi-conductor products, type faces, conditional access, access to cable of broadcasting services, protection of national treasures, legal deposit requirements, laws on restrictive practices and unfair competition, trade secrets, security, confidentiality, data protection and privacy, access to public documents, the law of contract.

Article 10
Application over time

1. The provisions of this Directive shall apply in respect of all works and other subject-matter referred to in this Directive which are, on 22 December 2002, protected by the Member States' legislation in the field of copyright and related rights, or which meet the criteria for protection under the provisions of this Directive or the provisions referred to in Article 1(2).

2. This Directive shall apply without prejudice to any acts concluded and rights acquired before 22 December 2002.

Article 11
Technical adaptations

1. Directive 92/100/EEC is hereby amended as follows:

(a) Article 7 shall be deleted;

(b) Article 10(3) shall be replaced by the following:

'3. The limitations shall only be applied in certain special cases which do not conflict with a normal exploitation of the subject-matter and do not unreasonably prejudice the legitimate interests of the rightholder.'

2. Article 3(2) of Directive 93/98/EEC shall be replaced by the following:

'2. The rights of producers of phonograms shall expire 50 years after the fixation is made. However, if the phonogram has been lawfully published within this period, the said rights shall expire 50 years from the date of the first lawful publication. If no lawful publication has taken place within the period mentioned in the first sentence, and if the phonogram has been lawfully communicated to the public within this period, the said rights shall expire 50 years from the date of the first lawful communication to the public.

However, where through the expire of the term of protection granted pursuant to this paragraph in its version before amendment by Directive 2001/29/EC of the European Parliament and of the Council of 22 May 2001 on the harmonisation of certain aspects of copyright and related rights in the information society (*) the rights of producers of phonograms are no longer protected on 22 December 2002, this paragraph shall not have the effect of protecting those rights anew.

Article 12
Final provisions

1. Not later than 22 December 2004 and every three years thereafter, the Commission shall submit to the European Parliament, the Council and the Economic and Social Committee a report on the application of this

Directive, in which, inter alia, on the basis of specific information supplied by the Member States, it shall examine in particular the application of Articles 5, 6 and 8 in the light of the development of the digital market. In the case of Article 6, it shall examine in particular whether that Article confers a sufficient level of protection and whether acts which are permitted by law are being adversely affected by the use of effective technological measures. Where necessary, in particular to ensure the functioning of the internal market pursuant to Article 14 of the Treaty, it shall submit proposals for amendments to this Directive.

2. Protection of rights related to copyright under this Directive shall leave intact and shall in no way affect the protection of copyright.

3. A contact committee is hereby established. It shall be composed of representatives of the competent authorities of the Member States. It shall be chaired by a representative of the Commission and shall meet either on the initiative of the chairman or at the request of the delegation of a Member State.

4. The tasks of the committee shall be as follows:

(a) to examine the impact of this Directive on the functioning of the internal market, and to highlight any difficulties;

(b) to organise consultations on all questions deriving from the application of this Directive;

(c) to facilitate the exchange of information on relevant developments in legislation and case-law, as well as relevant economic, social, cultural and technological developments;

(d) to act as a forum for the assessment of the digital market in works and other items, including private copying and the use of technological measures.

Article 13
Implementation

1. Member States shall bring into force the laws, regulations and administrative provisions necessary to comply with this Directive before 22 December 2002. They shall forthwith inform the Commission thereof.

When Member States adopt these measures, they shall contain a reference to this Directive or shall be accompanied by such reference on the occasion of their official publication. The methods of making such reference shall be laid down by Member States.

2. Member States shall communicate to the Commission the text of the provisions of domestic law which they adopt in the field governed by this Directive.

Article 14
Entry into force

This Directive shall enter into force on the day of its publication in the Official Journal of the European Communities.

Article 15
Addressees

This Directive is addressed to the Member States.
Done at Brussels, 22 May 2001.

Appendix 4

· Standard Clauses Decision (1) ·

Commission Decision 2001/497/EC of 15 June 2001 on standard contractual clauses for the transfer of personal data to third countries, under Directive 95/46/EC*

(Text with EEA relevance)

THE COMMISSION OF THE EUROPEAN COMMUNITIES,

Having regard to the Treaty establishing the European Community,

Having regard to Directive 95/46/EC of the European Parliament and of the Council of 24 October 1995 on the protection of individuals with regard to the processing of personal data and on the free movement of such data[1] and in particular Article 26(4) thereof,

Whereas:

(1) Pursuant to Directive 95/46/EC, Member States are required to provide that a transfer of personal data to a third country may only take place if the third country in question ensures an adequate level of data protection and the Member States' laws, which comply with the other provisions of the Directive, are respected prior to the transfer.

(2) However, Article 26(2) of Directive 95/46/EC provides that Member States may authorise, subject to certain safeguards, a transfer or a set of transfers of personal data to third countries which do not ensure an adequate level of protection. Such safeguards may in particular result from appropriate contractual clauses.

(3) Pursuant to Directive 95/46/EC, the level of data protection should be assessed in the light of all the circumstances surrounding the data transfer operation or set of data transfer operations. The Working Party on Protection of Individuals with regard to the processing of personal data established under that Directive[2] has issued guidelines to aid with the assessment[3].

(4) Article 26(2) of Directive 95/46/EC, which provides flexibility for an

---

* OJ 2001 L181/19

1 OJ L 281, 23.11.1995, p. 31.

2 The Internet address of the Working Party is:
http:www.europa.eu.intlcomm/internal_market/en/medial/dataprot/wpdocs/index.htm.

3 WP 4 (5020/97) 'First orientations on transfers of personal data to third countries working document – possible ways forward in assessing adequacy', a discussion document adopted by the Working Party on 26 June 1997.

organisation wishing to transfer data to third countries, and Article 26(4), which provides for standard contractual clauses, are essential for maintaining the necessary flow of personal data between the Community and third countries without unnecessary burdens for economic operators. Those Articles are particularly important in view of the fact that the Commission is unlikely to adopt adequacy findings under Article 25(6) for more than a limited number of countries in the short or even medium term.

(5) The standard contractual clauses are only one of several possibilities under Directive 95/46/EC, together with Article 25 and Article 26(1) and (2), for lawfully transferring personal data to a third country. It will be easier for organisations to transfer personal data to third countries by incorporating the standard contractual clauses in a contract. The standard contractual clauses relate only to data protection. The data exporter and the data importer are free to include any other clauses on business related issues, such as clauses on mutual assistance in cases of disputes with a data subject or a supervisory authority, which they consider as being pertinent for the contract as long as they do not contradict the standard contractual clauses.

(6) This Decision should be without prejudice to national authorisations Member States may grant in accordance with national provisions implementing Article 26(2) of Directive 95/46/EC. The circumstances of specific transfers may require that data controllers provide different safeguards within the meaning of Article 26(2). In any case, this Decision only has the effect of requiring the Member States not to refuse to recognise as providing adequate safeguards the contractual clauses described in it and does not therefore have any effect on other contractual clauses.

(7) The scope of this Decision is limited to establishing that the clauses in the Annex may be used by a controller established in the Community in order to adduce sufficient safeguards within the meaning of Article 26(2) of Directive 95/46/EC. The transfer of personal data to third countries is a processing operation in a Member State, the lawfulness of which is subject to national law. The data protection supervisory authorities of the Member States, in the exercise of their functions and powers under Article 28 of Directive 95/46/EC, should remain competent to assess whether the data exporter has complied with national legislation implementing the provisions of Directive 95/46/EC and, in particular, any specific rules as regards the obligation of providing information under that Directive.

(8) This Decision does not cover the transfer of personal data by controllers established in the Community to recipients established outside the territory of the Community who act only as processors. Those transfers do not require the same safeguards because the processor acts exclusively on behalf of the controller. The Commission intends to address that type of transfer in a subsequent decision.

(9) It is appropriate to lay down the minimum information that the parties

must specify in the contract dealing with the transfer. Member States should retain the power to particularise the information the parties are required to provide. The operation of this Decision should be reviewed in the light of experience.

(10) The Commission will also consider in the future whether standard contractual clauses submitted by business organisations or other interested parties offer adequate safeguards in accordance with Directive 95/46/EC.

(11) While the parties should be free to agree on the substantive data protection rules to be complied with by the data importer, there are certain data protection principles which should apply in any event.

(12) Data should be processed and subsequently used or further communicated only for specified purposes and should not be kept longer than necessary.

(13) In accordance with Article 12 of Directive 95/46/EC, the data subject should have the right of access to all data relating to him and as appropriate to rectification, erasure or blocking of certain data.

(14) Further transfers of personal data to another controller established in a third country should be permitted only subject to certain conditions, in particular to ensure that data subjects are given proper information and have the opportunity to object, or in certain cases to withold their consent.

(15) In addition to assessing whether transfers to third countries are in accordance with national law, supervisory authorities should play a key role in this contractual mechanism in ensuring that personal data are adequately protected after the transfer. In specific circumstances, the supervisory authorities of the Member States should retain the power to prohibit or suspend a data transfer or a set of transfers based on the standard contractual clauses in those exceptional cases where it is established that a transfer on contractual basis is likely to have a substantial adverse effect on the guarantees providing adequate protection to the data subject.

(16) The standard contractual clauses should be enforceable not only by the organisations which are parties to the contract, but also by the data subjects, in particular, where the data subjects suffer damage as a consequence of a breach of the contract.

(17) The governing law of the contract should be the law of the Member State in which the data exporter is established, enabling a third-party beneficiary to enforce a contract. Data subjects should be allowed to be represented by associations or other bodies if they so wish and if authorised by national law.

(18) To reduce practical difficulties which data subjects could experience

when trying to enforce their rights under the standard contractual clauses, the data exporter and the data importer should be jointly and severally liable for damages resulting from any violation of those provisions which are covered by the third-party beneficiary clause.

(19) The Data Subject is entitled to take action and receive compensation from the Data Exporter, the Data Importer or from both for any damage resulting from any act incompatible with the obligations contained in the standard contractual clauses. Both parties may be exempted from that liability if they prove that neither of them was responsible.

(20) Joint and several liability does not extend to those provisions not covered by the third-party beneficiary clause and does not need to leave one party paying for the damage resulting from the unlawful processing of the other party. Although mutual indemnification between the parties is not a requirement for the adequacy of the protection for the data subjects and may therefore be deleted, it is included in the standard contractual clauses for the sake of clarification and to avoid the need for the parties to negotiate indemnification clauses individually.

(21) In the event of a dispute between the parties and the data subject which is not amicably resolved and where the data subject invokes the third-party beneficiary clause, the parties agree to provide the data subject with the choice between mediation, arbitration or litigation. The extent to which the data subject will have an effective choice will depend on the availability of reliable and recognised systems of mediation and arbitration. Mediation by the supervisory authorities of a Member State should be an option where they provide such a service.

(22) The Working Party on the protection of individuals with regard to the processing of personal data established under Article 29 of Directive 95/46/EC has delivered an opinion on the level of protection provided under the standard contractual clauses annexed to this Decision, which has been taken into account in the preparation of this Decision.[4]

(23) The measures provided for in this Decision are in accordance with the opinion of the Committee established under Article 31 of Directive 95/46/EC,

HAS ADOPTED THIS DECISION:

Article 1

The standard contractual clauses set out in the Annex are considered as offering adequate safeguards with respect to the protection of the privacy and fundamental rights and freedoms of individuals and as regards the exercise of the corresponding rights as required by Article 26(2) of Directive 9/46/EC.

---

4 Opinion No 1/2001 adopted by the Working Party on 26 January 2001 (DG MARKT 5102/00 WP 38), available in the website 'Europa' hosted by the European Commission.

Article 2

This Decision concerns only the adequacy of protection provided by the standard contractual clauses for the transfer of personal data set out in the Annex. It does not affect the application of other national provisions implementing Directive 95/46/EC that pertain to the processing of personal data within the Member States.

This Decision shall not apply to the transfer of personal data by controllers established in the Community to recipients established outside the territory of the Community who act only as processors.

Article 3

For the purposes of this Decision:

(a) the definitions in Directive 95/46/EC shall apply;

(b) 'special categories of data' means the data referred to in Article 8 of that Directive;

(c) 'supervisory authority' means the authority referred to in Article 28 of that Directive;

(d) 'data exporter' means the controller who transfers the personal data;

(e) 'data importer' means the controller who agrees to receive from the data exporter personal data for further processing in accordance with the terms of this Decision.

Article 4

1. Without prejudice to their powers to take action to ensure compliance with national provisions adopted pursuant to chapters II, III, V and VI of Directive 95/46/EC, the competent authorities in the Member States may exercise their existing powers to prohibit or suspend data flows to third countries in order to protect individuals with regard to the processing of their personal data in cases where:

(a) it is established that the law to which the data importer is subject imposes upon him requirements to derogate from the relevant data protection rules which go beyond the restrictions necessary in a democratic society as provided for in Article 13 of Directive 95/46/EC where those requirements are likely to have a substantial adverse effect on the guarantees provided by the standard contractual clauses; or

(b) a competent authority has established that the data importer has not respected the contractual clauses; or

(c) there is a substantial likelihood that the standard contractual clauses in the Annex are not being or will not be complied with and the continuation of transfer would create an imminent risk of grave harm to the data subjects.

2. The prohibition or suspension pursuant to paragraph 1 shall be lifted as

soon as the reasons for the prohibition or suspension no longer exist.

3. When Member States adopt measures pursuant to paragraphs 1 and 2, they shall without delay inform the Commission which will forward the information to the other Member States.

Article 5

The Commission shall evaluate the operation of this Decision on the basis of available information three years after its notification to the Member States. It shall submit a report on the endings to the Committee established under Article 31 of Directive 95/46/EC. It shall include any evidence that could affect the evaluation concerning the adequacy of the standard contractual clauses in the Annex and any evidence that this Decision is being applied in a discriminatory way.

Article 6

This Decision shall apply from 3 September 2001.

Article 7

This Decision is addressed to the Member States.

Done at Brussels, 15 June 2001.

Annex
STANDARD CONTRACTUAL CLAUSES
for the purposes of Article 26(2) of Directive 95/46/EC for the transfer of personal data to third countries which do not ensure an adequate level of protection

Name of the data exporting organisation:..
....
Address:...
Tel.............................. fax................................. e-mail:...................................
Other information needed to identify the organisation:...................................

('the data exporter')

and

Name of the data importing organisation:...
Address:...
Tel.............................. fax................................. e-mail:...................................
Other information needed to identify the organisation:...................................

('the data importer')

HAVE AGREED on the following contractual clauses ('the Clauses') in order to adduce adequate safeguards with respect to the protection of privacy and fundamental rights and freedoms of individuals for the transfer by the data exporter to the data importer of the personal data specified in Appendix 1:

Clause 1
Definitions

For the purposes of the Clauses:

a) 'personal data', 'special categories of data', 'process/processing', 'controller', 'processor', 'data subject' and 'supervisory authority' shall have the same meaning as in Directive 95/46/EC of the European Parliament and of the Council of 24 October 1995 on the protection of individuals with regard to the processing of personal data and on the free movement of such data ('hereinafter the Directive');

b) the 'data exporter' shall mean the controller who transfers the personal data;

c) the 'data importer' shall mean the controller who agrees to receive from the data exporter personal data for further processing in accordance with the terms of these clauses and who is not subject to a third country's system ensuring adequate protection.

Clause 2
Details of the transfer

The details of the transfer, and in particular the categories of personal data and the purposes for which they are transferred, are specified in Appendix 1 which forms an integral part of the Clauses.

Clause 3
Third-party beneficiary clause

The data subjects can enforce this Clause, Clause 4(b), (c) and (d), Clause 5(a), (b), (c) and (e), Clause 6(1) and (2), and Clauses 7, 9 and 11 as third-party beneficaries. The parties do not object to the data subjects being represented by an association or other bodies if they so wish and if permitted by national law.

Clause 4
Obligations of the data exporter

The data exporter agrees and warrants:

(a) that the processing, including the transfer itself, of the personal data by him has been and, up to the moment of the transfer, will continue to be carried out in accordance with the relevant provisions of the Member State in which the data exporter is established (and where applicable has been notified to the relevant authorities of that State) and does not violate the relevant provisions of that State;

(b) that if the transfer involves special categories of data the data subject has been informed or will be informed transfer that this data could be transmitted to a third country not providing adequate protection;

(c) to make available to the data subjects upon request a copy of the Clauses; and

(d) to respond in a reasonable time and to the extent reasonably possible to enquiries from the supervisory authority on the processing of the relevant personal data by the data importer and to any enquiries from the data subject concerning the processing of this personal data by the data importer.

Clause 5
Obligations of the data importer

The data importer agrees and warrants:

(a) that he has no reason to believe that the legislation applicable to him prevents him from fulfilling his obligations under the contract and that in the event of a change in that legislation which is likely to have a substantial adverse effect on the guarantees provided by the Clauses, he will notify the change to the data exporter and to the supervisory authority where the data exporter is established, in which case the data exporter is entitled to suspend the transfer of data and/or terminate the contract:

(b) to process the personal data in accordance with the mandatory data protection principles set out in Appendix 2; or, if explicitly agreed by the parties by ticking below and subject to compliance with the mandatory data protection principles set out in Appendix 3, to process in all other respects the data in accordance with:

– the relevant provisions of national law (attached to these Clauses) protecting the fundamental rights and freedoms of natural persons, and in particular their right to privacy with respect to the processing of personal data applicable to a data controller in the country in which the data exporter is established, or

– the relevant provisions of any Commission Decision under Article 25(6) of Directive 95/46/EC finding that a third country provides adequate protection in certain sectors of activity only, if the data importer is based in that third country and is not covered by those provisions, in so far as those provisions are of a nature which makes them applicable in the sector of the transfer;

(c) to deal promptly and properly with all reasonable inquiries from the data exporter or the data subject relating to his processing of the personal data subject to the transfer and to cooperate with the competent supervisory authority in the course of all its inquiries and abide by the advice of the supervisory authority with regard to the processing of the data transferred;

(d) at the request of the data exporter to submit its data processing facilities for audit which shall be carried out by the data exporter or an inspection body composed of independent members and in possession of the required professional qualifications, selected by the data exporter, where applicable, in agreement with the supervisory authority;

(e)   to make available to the data subject upon request a copy of the Clauses
      and indicate the office which handles complaints.

Clause 6
Liability

1. The parties agree that a data subject who has suffered damage as a result of
   any violation of the provisions referred to in Clause 3 is entitled to receive
   compensation from the parties for the damage suffered. The parties agree
   that they may be exempted from this liability only if they prove that
   neither of them is responsible for the violation of those provisions.

2. The data exporter and the data importer agree that they will be jointly and
   severally liable for damage to the data subject resulting from any violation
   referred to in paragraph 1. In the event of such a violation, the data
   exporter or the data importer or both.

3. The parties agree that if one party is held liable for a violation referred to in
   paragraph 1 by the other party, the latter will, to the extent to which it is
   liable, indemnify the first party for any cost, charge, damages, expenses or
   loss it has incurred. (*).

Clause 7
Mediation and jurisdiction

1. The parties agree that if there is a dispute between a data subject and either
   party which is not amicably resolved and the data subject invokes the
   third-party beneficiary provision in clause 3, they accept the decision of the
   data subject:

(a)   to refer the dispute to mediation by an independent person or, where
      applicable, by the supervisory authority;

(b)   to refer the dispute to the courts in the Member State in which the data
      exporter is established.

2. The parties agree that by agreement between a data subject and the relevant
   party a dispute can be referred to an arbitration body, if that party is
   established in a country which has ratified the New York convention on
   enforcement of arbitration awards.

3. The parties agree that paragraphs 1 and 2 apply without prejudice to the
   data subject's substantive or procedural rights to seek remedies in
   accordance with other provisions of national or international law.

Clause 8
Cooperation with supervisory authorities

The parties agree to deposit a copy of this contract with the supervisory
authority if it so requests or if such deposit is required under national law.

Clause 9
Termination of the Clauses

The parties agree that the termination of the Clauses at any time, in any circumstances and for whatever reason does not exempt them from the obligations and/or conditions under the Clauses as regards the processing of the data transferred.

Clause 10
Governing Law

The Clauses shall be governed by the law of the Member State in which the Data Exporter is established, namely...

....

Clause 11
Variation of the contract

The parties undertake not to vary or modify the terms of the clauses.
On behalf of the data exporter:
Name (written out in full):...
Position:..
Address:...
Other information necessary in order for the contract to be binding (if any):

....

....

....
(signature)

(stamp of organisation)

On behalf of the data importer:
Name (written out in full):...
Position:..
Address:...
Other information necessary in order for the contract to be binding (if any):

....

....

....
(signature)

(stamp of organisation)

Appendix 1
to the standard contractual clauses

This Appendix forms part of the Clauses and must be completed and signed by the parties.

(The Member States may complete or specify, according to their national procedures, any additional necessary information to be contained in this Appendix).

Data exporter

The data exporter is (please specify briefly your activities relevant to the transfer):

....

....

....

Data importer
The data importer is (please specify briefly your activities relevant to the transfer):

....

....

....

Data subjects
The personal data transferred concern the following categories of data subjects (please specify):

....

....

....

Purposes of the transfer
The transfer is necessary for the following purposes (please specify):

....

....

....

Categories of data
The personal data transferred fall within the following categories of data (please specify):

....

....

....

Sensitive data (if appropriate)
The personal data transferred fall within the following categories of sensitive data (please specify):

....

....

....

Recipients
The personal data transferred may be disclosed only to the following recipients or categories of recipients (please specify):

....

....

....

Storage limit
The personal data transferred may be stored for no more than (please indicate)
.... (months/years)

Data exporter	Data importer
Name:..	Name:......................................
....	....
(Authorised signature)	(Authorised signature)

Appendix 2
to the standard contractual clauses

Mandatory data protection principles referred to in the first paragraph of Clause 5(b)

These data protection principles should be read and interpreted in the light of the provisions (principles and relevant exceptions) of Directive 95/46/EC.

They shall apply subject to the mandatory requirements of the national legislation applicable to the data importer which do not go beyond what is necessary in a democratic society on the basis of one of the interests listed in Article 13(1) of Directive 95/46/EC, that is, if they constitute a necessary measure to safeguard national security, defence, public security, the prevention, investigation, detection and prosecution of criminal offences or of breaches of ethics for the regulated professions, an important economic or financial interest of the State or the protection of the data subject or the rights and freedoms of others.

1. Purpose limitation: data must be processed and subsequently used or further communicated only for the specific purposes in Appendix I to the Clauses. Data must not be kept longer than necessary for the purposes for which they are transferred.

2. Data quality and proportionality: data must be accurate and, where necessary, kept up to date. The data must be adequate, relevant and not excessive in relation to the purposes for which they are transferred and further processed.

3. Transparency: data subjects must be provided with information as to the purposes of the processing and the identity of the data controller in the third country; and other information insofar as this is necessary to ensure fair processing, unless such information has already been given by the data exporter.

4. Security and confidentiality: technical and organisational security measures must be taken by the data controller that are appropriate to the risks, such as unauthorised access, presented by the processing. Any person acting under the authority of the data controller, including a processor, must not process the data except on instructions from the controller.

5. Rights of access, rectification, erasure and blocking of data: as provided for in Article 12 of Directive 95/46/EC, the data subject must have a right of access to all data relating to him that are processed and, as appropriate, the right to the rectification, erasure or blocking of data the processing of which does not comply with the principles set out in this Appendix, in particular because the data are incomplete or inaccurate. He should also be able to object to the processing of the data relating to him on compelling legitimate grounds relating to his particular situation.

6. Restrictions on onwards transfers: further transfers of personal data from the data importer to another controller established in a third country not providing adequate protection or not covered by a decision adopted by the Commission pursuant to Article 25(6) of Directive 95/46/EC (onward transfer) may take place only if either:

(a) data subjects have, in the case of special categories of data, given their unambiguous consent to the onward transfer or, in other cases, have been given the opportunity to object.

The minimum information to be provided to data subjects must contain in a language understandable to them:

–   the purposes of the onward transfer,

–   the identification of the data exporter established in the Community,

–   the categories of further recipients of the data and the countries of destination, and

–   an explanation that, after the onward transfer, the data may be processed by a controller established in a country where there is not an adequate level of protection of the privacy of individuals; or

(b) the data exporter and the data importer agree to the adherence to the Clauses of another controller which thereby becomes a party to the

Clauses and assumes the same obligations as the data importer.

7. Special categories of data: where data revealing racial or ethnic origin, political opinions, religious or philosophical beliefs or trade union memberships and data concerning health or sex life and data relating to offences, criminal convictions or security measures are processed, additional safeguards should be in place within the meaning of Directive 95/46/EC, in particular, appropriate security measures such as strong encryption for transmission or such as keeping a record of access to sensitive data.

8. Direct marketing: where data are processed for the purposes of direct marketing, effective procedures should exist allowing the data subject at any time to 'opt-out' from having his data used for such purposes.

9. Automated individual decisions: data subjects are entitled not to be subject to a decision which is based soley on automated processing of data, unless other measures are taken to safeguard the individual's legitimate interests as provided for in Article 15(2) of Directive 95/46/EC. Where the purpose of the transfer is the taking of an automated decision as referred to in Article 15 of Directive 95/46/EC, which produces legal effects concerning the individual or significantly affects him and which is based solely on automated processing of data intended to evaluate certain personal aspects relating to him, such as his performance at work, creditworthiness, reliability, conduct, etc., the individual should have the right to know the reasoning for this decision.

Appendix 3
to the standard contractual clauses
Mandatory data protection principles referred to in the second paragraph of Clause 5(b)

1. Purpose limitation: data must be processed and subsequently used or further communicated only for the specific purposes in Appendix 1 to the Clauses. Data must not be kept longer than necessary for the purposes for which they are transferred.

2. Rights of access, rectification, erasure and blocking of data: as provided for in Article 12 of Directive 95/46/EC, the data subject must have a right of access to all data relating to him that are processed and, as appropriate, the right to the rectification, erasure or blocking of data the processing of which does not comply with the principles set out in this Appendix, in particular because the data is incomplete or inaccurate. He should also be able to object to the processing of the data relating to him on compelling legitimate grounds relating to his particular situation.

3. Restrictions on onward transfers: further transfers of personal data from the data importer to another controller established in a third country not providing adequate protection or not covered by a decision adopted by the

Commission pursuant to Article 25(6) of Directive 95/46/EC (onward transfer) may take place only if either:

(a) data subjects have, in the case of special categories of data, given their unambiguous consent to the onward transfer, or, in other cases, have been given the opportunity to object.

The minimum information to be provided to data subjects must contain in a language understandable to them:

−   the purposes of the onward transfer,

−   the identification of the data exporter established in the Community,

−   the categories of further recipients of the data and the countries of destination, and

−   an explanation that, after the onward transfer, the data may be processed by a controller established in a country where there is not an adequate level of protection of the privacy of individuals; or

(b) the data exporter and the data importer agree to the adherence to the Clauses of another controller which thereby becomes a party to the Clauses and assumes the same obligations as the data importer.

· Standard Clauses Decision (2) ·

Draft Commission Decision on Standard Contractual Clauses under Article 26(4) of Directive 95/46/EC for the transfer of personal data to processors established in third countries

THE COMMISSION OF THE EUROPEAN COMMUNITIES,

Having regard to the Treaty establishing the European Community,

Having regard to Directive 95/46/EC of the European Parliament and of the Council of 24 October 1995 on the protection of individuals with regard to the processing of personal data and on the free movement of such data,[1] and in particular Article 26(4) thereof,

Whereas:

(1) Pursuant to Directive 95/46/EC Member States are required to provide that a transfer of personal data to a third country may only take place if the third country in question ensures an adequate level of data protection and the Member States' laws, which comply with the other provisions of the Directive, are respected prior to the transfer.

(2) However, Article 26(2) of Directive 95/46/EC provides that Member States may authorise, subject to certain safeguards, a transfer or a set of transfers of personal data to third countries which do not ensure an adequate level of protection. Such safeguards may in particular result from appropriate contractual clauses.

(3) Pursuant to Directive 95/46/EC the level of data protection should be assessed in the light of all the circumstances surrounding the data transfer operation or set of data transfer operations; the Working Party[2] on the Protection of Individuals with regard to the Processing of Personal Data

---

1 OJ 1995 L281/31.
2 The web address of the Working Party is:
   http://www.europa.eu.int/comm/internal_market/en/media/dataprot/wpdocs/index.htm.

established under that Directive has issued guidelines to aid with the assessment.[3]

(4)   These standard contractual clauses are only one of several possibilities under Directive 95/46/EC for lawfully transferring personal data to a third country together with Articles 25, 26(1) and (2), and will make it much easier for organisations to transfer personal data to third countries by incorporating the standard contractual clauses in a contract. The standard contractual clauses relate only to data protection. The Data Exporter and the Data Importer are free to include any other clauses on business related issues which they consider as being pertinent for the contract as long as they do not contradict the standard contractual clauses.

(5)   This Decision should be without prejudice to national authorisations Member States may grant in accordance with national provisions implementing Article 26(2) of Directive 95/46/EC. This Decision only has the effect of requiring the Member States not to refuse to recognise as providing adequate safeguards the contractual clauses described in it and does not therefore have any effect on other contractual clauses.

(6)   The scope of this Decision is limited to establishing that the clauses in the Annex may be used by a controller established in the Community in order to adduce sufficient safeguards for a transfer to a processor established in a third country within the meaning of Article 26(2) of Directive 95/46/EC.

(7)   Supervisory Authorities play a key role in this contractual mechanism in ensuring that personal data are adequately protected after the transfer. In specific circumstances, the Supervisory Authorities of the Member States retain the power to prohibit or suspend a data transfer or a set of transfers based on the standard contractual clauses in those exceptional cases where it is established that a transfer on contractual basis is likely to have a substantial adverse effect on the guarantees providing adequate protection to the data subject.

(8)   The Commission may also consider in the future whether standard contractual clauses for the transfer of personal data to processors established in third countries not offering an adequate level of data

---

3   Opinion No ?/2001 WP 4 (5020/97) "First orientations on Transfers of Personal Data to Third Countries – Possible Ways Forward in Assessing Adequacyî, a discussion document adopted by the Working Party on 26 June 1997; WP 7 (5057/97) Working document: "Judging industry self-regulation: when does it make a meaningful contribution to the level of data protection in a third country?", adopted by the Working Party on 14 January 1998; WP 9 (5005/98) Working document: "Preliminary views on the use of contractual provisions in the context of transfers of personal data to third countries", adopted by the Working Party on 22 April 1998; WP 12: Transfers of personal data to third countries: Applying Articles 25 and 26 of the EU data protection directive, adopted by the Working Party on 24 July 1998, available in the web site "europa.eu.int/comm/internal_market/en/media.dataprot/wpdocs/wp12/en" hosted by the European Commission;.

protection, submitted by business organisations or other interested parties, offer adequate safeguards in accordance with Article 26(2) of Directive 95/46/EC.

(9) A disclosure of personal data to a processor established outside the Community is protected under Chapter IV of Directive 95/46/EC. This Decision does not cover the transfer of personal data by controllers established in the Community to controllers established outside the Community which are not covered by a system recognised as offering an adequate level of data protection by the European Commission.

(10) The standard contractual clauses need to provide for the security measures that a processor established in a third country not providing adequate protection must apply ensuring a level of security appropriate to the risks represented by the processing and the nature of the data to be protected. Parties should provide in the contract those technical and organisational measures which, having regard to the state of the art and the cost of their implementation, are necessary in order to protect personal data against accidental or unlawful destruction or accidental loss, alteration, unauthorised disclosure or access or any other unlawful forms of processing. In addition to that, parties must provide for supplementary measures necessary to protect the personal data against the specific risks posed to the security of the data by transferring it to third countries for further processing after the transfer.

(11) In order to facilitate data flows from the Community, it is desirable that processors providing data processing services to several data controllers in the Community are allowed to put in place the same security measures irrespective of the Member State from which the data transfer originates, in particular in those cases where the Data Importer receives data for further processing from different establishments of the Data Exporter in the Community.

(12) It is appropriate to lay down the minimum information that the parties must specify in the contract dealing with the transfer. Member States should retain the power to particularise the information the parties are required to provide. The operation of this Decision should be reviewed in the light of the experience.

(13) The standard contractual clauses should be enforceable not only by the organisations which are parties to the contract, but also by the Data Subjects, in particular, where the Data Subjects suffer damage as a consequent of a breach of the contract.

(14) The Data Importer should process the transferred personal data only on behalf of the Data Exporter and in accordance with his instructions and the obligations contained in the clauses.

(15) The Data Subject is entitled to take actin and receive compensation from the Data Exporter who is the data controller of the personal data

transferred. Exceptionally, the Data Subject may also be entitled to take action and receive compensation from the Data Importer in those cases where a competent authority has determined that the Data Exporter cannot honour his responsibilities because he has disappeared, filed for bankruptcy or for whatever reasons and the Data Importer has violated his obligations under the contract.

(16) In the event of a dispute between the Data Subject, invoking the third party beneficiary and the Data Importer, which is not amicably resolved, the Data Importer agrees to provide the Data Subject with the choice between mediation, arbitration or litigation. The extent to which the Data Subject will have an effective choice will depend on the availability of reliable and recognised systems of mediation and arbitration. Mediation by the Supervisory Authorities of a Member State should be an option where they provide such a service.

(17) The governing law of the contract shall be the law of the Member State where the Data Exporter is established enabling a third party beneficiary to enforce a contract. Data Subjects should be allowed to be represented by associations or other bodies if they so wish and if authorised by national law.

(18) The Working Party on the Protection of Individuals with regard to the processing of Personal Data established under Article 29 of Directive 95/46/EC has delivered an Opinion on the level of protection provided under the standard contractual clauses annexed to this Decision, which has been taken into account in the preparation of the current decision.[4]

(19) The measures provided for in this Decision are in accordance with the opinion of the Committee established under Article 31 of Directive 95/46/EC.

HAS ADOPTED THIS DECISION:

Article 1

The standard contractual clauses set out in the Annex are considered as offering adequate safeguards with respect to the protection of the privacy and fundamental rights and freedoms of individuals and as regards the exercise of the corresponding rights as required by Article 26(2) of Directive 95/46/EC.

Article 2

This Decision concerns only the adequacy of protection provided by the standard contractual clauses for the transfer of personal data set out in the Annex. It does not affect the application of other national provisions

---

4 Opinion No ?/2001 adopted by the Working Party on 2001 (DG MARKET ...), available in the web site "Europa" hosted by the European Commission.

implementing Directive 95/46/EC that pertain to the processing of personal data within the Member States.

This Decision shall apply to the transfer of personal data by controllers established in the Community to recipients established outside the territory of the Community who act only as processors.

Article 3

1.For the purposes of this Decision:

(a) the definitions in Directive 95/46/EC shall apply;

(b) **"special categories of data"** means the data referred to in Article 8 of that Directive;

(c) **"Supervisory Authority"** means the Authority referred to in Article 28 of that Directive;

(d) **"Data Exporter"** means the Controller who transfers the Personal Data;

(e) **"Data Importer"** means the Processor who agrees to receive from the Data Exporter personal data intended for processing on the Data Exporterís behalf after the transfer in accordance with his instructions and the terms of this Decision and who is not subject to a third countryís system ensuring adequate protection;

(f) **"Applicable Data Protection Law"** means the legislation protecting the fundamental rights and freedoms of natural persons and, in particular, their right to privacy with respect to the processing of personal data applicable to a Data Controller in the Member State in which the Data Exporter is established.

Article 4

1. Without prejudice to their powers to take action to ensure compliance with national provisions adopted pursuant to Chapters II, III, V and VI of Directive 95/46/EC, the competent authorities in the Member States may exercise their existing powers to prohibit or suspend data flows third countries in order to protect individuals with regard to the processing of their personal data in cases where:

(a) it is established that the law to which the Data Importer is subject imposes upon him requirements to derogate from the relevant data protection rules which go beyond the restrictions necessary in a democratic society as provided for in Article 13 of Directive 95/46/EC where those requirements are likely to have a substantial adverse effect on the guarantees provided by the national legislation and the standard contractual clauses, or

(b) a competent authority has established that the Data Importer has not respected the contractual clauses, or

(c) there is a substantial likelihood that the standard contractual clauses in the annex are not being or will not be complied with and the continuing transfer would create an imminent risk of grave harm to the Data Subjects.

2. The prohibition or suspension shall be lifted as soon as the reasons for the suspension or prohibition no longer exist.

3. When Member States adopt measures pursuant to paragraphs 1 and 2, they shall inform the Commission which will forward the information to the other Member States.

Article 5

The Commission shall evaluate the operation of the present Decision on the basis of available information three years after its notification to the Member States. It shall submit a report on the findings to the Committee established under Article 31 of Directive 95/46/EC. It shall include any evidence that would affect the evaluation concerning the adequacy of the standard contractual clauses in the Annex and any evidence that this Decision is being applied in a discriminatory way.

Article 6

This Decision shall apply from (fixed date, ninety days from its notification to Member States).

Article 7

This Decision is addressed to the Member States.

Done at Brussels [........].

Annex
Standard contractual clauses

For the purposes of Article 26(2) of Directive 95/46/EC for the transfer of personal data to processors established in third countries which do not ensure an adequate level of data protection

Name of the data exporting organisation..
address..
tel:.................................... *fax:*............................... *e-mail:*....................................
Other information needed to identify the organisation..
("the Data Exporter")
and
Name of the data importing organisation...
address..
tel:.................................... *fax:*............................... *e-mail:*....................................
Other information needed to identify the organisation..
("the Data Importer")

HAVE AGREED on the following contractual clauses ("the Clauses") in order to adduce adequate safeguards with respect to the protection of privacy and fundamental rights and freedoms of individuals for the transfer by the Data Exporter to the Data Importer of the personal data specified in the Appendix.

The Parties agree and warrant that the data transfer is solely for the provision of data processing services by the Data Importer to the Data Exporter

Clause 1
Definitions

For the purposes of the Clauses:

(a) "**personal data**", "**special categories of data**", "**process/processing**", "**controller**", "**processor**", "**Data Subject**", "**Supervisory Authority**" and "**technical and organisational measures**" shall have the same meaning as in Directive 95/46/EC of 24 October 1995 on the protection of individuals with regard to the processing of personal data and on the free movement of such data ("the Directive");

(b) "**the Data Exporter**", who has been identified above, shall mean the Controller who transfers the Personal Data;

(c) "**the Data Importer**" who has been identified above, shall mean the processor who agrees to receive from the Data Exporter personal data intended for processing on his behalf after the transfer in accordance with his instructions and the terms of these Clauses and who is not subject to a third country's system ensuring adequate protection;

(d) "**the Applicable Data Protection Law**" shall mean the legislation protecting the fundamental rights and freedoms of natural persons and, in particular, their right to privacy with respect to the processing of personal data applicable to a Data Controller in the Member State in which the Data Exporter is established.

Clause 2
Details of the transfer

The details of the transfer, and in particular the categories of personal data and the purposes for which they are transferred, are specified in the Appendix 1 which forms an integral part of these Clauses.

Clause 3
Third party beneficiary clause

The Data Subjects can enforce this Clause and Clauses 4(b), (c), (d), (e), (f), (g) and (h), 5(a), (b), (c), (d), (f) and (h), 6(1), (2), 7, 8(2) and (3), 9 and 11 as third party beneficiaries. The parties do not object to the data subjects being represented by an association or other bodies if they so wish and if permitted by national law.

Clause 4
Obligations of the Data Exporter

The Data Exporter agrees and warrants:

(a that the processing including the transfer itself of the personal data by him has been and will continue to be carried out in accordance with all the requirements and relevant provisions of the applicable data protection law and where applicable has been notified to the relevant Authorities of that State;

(b) that he has instructed the Data Importer to process the personal data transferred only on his behalf and in accordance with the applicable data protection law and these clauses and that, if any, supplementary instructions such as those contained in a separate contract for the provisions of Data Processing Services or any other instructions given to the Data Importer, do not contradict these clauses, in

particular, the information contained in the Appendix annexed to this contract;
(c) that the Data Importer provides sufficient guarantees in respect of the technical security measures and organisational security measures specified in Annex 2 to this contract and that the Data Exporter will ensure compliance with these measures;
(d) that, if the transfer involves special categories of Data[5], the Data Subject has been informed or will be informed before the transfer that his data could be transmitted to a third country not providing adequate protection;
(e) to inform the Data Importer, where necessary and at a reasonable time, of the inquiries made by Data Subjects or the Supervisory Authority concerning processing activities carried out by him;
(f) to inform the Data Importer about those personal data that should be corrected, updated, deleted, blocked or whose use by determined purposes has been banned or restricted;
(g) to make available to the Data Subjects upon request a copy of these Clauses.[6]

Clause 5
Obligations of the Data Importer

The Data Importer agrees and warrants:
(a) to process the Personal Data only on behalf of the Data Exporter and in accordance with his instructions and these clauses and that in the event he could not provide such compliance for whatever reasons, he agrees to inform the Data Exporter of that, in which case the Data Exporter is entitled to suspend the transfer of data and/or terminate the contract;
(b) that he has no reason to believe that the legislation applicable to him prevents him from fulfilling the instructions received from the Data Exporter and his obligations under the contract and that in the event a change in this legislation which is likely to have a substantial adverse effect on the guarantees provided by the Clauses, he will notify the change to the Data Exporter and to the Supervisory Authority where the Data Exporter is established, in which case the Data Exporter is entitled to suspend the transfer of data and/or terminate the contract;
(c) that he shall use the personal data transferred solely for the provision of the data processing services on behalf of the Data Exporter and that he will not disclose the personal data transferred to third parties unless the Data Exporter has given prior written authorisation and the third party has entered into the same obligations than the Data Importer; that authorisation will be incorporated and form an integral part of this contract;
(d) that he shall immediately notify the Data Exporter of any request of disclosure of the personal data transferred from a public body that could eventually force him to disclose the data, unless such notification is forbidden by law as well as any disclosure or accidental or unauthorised access made by an employee, subcontractor or any other identified person as well as the known facts as regards the above mentioned disclosure or use;
(e) that he shall immediately notify to the Data Exporter any requests received directly from the data subjects acknowledging that he is not authorised to respond unless the Data Exporter has explicitly authorised that action or a competent authority has declared that the Data Exporter has disappeared or for whatever reason is unable to respond to requests from the data subjects;

---

5 Data revealing racial or ethnic origin, political opinions, religious or philosophical beliefs or trade union memberships and data concerning health or sex life and data relating to offences, criminal convictions or security measures.
6 Parties may decide to provide data subjects with the annexed security meaures or just a summary of them.

(f)　that he has implemented (please tick below the appropriate):

☐ (the technical and organisational measures of the national law of the Member State where the Data Exporter is established and appropriate supplementary security measures aimed at protecting personal data against the specific risks presented by the processing being carried out in a third country by the Data Importer, or
☐ (appropriate technical and organisational measures to protect personal data against accidental or unlawful destruction or accidental loss, alteration, unauthorised disclosure or access, in particular where the processing involves the transmission of data over a network, and against all other unlawful forms of processing, and appropriate supplementary measures aimed at protecting personal data against the specific risks presented by the processing being carried out in a third country by the Data Importer, or
☐ the appropriate technical and organisational measures set out in a system found as providing adequate protection in certain sectors of activity only by a Commission Decision under Article 25(6) of Directive 95/46/EC, provided that the Data Importer is based in that third country and not covered by those provisions and in so far as those provisions are of a nature which makes them applicable in the sector of the transfer,

which ensure a level of security appropriate to the risks presented by the processing and the nature of the data to be protected having regard to the state of the art and the cost of their implementation and are specified in Appendix 2 to this contract.

The relevant texts/documents are attached to these Clauses and form part of this contract.

(g)

(h)　to deal promptly and properly with all inquiries from the Data Exporter relating to processing of the Personal Data subject to the transfer and to co-operate with the competent Supervisory Authority in the course of all its inquiries and abide by the advice of the Supervisory Authority with regard to the processing of the data transferred;
(i)　at the request of the Data Exporter to submit its data processing facilities for audit which shall be carried out by the Data Exporter or an inspection body composed of independent members and in possession of the required professional qualifications, selected by the Data Exporter, where applicable, in agreement with the Supervisory Authority;
(j)　to make available to the Data Subjects upon request a copy of these Clauses in those cases where the Data Subject is unable to obtain a copy from the Data Exporter and indicate the Data Exporterís office which handles complaints.

Clause 6
Liability

1.　The Parties agree that a Data Subject who has suffered damage as a result of any violation of the clauses covered by Clause 3, committed by the Data Exporter, or the Data Importer, is entitled to receive compensation from the Data Exporter for the damage suffered.
2.　The Parties agree that the Data Importer can also be considered liable for damages caused to the Data Subjects in those cases where the Data Exporter has disappeared, filed for bankruptcy or for any other reasons a competent authority of the Data Exporterís country has determined that the Data Exporter cannot face his responsibilities and the Data Importer has violated some of his obligations under this contact.

Clause 7
Mediation and jurisdiction

1. The Data Importer agrees that if there is a dispute between a Data Subject and him as provided for in Clause 6(2), which is not amicably resolved and the Data Subject invokes the third party beneficiary provision in Clause 3, the Data Importer accepts the decision of the Data Subject:

(a) to refer the dispute to mediation, by an independent person or, where applicable, by the Supervisory Authority;

(b) to refer the dispute to the courts in the Member State where the Data Exporter is established.

2. The Data Importer agrees that by agreement with the Data Subject, the resolution of a specific dispute can be referred to an arbitration body if the Data Importer is established in a county which has ratified the New York Convention on enforcement of arbitration awards.

3. The Parties agree that the available above options will not prejudice the Data Subjectís substantive or procedural rights to seek remedies in accordance with other provisions of national or international law.

Clause 8
Co-operation with Supervisory Authorities

1. The Parties agree to deposit a copy of this contract with the Supervisory Authority if it so requests or if such deposit is required under national law.

2. The Parties agree that the Supervisory Authority has the right to audit the Data Importer with the same extension and conditions the Authority would have to audit the Data Exporter under national law.

3. The Parties agree that they will inform the Supervisory Authority of any loss, corruption or substantial bad use of the personal data transferred that cannot be rectified in a reasonable time without creating prejudice to the data subjects.

Clause 9
Governing law

The Clauses shall be governed by the law of the Member State where the Data Exporter is established, namely.............................

Clause 10
Variation of the contract

The Parties undertake not to vary or modify the terms of the Clauses.

Clause 11
Obligation after the termination of the Clauses

1. The Parties agree that at the termination of the provision of Data Processing Services, at the choice of the Data Exporter, the Data Importer shall return all personal data transferred and its copies to the Data Exporter or shall destroy all personal data and certify to the Data Exporter that he did so, unless legislation imposed upon the Data Importer prevents him from the devolution or destruction of whole or part of the personal data transferred. In that case, the Data Importer warrants that he shall guarantee the confidentiality of the personal data transferred and shall not actively process the personal data transferred anymore.

2. The Data Importer warrants that upon request of the Data Exporter and/or of the Supervisory Authority, he shall submit his data processing facilities for audit of the above mentioned measures.

On behalf of the Data Exporter:

Name (written out in full:...

Position:...

Address:..

Other information necessary in order for the contract to be binding (if any):

Signature..
(stamp of organisation)

On behalf of the Data Exporter:

Name (written out in full:)...

Position:...

Address:..

Other information necessary in order for the contract to be binding (if any):

Signature..
(stamp of organisation)

On behalf of the Data Importer:

Name (written out in full:..

Position:...

Address:..

Other information necessary in order for the contract to be binding (if any):

Signature..
(stamp of organisation)

APPENDIX 1 to the Standard Contractual Clauses

This appendix forms part of the Clauses and must be completed and subscribed by the Parties

(*The Member States may complete or specify, according to their national procedures, any additional necessary information to be contained in this Appendix)

Data Exporter

The Data Exporter is (please specify briefly your activities relevant to the transfer):

....

Data Importer

The Data Importer is (please specify briefly your activities relevant to the transfer):

....

Data Subjects

The Personal Data transferred concern the following categories of Data Subjects (please specify):

....

Categories of data

The Personal Data transferred concern the following categories of data (please specify):

....

Sensitive Data (if appropriate)

The Personal Data transferred concern the following categories of sensitive data (please specify):

....

Processing Operations

The Personal Data transferred concern the following categories of sensitive data (please specify):

....

DATA EXPORTER   DATA IMPORTER

Name:..   ....

Authorised
Signature....................................   ....

APPENDIX 2 to the Standard Contractual Clauses

Description of the technical and organisational measures implemented by the Data Importer in accordance with Clause 5(f), first, second or third indent (or document/legislation attached):

....

Description of the supplementary technical and organisational measures implemented by the Data Importer aimed at protecting personal data against the specific risks presented by the processing being carried out in a third country (or document attached):

· Index ·

Advanced Research Project Agency (ARPA),
   work associated, with, 1
Advertising, 119 *et seq*
   advertising codes, application of, 120, 135
   data protection, relating to, 119
   differing standards, dealing with, 121
   jurisdictional issues, connected with, 47
   legal implications, involving, 119
   telecommunications, used for, 123
Advertising Standards Agency (ASA), role of, 120
ARPANET,
   development of, 1,2
Authors,
   copyright protection, for, 137, 138
   moral rights, of, 141, 142, 157

Banks. *See also* **Electronic money institutions, Financial services**
   EU law, relating to, 57, 60, 65
   smartcards, use of, 56
Banner ad keying,
   practice, relating to, 158, 163
Billing data,
   regulations affecting, 127
Biometric signatures,
   use of, 28
Brussels Convention,
   effect of, 38, 40, 43
Brussels Regulation,
   effect of, 38, 40, 42
Bulletin boards,
   monitoring, need for, 25
Business to business,
   contracts,
      jurisdiction governing, 41, 42
      VAT position, 167
Business to consumer,
   contracts,
      jurisdiction governing, 42, 43, 47

Business to consumer, *cont.*
      VAT position, 167

CCTLD,
   jurisdiction, issues involving, 75
   meaning of, 74
Chat rooms,
   monitoring, need for, 25
Choice of law. *See also* **Jurisdiction**
   asserting, practical steps towards, 47, 51
   jurisdictional clauses, use of, 37, 38, 40, 46, 47
Click wrap agreements,
   effect of, 11-13
Companies. *See also* **Multinational companies**
   country of origin, importance of, 65, 164
   domicile, attributed to, 40
   employees, benefits for, 170
   enterprise management incentives, 173, 174
   initial public offering, managing, 164, 165
   offshore, setting up, 166, 169
   "permanent establishment",
      ISP, whether, 165
      meaning of, 165, 169
      server location, 165, 169
      website, whether, 165
   setting up, issues involving, 164
   share option schemes, in, 171-173
   subsidiaries,
      development of, 164
      offshore, setting up, 166, 169
      transactions between, 166
   tax considerations, for, 164-166
Competition law,
   intellectual property, concerned with, 150
Computer systems,
   supply of, 14

Confidential information,
    breach of confidence, proof of, 149
    confidentiality agreements, effect
      of, 148, 149
    disclosure of, 148
    protection of, 148
Consent,
    data protection, issues involving,
      99-101, 110, 113, 118, 122, 127
Consumer protection,
    contract terms, covering, 16, 17,
      66, 67
    customers, attention paid to, 19
    distance selling, issues involving,
      17
    information supplied, requirements
      as to, 19, 20, 66
    mandatory laws, assisting, 45
    representational actions, directed
      towards, 47
    supply of goods, rules governing,
      16, 17
    unfair terms, provisions covering,
      14, 16, 17
Contract law. *See also* **Contract terms,
Online contracts**
    breach of contract, where, 17
    cancellation, issues concerning, 20-
      23
    consideration, existence of, 10
    exclusion clauses, effect of, 14
    governing law, 4, 38, 51
    invitation to treat, 8, 9
    jurisdictional clauses,
      absence of, 41-43
      effect of, 37, 38, 40, 46, 51
    offer and acceptance, rules on, 8, 9
    liability, exclusion of, 14, 17
    principles applied, 4
    standard terms, use of, 6, 10, 26
    unfair terms, use of, 17
    writing, requirement as to, 6, 8
Contract terms. *See also* **Standard terms**
    consumer protection, provided by,
      16
    exclusion clauses, use of, 14, 17
    implied terms, use of, 10, 11, 16
    legislation, governing, 16
    reasonable, nature of, 14
    unfair terms, effect of, 14, 16, 17
Copyright 136 *et seq. See also* **Intellectual
property, Trade mark**
    databases, position as to, 140

Copyright, *cont.*
    duration of, 138
    employee, created by, 138
    EU Directive on, 239 *et seq*
    exploitation of 137, 138
    infringement, nature of, 139, 156,
      157
    ownership, extent of, 138
    legislative provisions, covering,
      137, 138
    moral rights, protection of, 141,
      142, 157
    protection, afforded by, 137
    website content, position on, 139,
      140
Country of origin,
    rules, relating to, 64, 65
Credit card,
    administration fees, 53
    fraud, associated with, 52, 53, 56, 62
    payments by, 28, 52, 53
    risks, associated with, 53
Cryptography,
    EU law, relating to, 34, 36
    loss, recovery of, 34, 36
    service providers,
      certification facilities, 33
      liability of, 33, 34
      provisions covering, 33
      registration facilities, 33
Customs duties,
    chargeable, where, 168, 169
Cyber squatting,
    case decisions, on, 79, 80
    regulations, dealing with, 78

Data controllers. *See also* **Data
processing, Data protection**
    fees, charged by, 103
    information, required from, 101,
      102
    meaning, given to, 94
    notification procedures, involving,
      97
    personal data, handled by, 97, 98
Data processing. *See also* **Data
controllers, Data protection**
    administration of justice,
      involving, 99
    consent, requirements as to, 99-
      101, 110, 113, 118, 122, 127
    contractual relations, covering, 99,
      105, 110, 111

Data processing, *cont.*
  data processors, provisions
    covering, 95, 96, 106, 107
  fair and lawful, 98, 99, 101
  legal obligations, compliance with,
    99, 106, 107
  legitimate interest, pursuing, 99,
    100, 105, 122
  processing, meaning given to, 94
Data protection, 89 *et seq. See also* **Data
controllers, Data processing, Personal
data**
  access to data, 103, 104, 118
  advertising, affected by, 119
  automated decision-making,
    where, 105
  data, meaning of, 90, 91
  data subject,
    compensation, entitlement
      to, 106
    damage, caused to, 105, 106
    distress, caused to, 105, 106
    financial assessment of, 105
    meaning of, 96
    rights of, 103, 104, 118
  destruction of data, 106
  direct marketing, affected by, 122,
    123
  enforcement procedures, 112, 113
  EU personal data Decision, 260 *et
    seq*
  identity, disclosure of, 104
  Information Commissioner, role of,
    17, 90
  legislation, relating to, 5, 89, 90, 97
  mailing lists, purchase of, 102
  non-automated data, position
    regarding, 91
    principles governing, 97, 98,
      118
  notification,
    data controllers, affecting,
      97
    notification fees, 97
    procedures, for, 97
    processing operations,
      exempt from, 97
    requirements for, 96, 118
  privacy policy, use of, 113, 114,
    118
  rectification of data, 106
  relevant filing systems, for, 90-92
  sensitive data, involving, 96

Data protection, *cont.*
  vital interests, protection of, 99,
    100, 111
  website, information held on, 91
Databases,
  copyright, position regarding, 140
  EU law, applied to, 141
  legislative provisions, affecting,
    141
  "maker", importance attached to,
    141
  meaning, attributed to, 140
Defamation,
  liability for, 25, 69
Digital certificates,
  use of, 30-32
Digital signatures,
  legal position, regarding, 31, 32
  use of, 30
Direct marketing, 119 *et seq*
  automated calling systems, 124
  data protection, affecting, 119,
    122, 129, 130
  e-mail, by means of, 121, 128, 130
  faxes, use of, 125, 126
  jurisdictional issues, involving, 47
  legislative controls, over, 121
  mail, use of, 126
  personal data, removal of, 122, 123
  telecommunications, used for, 123
  unsolicited communications,
    where, 124, 125
Direct Marketing Association,
  role of, 125, 129, 133
Director General of Fair Trading,
  powers of, 17, 120
Dispute resolution,
  domain names, over, 75-77, 85, 87
  EU law, dealing with, 71, 72
Dispute settlement,
  jurisdiction, issues concerned with,
    37
Distance communication,
  definition of, 17
Distance selling,
  cancellation of contract, 20, 21, 67
  consumer protection, issues
    involving, 17, 19, 20
  credit agreements, involving, 23
  definition of, 17
  exempt contracts, categories of, 18
  information supplied, requirements
    as to, 19, 20, 66

Distance selling, *cont.*
    regulations, affecting, 17, 18, 26, 66
    withdrawal, right of, 20, 21, 67
Domain name disputes,
    bad faith, registration in, 83, 85, 88
    brand names, protection of, 80
    commercial gain, registration for, 81
    complaints procedures, involving, 77
    dispute resolution, procedures for, 75-77
    false representation, where, 80
    good faith, importance of, 81
    goodwill, assessment of, 80, 82, 84
    ISP, involvement of, 85
    loss of business, whether, 83
    mediation procedures, for, 77
    unjustified threats, risk of, 86
    wrongful registration, where, 78, 79
Domain names, 74 *et seq. See also* **Domain name disputes**
    confusion between, where, 79 *et seq*
    instrument of fraud, whether, 80, 82
    litigation, involving, 78, 85
    passing off, action for, 78, 80, 82
    portfolio, use of, 86, 88
    product launches, difficulties with, 79
    protection of, 77-82
    registration system, for, 74, 75, 88
    services offered, nature of, 79, 84
    trade mark, infringement of, 78, 79
    use, requirements as to, 79
Domicile,
    companies, attributed to, 40
    jurisdiction, influenced by, 40
    meaning given to, 40

E-Commerce Directive 63 *et seq*, 203 *et seq*
    commercial communications, identification of, 68
    contractual rules, dealing with, 66, 73
    dispute resolution, under, 71, 72
    electronic transactions,
        legal framework for, 64, 66

E-Commerce Directive, *cont.*
    e-tailers, information required from, 66-68
    formation of contract, under, 67, 73
    harmonisation, need for, 66
    home state regulation, 64, 65, 73
    implementation of, 63, 64
    importance, attached to, 63, 73
    intermediaries,
        liability, extent of, 69-71, 73
        publication, responsibility for, 70, 71
        status of, 68, 69
    objectives of, 63, 64
    scope of, 64
EFTA countries,
    jurisdiction, issues concerning, 38, 40
Electronic money, 52 *et seq*
    "cash", transfer of, 54, 58
    credit institutions, legislation covering, 56, 57
    definition of, 57, 58, 62
    electronic cheques, position regarding, 59
    electronic devices,
        examples of, 58
        use of, 57, 58
    EU law, relating to, 52, 56, 57, 58, 230 *et seq*
    micro payments, problems with, 52, 53
    payment systems, involving, 52, 53
    software-based virtual cash,
        loyalty points, 54, 55
        "tokens", 54
        use of, 54, 58
        "wallets", 54
Electronic Money Institutions (EMIs)
    capital requirements, for, 59, 61
    compliance rules, affecting, 60
    credit institutions, regards as, 57
    deposit-taking, position as to, 57, 62
    EU law, relating to, 56, 57, 60-62
    funds,
        received by, 57, 62
        redemption of, 58
    "grandfathering", practice as to, 60
    information, required from, 60
    investments, restrictions on, 59-61
    licensing procedures, for, 59, 62

Electronic Money Institutions, *cont.*
  meaning of, 56
  regulatory regime, affecting, 59, 62
  third parties, position regarding, 58
Electronic signature, 27 *et seq*
  advanced electronic signature, use
    of, 32, 33
  credit card, payments by, 28
  customer identity, establishing, 28
  EU law, relating to, 32, 36
  legal issues, relating to, 31, 32
  legislation, applying to, 34, 35
  meaning of, 27, 28, 32, 36
  order forms, completion of, 28, 32
  verification of, 32
E-mail. *See also* **Spamming**
  correspondence, contractual
    implications, 15
  direct marketing, by, 121, 128,
    130, 135
  EU law, applying to, 128, 135
  preference services, operation of,
    129
  telecommunication regulations,
    affecting, 128-130
  unsolicited communications, 130
Employee benefits, 170 *et seq*
  enterprise management incentives,
    173, 174
  ESOPs, information on, 178
  Inland Revenue, approval for, 170,
    175
  Long Term Incentive Plans (LTIPs),
    177
  National Insurance, contributions,
    176, 179
  PAYE, position regarding, 176
  profit sharing schemes, 174, 175
  shares,
      all employee share plan,
        172, 173
      granting of, 170
      savings related schemes,
        171, 172
      share option plans, 171, 176
      share ownership trusts, 178,
        179
  tax consequences, for, 170, 175,
    179
Encryption,
  asymmetric key encryption, 29, 36
  digital certificates, use of, 30-32
  digital signatures, use of, 30-32

Encryption, *cont.*
  meaning of, 28, 36
  symmetric key encryption, 29, 36
Enforcement of judgments,
  jurisdiction, issues relating to, 39
Enterprise management incentives,
  employee benefits, derived from,
    173, 174
ESOPs,
  employee benefits,
      information on, 178
      meaning of, 178
E-tailers,
  advertising rules, affecting, 119, 121
  fax, marketing by, 126
  EU law, affecting, 66-68
  profits, taxation of, 165, 166
EU law. **See also E-Commerce Directive**
  cryptography, involving, 34, 36
  databases, provisions covering, 141
  data protection, under, 100
  e-commerce, developments relating
    to, 63 *et seq*
  electronic money, relating to, 52,
    56-58
  electronic money institutions,
    affecting, 56, 57, 60-62
  electronic signature, position
    regarding, 32, 36
  electronic transactions, framework
    for, 64
  e-mail marketing, affected by, 128,
    135
  financial services, involving, 57,
    62, 65
  harmonisation of, 130, 133
  spamming, position as to, 130, 133
EU Member States,
  jurisdiction, position as to, 38
European Economic Area,
  personal data, transferred outside,
    107, 108, 118
European Patent Office,
  work of, 148

Fax,
  direct marketing, use of, 125, 126
  unsolicited faxes, position as to,
    125
Fax Preference Service,
  function of, 125, 126, 128
Financial services. *See also* **Electronic
Money Institutions**

Financial services, *cont,*
 deposit, definition of, 57
 EU law, relating to, 57, 60, 65
 funds, receipt of, 57
 regulatory regime, covering, 59, 60
Framing,
 issues involving, 24, 157, 163
Fraud,
 credit cards, linked to, 52, 53, 56,
  62

GTLDs,
 meaning of, 74
 registration of, 74, 88

Home State Regulation,
 contractual rules, relating to, 65
 EU law, establishing, 64, 65, 73
 land ownership, position
  regarding, 65
 operational base, companies for,
  64, 65
Hyperlinks. *See also* Linking
 contract acceptance, through, 11,
  13, 24

Information. *See* Confidential
 information
Information Commissioner,
 direct marketing, as defined by, 123
 e-mail marketing, guidance from,
  128
 powers of, 17, 90
 preference services, supported by,
  126
 telecommunication regulations,
  enforced by, 129
Initial Public Offering (IPO),
 company management, of, 164, 165
Inland Revenue,
 share schemes,
  approved by, 170
  information, provided by,
   178
  unapproved by, 175
Insurance transactions,
 legal position, regarding, 65
Intellectual property, 136 *et seq. See also*
  Copyright, Patents, Trade mark
 exploitation of, 149
 licensing,
  competition law, concerned
   with, 150

Intellectual property, *cont.*
  criteria, required for, 149,
   150
  licensing agreements, 150
 online business, significance for,
  136
 ownership rights, relating to, 136,
  162
 scope of, 136
Interactive TV,
 regulations affecting, 128, 129
Intermediaries,
 EU law, position regarding, 68, 69,
 liability of, 69-71, 73
Internet,
 copyright issues, involving, 139,
  140
 development of, 3
 glossary of terms, 180 *et seq*
 information, distributed through,
  1, 2
 publication, restrictions on, 70, 71
 security, issues relating to, 27, 52,
  56, 60
Internet Service Providers (ISPs),
 domain name disputes, involving,
  85
 EU law, affecting, 68, 69
 liability of, 69-71, 73
 spamming, difficulties for, 131
 tax issues, consideration of, 165
 useful sites/sources, 186 *et seq*
  broadcasting, 192
  competition law, 186
  corporate information, 186
  directories, 188
  e-commerce, 190
  EU information, 189
  government sources, 195
  information technology, 190
  intellectual property, 197
  international trade, 199
  legal resources, 199, 201
  taxation, 202
  telecommunications, 192
  trade associations, 193
Inventions. *See also* Patents
 industrial application, required for,
  146, 147
 inventive step, necessary for, 147
 "new", as requirement for, 146
 priority date, relating to, 146
 protection, measures for, 146

Junk mail,
sending of, 126
Jurisdiction, 37 *et seq*
business to business contracts, 41,
42
business to consumer contracts,
42, 43, 47
contract, jurisdictional clauses, 37,
38, 40, 42, 43, 46, 51
choice of law, determining, 38, 47
domicile rule, operation of, 40
e-commerce activities, directed
towards, 43
EFTA countries, position
regarding, 38, 40
enforcement of judgments, 39
EU Member States, position
regarding, 38
governing law, relating to, 38, 51
importance, attached to, 4, 37
international conventions,
covering, 38, 40, 42-44
mandatory laws, effect of, 45
risk, associated with, 45-47, 49, 50
website, international access to, 37

Legislation. *See also* **EU law**
development of, 3, 7
harmonisation, need for, 5
Liability,
contract law, exclusion of, 14, 17
defamation for, 25, 69
Linking, 152 *et seq*
affiliated contracts, 159 *et seq*
benefits, derived from, 162
click through payment
structure, 160
commission payment
structure, 159, 160
fee payment structure, 161
intellectual property rights,
ownership of, 162
legal issues involving, 161, 162
sales reporting, 160
judicial decisions, involving, 154-156
meaning of, 24, 152, 153
practice relating to,
deep linking, 157, 163
defamation, 156, 163
framing, 157, 163
registered trade marks, 157,
163

Linking, *cont.*
UK, position on, 155
USA, position regarding, 153, 154
Long Term Incentive Plans (LTIPs),
employees benefits, derived from,
177
Lugano Convention,
effect of, 38, 40

Mail. *See* **E-mail, Junk mail, Mailing lists**
Mail Preference Service,
function of, 126
Mailing lists,
personal data,
protection of, 97, 98, 118
removal of, 122, 123
purchase of, 102
Mandatory laws,
consumer protection, effect of, 45
Marketing. *See* **Direct marketing**
M-commerce,
payment for, 53
Metatags,
practice regarding, 158, 163
Micropayments,
problems, associated with, 52, 53
Minimum orders,
imposition of, 53
Mobile telephones,
location of calls, 130
Moral rights,
protection of, 141, 142, 157
Multi-national companies,
operational base, for, 40, 64, 65

National Insurance,
payment of, 176, 179
Nominet UK,
complaints procedures, involving,
77
dispute resolution,
mediation procedures, 77
policy, operated by, 76, 77
service, organised by 76, 85,
87
registration procedures, 77
role of, 74

Obscenity,
liability for, 25
Offshore,
companies, setting up, 166, 169

Online contracts, 6 *et seq. See also*
   Contract law, Contract terms
     acceptance, validity of, 8
     cancellation,
         effect of, 23
         goods returned, 23
         money refunded, 23
         period for, 21, 22
     click wrap agreement, effect of, 11-
       13
     consumer confidence, need for, 27,
       56, 60
     display of goods, 8, 9
     dispute resolution, affecting, 48
     distance selling, issues involving,
       17-21, 26
     e-mail correspondence, position
       regarding, 15
     evidence, requirements as to, 15
     formation of contract, 6, 66, 67
     governing law, applied to, 38, 51
     hyperlink, acceptance through, 11,
       13, 24
     insurance cover, extent of, 49
     jurisdiction, relating to, 41-43, 47
     legislation covering, 7, 8
     negotiation, importance of, 14, 15
     offer, validity of, 8, 9, 26
     price displayed, 9, 10
     signature, requirements for, 7
     special offers, condition affecting,
       10
     standard terms, validity of, 6, 10
     terms,
         implied terms, use of, 10,
           11, 16
         reasonable, nature of, 14
         terms displayed, where, 11,
           15, 24
         unfair terms, effect of, 14,
           16, 17
     writing, meaning given to, 7
Origin. *See* **Country of origin**

Passing off,
     action for, 78, 80, 82, 143, 144, 157
Patents, 145 *et seq. See also* **Copyright,**
   Intellectual property, Trade mark
     applications, requirements for,
       146, 147
     EU law, position regarding, 148
     international protection, for, 147,
       148

Patents, *cont.*
     protection, extent of, 146-148
     purpose of, 145
     USA, position regarding, 146, 147
PAYE,
     position, as to payment, 176
Payments. *See also* **Micropayments**
     credit cards, through, 28
     m-commerce, for, 53
     t-commerce, for, 53
Personal data,
     access to, rights over, 103, 104,
       118
     billing data, position regarding,
       127
     data controllers, handled by, 97,
       98
     direct marketing, involving, 122,
       123
     EU Decision on, 260 *et seq*
     individuals, data identifying, 92, 93
     legislative requirements, covering,
       97, 98, 118
     meaning, given to, 92, 93
     retention, time limits for, 127
     sensitive data, processing of, 96,
       102
     telecommunications, use of, 127
     transfer, issues involving, 107, 108,
       118
Price,
     incorrect, where, 9, 10
Privacy,
     data protection, rules as to, 113,
       114, 118
     telecommunications, involving,
       129, 130

QUEST,
     share ownership trusts,
       requirement for, 178

Refunds,
     cancelled contract, where, 23
Regulation,
     development of, 3
Return of goods,
     provisions covering, 23
Rome Convention,
     choice of law, under, 44
     consumer contracts, under, 45
     effect of, 43, 44
     governing law, applied, 44

Security,
consumer concerns, over, 27, 52, 55, 56
smartcards, use of, 55
Share options schemes
employee benefits, derived from 171, 172, 176
tax consequences for, 175
Share ownership trusts,
employee benefits, derived from, 178, 179
Signature. *See also* **Digital signatures, Electronic signature**
requirements, as to, 7
verification, need for, 28, 31
Smartcards,
banking regulations, affecting, 56
security programs, within, 55
use of, 55, 58
Software systems,
supply of, 14
Spamming,
costs, relating to, 131
EU law, harmonisation of, 130, 133
ISPs, position regarding, 131
judicial action, against, 133
opt-out registers, use of, 133
practice, relating to, 131
regulations, dealing with, 130, 135
self-regulation, schemes involving, 133
Standard terms. *See also* **Contract law, Contract terms**
case decisions, involving, 11
incorporation of, 13
reasonable, nature of, 14
use of, 6, 10, 26
validity of, 6, 10

Tax, 164 *et seq. See also* **VAT**
business considerations,
company location, 164
company structure, 164
setting up, 164
employee benefits, subject to, 170, 175, 179
offshore, companies located, 166, 169
overseas sales, profits from, 165
"permanent establishment", criteria for, 165, 169
server, location of, 165, 169

Tax, *cont.*
website, location of, 165
T-commerce,
payment for, 53
Telecommunications,
advertising, regulation of, 123
automated calling systems, use of, 124
billing data, provisions covering, 127
direct marketing, involving, 123
enforcement procedures, relating to, 129
legislative provisions, affecting, 123, 128-130
mobile telephones, location of calls, 130
"subscribers", status of, 124
traffic data, regulation of, 127
unsolicited communications, 124, 125
Telephone Preference Service,
function of, 125, 126
Text messaging,
regulations affecting, 128, 129
Trade mark, 142 *et seq. See also* **Copyright, Intellectual property, Patents**
application procedures, for, 85
infringement of, 78, 79, 143
legislation protecting, 142
meaning of, 142
product launches, difficulties with, 79
registration,
eligibility, for, 142, 143
period of, 145
procedures, for, 144, 145
reasons for, 144
services offered, distinctive nature of, 79, 84
Traffic data,
regulations affecting, 127

UDRP,
operation of, 75, 76, 85, 87
USA,
jurisdictional reach, of, 46
linking, practice as to, 153, 154
patents, position regarding, 146, 147

Value Added Tax,
eligibility, for, 167-169

Value Added Tax, *cont.*
    transactions liable for,
        business to business, 167
        business to consumer, 167
Venue,
    jurisdiction, affected by, 48

Website,
    advertising, placed on, 119, 121
    applicable law, issues relating to,
        37
    content, protection of, 24
    copyright, protection of, 24, 139,
        140
    data protection, covering
        information, 91
    design, protection of, 24
    distance communication, through,
        17, 18
    framing, issues concerning, 24
    interactivity, importance attached
        to, 46
    international access, consequences
        of, 37, 43

Website, *cont.*
    jurisdiction, covering, 37, 41-43,
      46, 48
    licence, limits on, 24
    linking, issues concerning, 24
    multiple websites, jurisdiction
        governing, 48
    online contracts,
        contract terms displayed,
          11, 13, 15, 20, 24
        earlier versions, retained, 15
        goods displayed, 8, 9, 15
    "permanent establishment",
        whether, 165
    privacy policy, use of, 113, 114, 118
    registration processes, 24
    venue, choice stated, 48, 51
World Intellectual Property Organisation
    (WIPO),
    work of, 148
World Wide Web,
    origins of, 1, 2
Writing,
    contract law, requirements under, 7